MISSIONARY COSMOPOLITANISM IN
NINETEENTH-CENTURY BRITISH LITERATURE

LITERATURE, RELIGION, AND POSTSECULAR STUDIES
Lori Branch, Series Editor

MISSIONARY COSMOPOLITANISM IN NINETEENTH-CENTURY BRITISH LITERATURE

Winter Jade Werner

THE OHIO STATE UNIVERSITY PRESS
COLUMBUS

Copyright © 2020 by The Ohio State University.
All rights reserved.

Library of Congress Cataloging-in-Publication Data
Names: Werner, Winter Jade, author.
Title: Missionary cosmopolitanism in nineteenth-century British literature / Winter Jade Werner.
Description: Columbus : The Ohio State University Press, [2020] | Series: Literature, religion, and postsecular studies | Includes bibliographical references and index. | Summary: "Examines the effects of missionary evangelicalism on cosmopolitanism through the nineteenth-century novel, including works such as Charlotte Brontë's *Jane Eyre*, Charles Dickens's *Bleak House*, and lesser-known works by Robert Southey and Sydney Owenson"—Provided by publisher.
Identifiers: LCCN 2019052454 | ISBN 9780814214268 (cloth) | ISBN 0814214266 (cloth) | ISBN 9780814277973 (ebook) | ISBN 0814277977 (ebook)
Subjects: LCSH: English fiction—19th century—History and criticism. | Cosmopolitanism in literature. | Missionaries in literature. | Evangelicalism in literature.
Classification: LCC PR868.C664 W47 2020 | DDC 823/.8093827—dc23
LC record available at https://lccn.loc.gov/2019052454
Other identifiers: ISBN 9780814255889 (paper) | ISBN 0814255884 (paper)

Cover design by Laurence J. Nozik
Text design by Juliet Williams
Type set in Adobe Minion Pro

CONTENTS

Preface		*vii*
Acknowledgments		*ix*
INTRODUCTION	The Only True Cosmopolite	1
CHAPTER 1	The Cosmopolitan Idea in Early Nineteenth-Century Missionary Societies	39
CHAPTER 2	Robert Southey and the Case for Christian Colonialism	69
CHAPTER 3	Universal Kinship and *Jane Eyre*	109
CHAPTER 4	*The Missionary, Luxima,* and the Forging of a Post-"Mutiny" Cosmopolitanism	139
CODA	The Afterlives of Missionary Cosmopolitanism	169
Works Cited		*181*
Index		*201*

PREFACE

IN A WAY, this book starts with my name, Winter Jade Werner. People often ask me about it, and I've asked my mother many times, too, why this name? She is generally evasive in her answers, and the closest I've gotten to an explanation goes something like this: My name is Yoke Hong, she says. This means "Fragrant Jade" in English. So, you are "Winter Jade." What strikes me in this story is the feat of translation it represents. My name is an English iteration (my mother's third language) of her Cantonese name (her first language). And this strange path by which I ended up with my name inevitably makes me think about the origins of my mother's multilingualism.

Her story starts with British Methodist missionaries in Tanjung Malim, Malaysia, in a kampong, or village, outside of Kuala Lumpur. My mother was born in 1956, the youngest of eleven children. Before she turned one year old, the Federation of Malaya would get its independence from Britain. But, of course, independence didn't mean an end to British influences. The legacy of British imperialism would still persist in everyday life, even in a kampong as small as the one where my mother lived. For her, this legacy was embodied in these missionaries, in the games (Snakes and Ladders), hymns ("What a Friend We Have in Jesus"), and stories they taught her ("I learned about snow from them, and this had no application to my life," my mother tells me).

Most of all, these missionaries introduced my mother to English, a language she would go on to study when she moved with her family to the capital of Kuala Lumpur and enrolled there in the Methodist Girls School (or MGS, which started as a government school, but was brought under the control of the Methodist Mission from the United States in 1899). The influence of missionaries on my mother's life, then, has been profound. Thanks in significant part to her proficiency in English and her education at MGS, she would become the first in her family to graduate from university and, afterwards, become a flight attendant ("And would see snow for the first time," my mother adds). She would meet my American father, and I would eventually be born and receive my name, Winter Jade Werner.

It is difficult for me to parse the unexpectedly significant role missionaries have played in my family. On the one hand, it seems my mother's life was shaped by the lingering presence of British imperialism. But, on the other hand, my mother seems to have experienced the missionary presence as a curiosity ("They were always serious and unhappy," she has said) and a window into a larger world, one she hoped to explore when she grew up.

While all this strangeness has kept me from writing about the missionary encounter with the so-called natives (because what do I say? What do I think? It's difficult to get critical distance from the questions), it did alert me to the fact that there were stories to be told about missionaries that I hadn't yet heard, intellectual histories about missionaries and their global influences that perhaps hadn't been excavated. *Missionary Cosmopolitanism* is my effort to tell one of those stories. It's a limited effort to realize a "capacious historicism" (Goodlad and Sartori 596); I hope it might represent something of a starting point for other stories in the future.

This book is dedicated to my family.

ACKNOWLEDGMENTS

IN MANY WAYS, this is the easiest and most difficult section to write. Easy, because there are so many people to whom I'm so grateful. And difficult, because I can't put the immensity of the feeling and the debt I owe into proper words. I hope the following people will excuse the inadequacy of these thanks.

First is Christopher Herbert, without whose mentorship I'd be nowhere. His unfailingly good advice has guided this body of research and writing from its earliest stages to the final form it takes now. He embodies generosity, intelligence, and tact, and my earnest wish for the world is that everyone could be so lucky as to have a Chris Herbert in their life. Jules Law and Christopher Lane offered crucial, always incisive feedback as this project first took shape, and I would be remiss if I didn't acknowledge the other brilliant minds who supported me during this formative period: Jim Farr, Mary Dietz, Holly Clayson, Barbara Newman, Helen Thompson, Julia Stern, Regina Schwartz, Josh Honn, Bart Scott, Liz McCabe, Maha Jafri, Christie Harner, and Jim Kincaid played larger roles in shaping my intellectual development than I think any of them are aware. And, way back in 2013, Brian Stanley invited me to the History of World Christianity Research Seminar in Edinburgh to present early research; I still think of this experience as one of the most influential in my approach to missionary writing and culture.

I cannot say enough good things about Wheaton College and the broader Boston-Providence community, where I live and work now. Beverly Lyon

Clark has thoughtfully read this entire manuscript, and Claire Buck is a font of good advice. My students at Wheaton continually inspire me, and I'm especially grateful for the research assistance of Carly Lewis ('18). Joel Simundich and Greg Vargo provided much needed advice at just the right time. And the VLC Seminar at the Mahindra Center and the Boston-area Works-in-Progress Group led by Martha Vicinus have become new intellectual homes—huge thanks to Martha, Carolyn Betensky, Aeron Hunt, Mary Carpenter, Laura Green, Kelly Hager, Anna Henchman, Jim Buzard, John Plotz, Louise Penner, Deb Gettelman, Maia McAleavey, James Najarian, Daniel Williams, and Christie (again) for helping me find my way through chapters 2 and 3 (as well as in thinking through the title for this book).

In 2016, I had the good fortune to participate in an NEH seminar on "Postsecular Studies and the Rise of the English Novel, 1719–1897," led by Lori Branch and Mark Knight. It was during these four weeks that my research started cohering into some incipient book-like form. I'm indebted to Christine Colón, John Wiehl, Stephanie Hershinow, Jessica Ling, Kevin Seidel, Ariana Reilly, Dwight Codr, Sean Dempsey, Lauren Matz, Joanne Janssen, Jeffrey Galbraith, Ioana Patuleanu, Haien Park, Cheri Larsen Hoeckley, and Deidre Lynch for providing fresh new perspectives on my work. Mimi Winick, especially, has been an unparalleled interlocutor on all things related to religion and literature. Mark has been, and continues to be, an unwavering source of support, and I'm grateful for Lori's belief in this project, as well as for the warm and hospitable home she created for it as editor of the "Religion, Literature, and Postsecular Studies" series at The Ohio State University Press.

An equally important community sprang up in preparing my co-edited volume with Joshua King, *Constructing Nineteenth-Century Religion* (OSUP 2019). I've heard from some people how ill-advised it can be for an assistant professor to work on an edited volume. But I can't bear to imagine how impoverished this book would have been without the model of brilliance and kindness that is Josh King. And, similarly, I can't express how much I've learned from our contributors. My gratitude goes out to them for providing object lessons in how to think and write about nineteenth-century religion.

As the above acknowledgments suggest, I am fortunate to be working with the Ohio State University Press. The insights of editors Lindsay Martin and Ana M. Jimenez-Moreno have sharpened mine, and the outside readers helped clarify my arguments in crucial ways. This book has been greatly improved because of their contributions. I should add, too, that none of this work would have been possible without the librarians and resources of SOAS, the British Library, the Crowther Mission Studies Library, the University of Birmingham, the University of Aberdeen, the University of Edinburgh, and the Styberg Library at Northwestern—visits to which were supported by the Woodrow Wilson Foundation, the Josephine de Karman Fellowship Trust, and grants from Wheaton College.

There are also those scholar-friends who really defy all categorization, so complete and wonderful are their presences in my life. Jocelyn Sczcepaniak-Gillece has been there every step of the way; Emily Rohrbach is forever the best running partner and gin-and-tonic maker; and Ashton Lazarus is a rock in my life. Their books set a high bar for this one, and I hope I've done them proud. My profound gratitude and love to my family, too: Lily Werner, Krissy Werner, and Robert Ewen have always been my cheerleaders. My toddler, Addy, was born the day before I was awarded my book contract. In truth, she contributed pretty much nothing, but I've always thought the two events a remarkable coincidence worth acknowledging. Finally, my father, Tony Werner, who passed away in 2015, would have been thrilled to see this book and doubtless would have bought ten copies.

My biggest thanks are for my husband, Nick Dorzweiler. He has looked over every page, and each word, each sentence, each paragraph is all the more precious to me for the attention he has given it. It can be hard to see an academic monograph as an act of love (could any form of writing be more impersonal?). But when I look at this one, I see it suffused with the love and care we have for each other.

An earlier version of chapter 3 was published in *Nineteenth-Century Literature* as "All in the Family? Missionaries, Marriage, and Universal Kinship," and parts of chapter 1 and the coda appeared in other essays in the *Victorians Institute Journal* and *Nineteenth-Century Literature*.

INTRODUCTION

The Only True Cosmopolite

"TO THE EAR of a Christian there is a peculiar meaning in the trite expression of the poet,—'The proper study of mankind is man,'" proclaimed the introduction to the American edition of the British missionary John Williams's *A Narrative of Missionary Enterprises in the South Sea Islands* (1837). "Every thing connected with man's condition, and habits, and history, mental or physical, is in his view invested with real importance," it continued. "Especially should Christians, at this day, be familiar with the condition, and changes, and prospects, of every people, among whom missionary labours have been commenced. They should be at home on missionary ground. The Christian is the only true cosmopolite" (xi).

The passage is worth quoting at length, as it profoundly impressed me when I first encountered it years ago. I had just finished Amanda Anderson's *The Powers of Distance*, I remember, and I had thought about missionaries cursorily. Armed with this formidable body of knowledge built on light reading and conjecture, I naturally felt certain of my expertise on both missionaries ("enthusiasts and imperial functionaries") and cosmopolitanism ("mostly good"). But reading this passage again and again, it struck me that there were a number of ideas being presented, which, as I mulled them over, perhaps stood to unsettle my understanding of cosmopolitanism and my preconceptions of the nineteenth-century missionary movement.

First, the introduction implied that in some sense missionaries were humanists par excellence. The term seemed strange applied to some missionaries; I had imagined their primary loyalties belonging mostly to the next world rather than this one. Yet, I eventually found that the nineteenth-century missionary more often than not saw himself as particularly embedded in the human society. As much as he regarded the "heathen" with condescension, as "a creature to be pitied, to be saved from slavery and also from his own darkness, his savagery" (Brantlinger, *Rule* 182), the missionary often also positioned himself to be a sympathetic and keen observer of human culture,[1] not to mention an agent for its betterment. That missionaries saw themselves not just *of* the world, but took it upon themselves to regard all human matters as "invested with real importance," in no small way troubled my received view of them as simply narrow-minded religious zealots or "little detachments of maniacs," to use Sydney Smith's enduring characterization of the Baptist Missionary Society (BMS) missionaries in the *Edinburgh Review* in 1807 (61). Hence one of the points of inspiration for this book. If accounts of British imperialism have tended to presume the "marginality, if not . . . insanity" of missionaries (Cox, *Imperial* 8), I instead interrogate what the opening paragraph of this introduction makes clear: Missionaries consciously tried—and, to a remarkable degree, actually succeeded—in their efforts to become savvy social, cultural, and political players in a rapidly globalizing world (8).

Second (and the inspiration for the line of research that would eventually result in this book), I was fascinated by what I perceived to be Christian missionaries' claim to being true cosmopolites. My initial instinct was to treat the claim with skepticism and dismiss it as little more than an empty rhetorical flourish, evidence of nothing but the "contradictory and overlapping" ways that cosmopolitanism was deployed in the nineteenth century (Agathocleous, *Urban Realism* 2). What was this statement, after all, but another bad-faith effort to legitimate the project of British imperialism, yet another instance in which "humanitarian aims" did little but "contribute to imperialist encroachment" (Brantlinger, *Rule* 181)?

However, closer examination of missionary societies alongside the recent history of cosmopolitanism suggests that such assertions of being "cosmopoli-

---

1. Scholars of Victorian ethnographic and anthropological practice often remark on its indebtedness to missionary work. George Stocking, for instance, observes that the Methodist missionary Thomas Williams's *Fiji and the Fijians* (1858) played a central role in the creation of Victorian anthropology (*Victorian* 89). Christopher Herbert's *Culture and Anomie* extends Stocking's line of inquiry in its examination of the "early ethnography of the South Pacific" penned by London Missionary Society (LMS) missionaries in the early nineteenth century (155). And Brantlinger's more recent *Taming Cannibals* notes missionaries' "detailed, surprisingly sympathetic accounts of the cultures of those they sought to convert" (33).

tan" were not insignificant. In calling themselves "cosmopolites" or "citizens of the world," missionaries participated in charged political and moral conversations concerning the relationship between British Christianity and (what we now take to be) Enlightenment ideas—ideas that included British responsibility to foreign peoples and nations, the "proper" reach of global commerce, the meaning and practicability of the "universal family of mankind," and the existence (or not) of an essential "human nature." Missionary claims of being "true cosmopolites" thus were not only attempts to capitalize on the term's positive connotations to advance religious and imperial expansionism (though this was certainly a motivating factor). They were also earnest efforts to square an Enlightenment humanist ethos with evangelical Christianity, with consequences that proved—and continue to prove—influential and enduring.

Animating my arguments, then, is a simple idea. What would happen were I to take missionaries' cosmopolitan sentiments seriously? What would follow if I commenced a study of imperial history and literature not with a presumption of missionary backwardness but rather with careful consideration of those values that missionaries themselves claimed to be central to their work? What might this history tell us about how religion and imperialism together influenced cosmopolitanism in the nineteenth century and beyond? And what might it reveal about the outsized role—especially when one considers their supposed "marginality" in nineteenth-century culture—missionaries end up playing in some of the most beloved and best-selling works in the period?[2]

In the chapters that follow, I tell two stories about nineteenth-century cosmopolitanism. First, I demonstrate that cosmopolitanism both fueled and found an unlikely champion in the modern missionary movement, and I highlight in particular the disjunction between missionaries' cosmopolitan schemes and their participation in the consolidation of empire. Thus I identify the subtle processes by which missionaries and their interlocutors manipulated the concept of cosmopolitanism in order to align it with various religious, colonial, and commercial interests.

However, I *also* explore how the Enlightenment idea inevitably complicated and was complicated by these interests. It is these moments of friction that are the groundwork for my second story. While originally drawing upon the universalism of Enlightenment thought, the missionary conception of cosmopolitanism over time—and after the so-called Indian "Mutiny" of 1857 in

---

2. Observing that "missionaries figure prominently in Victorian fiction," Brantlinger, for instance, lists the many authors who drew inspiration from missionaries, including Sydney Owenson, Charlotte Brontë, Charles Dickens, Robert Ballantyne, Charlotte Yonge, and Robert Louis Stevenson (*Victorian Literature* 22).

particular—was compelled by such difficulties to develop a sense of racial difference that resulted in a *new* post-Mutiny cosmopolitanism. Surprisingly, this post-Mutiny missionary cosmopolitanism in no small way resembles the "new cosmopolitanisms" of late-1990s and 2000s scholarship, which were celebrated for correcting the Eurocentric normativity of Enlightenment cosmopolitanism. Thus a key contention of this book, one I explore especially in chapter 4 and the coda: In the nineteenth century, global evangelicalism helped precipitate the shift away from the universalism of Enlightenment cosmopolitanism to a *new* post-Mutiny cosmopolitanism, one that displayed awareness of the "inadequacy of the totalizing vision even while that ideal [was] being asserted" (Agathocleous, *Urban Realism* 120). Hand in hand with those more secular nineteenth-century globalisms including free trade (Goodlad, *Victorian Geopolitical*), the aspiration to scientific objectivity (A. Anderson, *Powers*), and improved technologies for global communication, global evangelicalism represents something of a taproot for the "new" cosmopolitan views that proliferate today. In this capacity, tracing the cosmopolitan thought of missionary societies potentially helps explain why twenty-first-century religious projects frequently prove not the "backwardly or defensively parochial" antitheses of the savvy, self-reflexive, and secular "new cosmopolitanisms" but instead avid and acute rivals (Calhoun, "Cosmopolitanism").

I name the different ways that nineteenth-century missionaries took up, instantiated, and transfigured Enlightenment-influenced cosmopolitan ideas "missionary cosmopolitanism." Missionary cosmopolitanism, I submit, holds a special place in the nineteenth-century British literary imagination, not least because it was where the ideological contradictions of missionaries' cosmopolitan sentiments were distilled to their essence. In her overview of "Form and Global Consciousness," Ayşe Çelikkol neatly summarizes one of those engrained critical truisms of the Victorian novel: "Holding together irreconcilable difference, individual forms often manifest contradictory aspects of an ideological system or manage them" (274). The observation is commonplace, even axiomatic at this point, but it highlights one way in which a literary critical study might yield different insights than historical, sociological, or anthropological accounts of the same phenomena. For, if missionary publications as a whole mostly functioned as "propaganda," suppressing or smoothing over ideological contradictions all the better to claim "divine approval for the British colonial project" (Thorne 38; see Comaroff and Comaroff 37), literary representations of missionary cosmopolitanism instead seized and mulled on these contradictions, bringing them into focus. Thus a double thrust to my project: While I read the archive of missionary writing to explain the social context of literary texts, I also emphasize that Romantic and Victorian literature illuminates the grit in the "well-oiled publicity machine" of missionary propaganda (Elbourne 14). The literary stages explicitly what the voluminous archive of missionary publications might otherwise obscure.

Such a pronouncement cannot and is not meant to extend to the entirety of nineteenth-century literature, though. In a number of cases, after all, the missionary serves as the idealized (not to mention, usually paternalistic) model of intercultural relations, as illustrated in the nameless missionary of R. M. Ballantyne's *The Coral Island* (1858) or Rev. Colin Morton and his daughter Agnes in Charlotte Yonge's *New Ground* (1868). But it would be a mistake to see Ballantyne's or Yonge's almost saintly missionaries as representative of some broad nineteenth-century tendency to romanticize the vocation. For in several prominent instances, missionary work functioned as the negative example against which a more moral and (the novels suggest) more genuinely Christian model of global engagement might begin to take shape, as in Jane Eyre's opposition to her missionary cousin St. John, *Bleak House*'s scathing takedown of "telescopic philanthropy," or Sydney Owenson's titular missionary, whose love for a Hindu prophetess leads him finally to adopt a new syncretic religion, which, the novel hints, better fulfills the spirit of Christianity than the dogmatic Catholicism the missionary had previously practiced.

It is these works that interest me. In them, the contradictions inhering in missionary work serve as occasions for grappling with the nature and consequences of a given set of responsibilities the British Christian might bear to other countries and people in an era of rapid globalization—a grappling that sparked an array of formal strategies to make imaginable and more fully perceptible this "complex, incoherent web of interconnections" (Agathocleous, *Urban Realism* xv).[3] As we will see, cosmopolitanism in these texts is not the moral substitute for Christianity in decline. Instead, they treat cosmopolitanism and its correlated concepts as inescapably mediated by religion and religiously informed philanthropic efforts on behalf of the "family of mankind."

Because he stood at the nexus of those issues that preoccupied Romantic and Victorian writers—the extent of Christian responsibility, the viability of Enlightenment ideals, and the moral character of imperialism and globalization—the missionary emerged as a crucial figure in this representational challenge. What interested these writers specifically were the ways that the missionary found himself beholden to *two* sets of principles and directives in

---

3. For Agathocleous and Goodlad, the endeavor to make concrete and representable those abstract global connections "beyond individual experience and cognition" constitutes the cosmopolitan imagination of nineteenth-century literary realism (Goodlad, *Victorian Geopolitical* 9).

his efforts to navigate global interconnectedness: the first born of the injunction that the will of the Lord "be done on earth as it is in heaven," and the second derived from the history of interaction between Protestantism—especially eighteenth-century Dissent—and the values of the "secular" Enlightenment (i.e., a commitment to a politics grounded in the belief in the universal capacity for reason, the fundamental equality and kinship of mankind, and the necessity of a tolerant state to ensure individual liberties).[4] While these sets of principles and directives sometimes overlapped so as to seem indistinguishable, they sharply diverged at other times. Authors such as Charles Dickens, Robert Southey, Charlotte Brontë, and Sydney Owenson, I suggest, were especially quick to seize on the divergences, finding rich material in the missionary's conflicted position to reflect on and represent the potential lived consequences of various instantiations of cosmopolitan feelings (one imagines often to the dismay of missionary societies themselves). Hence *Jane Eyre*, for instance, dwells on the sizeable gap that emerged between the ideal of universal kinship in principle and the missionary practice of policing missionary marriages according to ever-stricter racial lines.

By distilling such strands of thought from the mammoth textual output of missionary societies and their supporters, Romantic and Victorian literature lights an unexpected path taken by post-Enlightenment cosmopolitanism. The genealogy of the idea, it turns out, wends as much through nineteenth-century global evangelicalism as it does more "secular" globalisms. In my chapter descriptions below, I expand on and clarify these lines of thought. However, before I continue, I want to make clear some of the key terms and concepts informing this book: the modern missionary movement, cosmopolitanism, and religion and globalization.

The Modern Missionary Movement

The "modern missionary movement" designates the sudden enthusiasm in the 1790s and early 1800s for missionary work, an enthusiasm characterized by remarkable cooperation and coordination of efforts among missionary societies despite their individual denominational leanings.[5] Two Anglican societies, the Society for the Propagation of the Gospel in Foreign Parts (SPG) and Society for Promoting Christian Knowledge (SPCK), had dominated the British

---

4. See Canuel, chapter 1; White, *Early Romanticism*; and Stanley, *Christian Missions*.
5. See Porter, *Religion* 40–41. For an overview on the difference between denominationalism and sectarianism, see White, *Early Romanticism* 6.

missionary landscape in the 1700s.[6] Yet these societies, as noted by an 1801 sermon preached before the newly founded Society for Missions to Africa and the East (renamed the Church Missionary Society [CMS] in 1812), were less interested in the task of evangelizing than they were in the "maintenance of a learned and orthodox Clergy" in the colonies ("A Sermon" 6). Hence evangelicals saw "room . . . left for the institution of [societies], which shall consider the Heathen as [their] principal care" (7). In very short order, a number of societies were founded to fill this "room." These included the Baptist Missionary Society (BMS) in 1792, the Missionary Society in 1795 (renamed the London Missionary Society [LMS] in 1818), the Edinburgh (Scottish) and Glasgow Missionary Societies in 1796, and the Society for Missions to Africa and the East (later CMS) in 1799. In this sense, the missionary movement of the turn of the century defined itself as distinct from the missionary efforts that had preceded it in making the conversion of the foreign "heathen" its primary goal.

But what made this movement "modern"? Why did *this* particular moment, in the words of the declaration that opened the LMS missionary William Ellis's *Polynesian Researches* (1829), mark the "beginning of a new era in the Missionary efforts of modern times" (1:140)? Historians have pointed to a few characteristics of the turn-of-the-century missionary movement that differentiates it from those in the past. Hilary Carey, for one, observes that the new missionary societies shared with nineteenth-century British culture more generally an unprecedented broad-mindedness born of (what we today might consider) relatively secular political values when it came to denominational differences: "Unlike Britons in the eighteenth century, Greater Britons in the new century tended to define themselves less by their belligerent Protestantism than by their religious toleration and love of liberty" (10). And whereas the Catholic Church responded to the events of the French Revolution by "set[ting] its face firmly against the values of modernity," missionary Protestantism generally had the opposite reaction, as its churches to different degrees "appropriated the intellectual legacy of the Enlightenment," thereby blending "the doctrines of grace and the canons of empiricism and common-sense philosophy" (Stanley, "Christian Missions" 2, 3). For these reasons, according to missiologist David J. Bosch, "the entire modern missionary movement is, to a very real extent, a child of the Enlightenment" (280).

Such pronouncements make clear the imbrication of the perceived "modernity" of the missionary movement and the intellectual movement we

---

6. But despite their existences, "there was no consistent acceptance of the missionary obligation by either Anglicanism or Dissent" before the Evangelical Revival (Stanley, *Bible* 55–56).

call the Enlightenment. But describing the values and ideas of the modern missionary movement as influenced by or possessing an "Enlightenment" ethos is inevitably problematic. For one thing, the term is anachronistic: "'Enlightenment' as an English rendering of the German term *Auklärung* first appears in 1865, followed in 1889 by the first use by Edward Caird of the phrase 'the Age of Enlightenment'" (Stanley, "Christian Missions" 6). Even if the term *had* existed in the early to mid-nineteenth century, evangelicals doubtless would have resisted "the implication that their brand of godliness had anything in common with the thought of Voltaire and Rousseau" (7). Further complicating the matter is historians' skepticism of "the image of a unitary secular Enlightenment project" (Sorkin 3). In this vein, scholars such as J. G. A. Pocock advocate for a "plurality of Enlightenments," comprising vastly different intellectual positions and ranging from (in David Sorkin's words) "the genuinely religious to the genuinely antireligious" (Pocock 138; Sorkin 3).

My lodestar for navigating the pitfalls attending the terms "Enlightenment" and "modern" with respect to Protestantism and the missionary movement is derived from scholars such as Webb Keane and J. Barton Scott. Emphasizing the Kantian definition of the term, each identifies the modernity of "Enlightenment" thinking as obtaining (more or less) from its self-conscious "rupture from a traditional past" and accompanying faith in mankind's "progress into a better future" (Keane 48). The necessary precondition of this rupture (drawing on Adorno and Horkheimer's formulation, inherited from Kant) was the subject's "unconditional freedom from tutelage," his "emergence from his . . . inability to use [his] own understanding without the guidance of another" (qtd. in Scott 2; see Scott 40–42; Kant, "An Answer" 54). While this narrative typically is "taken to lean inexorably to the secular vision of modernity, replacing gods with humans at the center of the action," there is also no mistaking its resemblance to Protestantism (Keane 49). "The thought of freedom . . . of the autonomous self" at the center of much Enlightenment writing converges with Protestantism's emphasis on "liberating individuals from the domination of illegitimate clerics and their rituals," thereby "restoring agency to . . . proper subjects" (Keane 49; Scott 2). Indeed, there is some historical credence for the connection between Protestant and Enlightenment sensibilities in this regard. The "fervent conviction of man's inward sense of morality" on which Kant built his narrative of Enlightenment self-liberation probably originated in the values promulgated by German Pietism—a religious movement that itself anticipated and profoundly influenced British foreign missionary societies (Reiss 8; see Walls, "Eighteenth-Century").[7]

---

7. As Walls argues, the modern missionary movement in Britain and the German Enlightenment therefore share common genealogical roots in the sensibilities of continental

This formulation of modernity qua "Enlightenment anticlericalism" is helpful, for it highlights two important dynamics that are crucial to my arguments regarding missionary cosmopolitanism (Scott 43). First, despite their many differences, Enlightenment thinkers and movements generally shared a commitment to the ideal of a "free" individual whose exercise of autonomous reason would better self and society. Second, it is in this manner that Enlightenment humanism and Protestantism could work in concert to valorize the ideal of "the self-governing individual" while simultaneously affirming "the *intrinsic* unity and equality of all humanity" (Scott 3; Stanley, "Christian Missions" 11).[8]

The result was an Enlightenment-influenced ethos of Protestantism, which encouraged the modern missionary movement to modify "long-established Christian patterns of thinking about the Christian encounter with non-Christian faiths and cultures" (Stanley, "Christian Missions" 8).[9] The primary upshots of this modification were (1) missionaries' insistence—one unmatched by "predecessors in Christian history"—"on the fundamental unity of humanity as a foundational principle in biblical teaching" and (2) their "immense confidence in the elevating and illuminating capacity of knowledge and rational

---

Pietism. For more on Pietism's influence on the cosmopolitanism of the German Enlightenment writer Christoph Martin Wieland, see chapter 3.

8. Scott reminds us of Eric Stokes's claim that "utilitarianism and Evangelicalism were both 'movements of individualism' that sought 'to liberate the individual from the slavery of custom and from the tyranny of the noble and the priest'" (qtd. in Scott 10). But Scott notes the contradiction that attends this "liberal ideal" of the autonomous subject. "Only insofar as the liberal subject can lay claim to a position of abstract generality [can it] serve as the conceptual basis of the modern state," he observes. But "in assuming a position of generality, any given subject necessarily renounces a portion of its lived particularity" (10). Enlightenment cosmopolitanism is structured around a similar tension. It has a tendency to stress individual freedom (particularly from national traditions and customs) while nevertheless implying such individuality matters little, as all humanity is intrinsically unified and equal once the surface of "culture" is scratched away. I discuss these themes further in chapter 4.

9. According to Stanley, the following are the five main features of the missionary movement: (1) "an almost universal belief that non-Western peoples were 'heathens' . . . in need of salvation"; (2) "a parallel tendency to dismiss other religious systems either as 'heathen idolatry' or as at best superstitions and not religions at all"; (3) "a belief in the manifest superiority and liberating potential of Western 'civilization'"; (4) "an unshakeable confidence in the regenerative capacity of rational knowledge, always provided this was linked to Christian proclamation"; and (5) "an assumption that the Christian message was addressed principally to individuals, calling them to undergo a conscious and identifiable inner experience of personal 'conversion'" ("*Christian Missions*" 8). These features cannot be attributed to Enlightenment thinking, of course. However, the particular manner by which modern missionary societies *enacted* such convictions can be "partially, or in some instances even wholly" attributed to the intellectual milieu of the Enlightenment (8).

argument" (11, 12).[10] Fascinatingly, the unprecedented stress placed by missionary societies on these "Enlightenment" values attracted rather than alienated a startling breadth of supporters, as societies eventually found contributors and recruits not only among working-class religious "enthusiasts" but also deistic rationalists—a phenomenon I explore in chapter 2 (Walls, "Eighteenth-Century" 39). In these ways, as Stanley notes, the missionary movement troubles the assumption that the resurgence of evangelical Christianity at the turn of the century represented but "an enthusiastic, heartwarming, and experiential reaction against the aridity and skepticism of the Age of Reason" ("Christian Missions" 2).

The "modern" ethos among missionary societies manifested itself in one especially key way: namely, in the remarkable interdenominational cooperation among the newly established foreign missionary societies.[11] Leading members of the BMS were connected to "Anglicans such as John Venn, Thomas Scott, and John Newton" by "family ties, personal friendships and correspondence and geographical proximity" (Porter, *Religion* 40), and William Carey, the renowned BMS missionary often credited with jump-starting the modern missionary movement, found that "of all the publicists in the United Kingdom during [his] long career the foremost was William Wilberforce" (the prominent politician and Clapham Sect member, who himself was profoundly influenced by the evangelical spirit of nonconformity) (G. Smith, *The Life* 343). Moreover, despite its Congregationalist leanings, the LMS saw itself as reflecting a newly emergent, religiously tolerant attitude that all members of the Reformed church were "bound together in an 'imagined com-

---

10. Hence the missionary propensity for establishing schools, colleges, and hospitals in the fields where they worked. Hence, too, the profound dedication to education *for* missionaries (Stanley, "*Christian Missions*" 17-19). Indeed, one need only look to the two most prominent missionary academies—the one in Gosport, run by the LMS director Rev. David Bogue, and the other, by Johannes Jänicke in Berlin, which was modeled after Bogue's and which trained LMS and CMS missionaries—to see this emphasis on rigorous education (Herppich 58-59). The curricula covered "reading, writing, arithmetic, basic sciences," and "English, Latin, Greek, Hebrew, Systeatic Theology, writing sermons, music, and drawing" (59).

11. It is important to note that the SPCK, founded in 1698, also embraced a "Protestant internationalism" that sought to downplay denominational differences (Carté Engel 81-84). But despite SPCK membership including some Dissenters domestically (such as the Unitarian Theophilus Lindsey), the evangelical movement in England before the 1790s mainly "stayed within the national Church, though often acting in considerable independence of it" (Neill 214). The mission societies of the modern missionary movement, by contrast, were composed of Dissenters *and* Church evangelicals. With the LMS leading the way, many of these mission societies made nondenominationalism a foundational principle of mission societies, thus formalizing the ecumenicalism displayed by the SPCK in the eighteenth century. It is in this capacity that the "interdenominational or undenominational missionary society" represented a "new phenomenon of the nineteenth century" (214).

munity' of shared Protestantism" (Elbourne 34). So vital was this sentiment to the LMS that it was restated in no subtle terms in several LMS publications and speeches. Thus the opening of Williams's bestselling *Narrative of Missionary Enterprises* declares, "As the union of Christians of various denominations, in carrying on this great work, is a most desirable object, so to prevent, if possible, any cause of future dissensions, it is declared to be a *fundamental principle* of the Missionary Society" (i). And, in a 1795 sermon celebrating the founding of the LMS, Rev. David Bogue—a leading figure in the missionary movement—praised the confederation of Protestant denominations as "the funeral of bigotry. . . . And may she be buried so deep that not a particle of her dust may ever be thrown upon the face of the earth" ("Objections" 181). Indeed, the first board of directors of the LMS reflected this dedication to nondenominationalism, with members hailing from Independency (Congregationalism), Methodism, Anglicanism, and others.

When one considers the antipathy regularly exhibited between Dissenters and the Church of England in the eighteenth century,[12] it might seem surprising that the Anglican CMS followed the lead of the LMS and BMS in championing nondenominationalism. In an 1801 sermon preached at St. Andrews parish, the CMS stated its intention to adhere to the "regular constitution of the Church of England" ("A Sermon" 8). Yet it also announced that it wished to cooperate fully with other denominations. "Let not this Society be considered, as opposing any that are engaged in the same excellent purpose," the CMS stated. "From the very constitution of the human mind, slighter differences of opinion will prevail, and diversities in external forms; but, in the grand design of promoting Christianity, all these should disappear. Let there be cordial union amongst all Christians, in promoting the common salvation of their Lord and Saviour" (13). In line with these sentiments, the CMS endorsed a multi-denominational reading list for prospective missionaries (which even included an account of Jesuitical missions)[13] and recruited its first two missionaries, Melchior Renner and Peter Hartwig, based on the recommendations of the LMS.[14]

---

12. Such antagonism was enshrined in the eighteenth-century cultural memory of the English Civil War. Therefore "across eighteenth-century England," notes John Seed, "Dissenters continued to carry the stigma of regicide ancestors," which led to the creation of anti-Dissenting legislation such as the Test and Corporations Act, the Occasional Conformity Act (1711), and the Schism Act (1714) (3, 6).

13. The CMS deemed "useful for the purpose of the Society" works including *Moravian Periodical Accounts, Baptist Periodical Accounts*, the *Missionary Magazine*, and *Jesuits Missions in Paraguay* ("Minutes Nov 4th, 1799").

14. The history of cooperation between the CMS and LMS is downplayed in Eugene Stock's *History of the Church Missionary Society* (1899). Thus Stock neglects to mention that

In part, economic considerations help explain this denominationally tolerant attitude. As Anna Johnston notes, "Missionary societies were very expensive and relied heavily upon donations from British congregations, so nascent mission societies appear to have assessed the difficulties of competing for funds as well as souls" (15). Yet financial exigency alone cannot fully account for moments when, for instance, the CMS donated funds to the LMS to help the latter cope with the disaster of losing its missionary ship, the *Duff,* to French pirates off the Brazilian coast ("Minutes August 5th, 1799"). Evidence suggests that we would be remiss to take the missionary societies' interdenominational cooperation as anything less than a structuring principle of the movement as a whole.

The dedication to interdenominational cooperation instead can be traced with reference to a broader Dissenting culture that was deeply intertwined with humanist discourses of the Enlightenment—a history of interaction that also provides a starting point for explaining the missionary attraction to cosmopolitan ideas. No doubt this history will be familiar to some. In the eighteenth century, the marginalization experienced by Dissenting Christians, particularly their legal exclusion from political and civic institutions, fed a religious revivalism that saw itself as a natural extension of the political and social insights of Enlightenment philosophers (Elbourne 12). Dissent thus cast religion as an "ideology of liberation rather than one of repression," one "naturally and increasingly appropriate to a civil order grounded in the preservation of individual liberties central to constitutional history: protection of private property, habeas corpus, trial by jury, freedom of election, and liberty of the press" (Ryan qtd. in White, *Early* 3; White, *Early* 20). Freedom of conscience in particular composed "the true spirit of the modern British nation," and these Dissenters (and not the aristocratic holdovers of the ancien régime) were the ones who were "perfectly rational," "naturally middle-class, anti-establishmentarian . . . mercantilist and abolitionist, and dedicated to the causes of 'Liberty' throughout Europe" (79, 61, 79). Notions of "inalienable rights" and "civil liberties" as the foundations of *all* just states became, in short, an "Enlightened" means to argue for governmental and cultural recognition of the legitimacy of non-Church faith. So effective was this rhetoric of

---

the minutes of a CMS meeting contain the following interesting instance of intersocietal cooperation: "The Secretary Reported that he had received a letter from Joseph Hardcastle Esq. [of the LMS] assuring the Committee of the cordial concurrence of the London Missionary Society with the views of this Committee; and mentioning two young men, in the Society at Berlin, are now ready to be sent out as Missionaries, of whom a very good account is given; who might be engaged by this Society; but if it declined to employ them, the London Missionary Society intended to do" ("Minutes May 4th, 1802").

rights, reason, and liberation that it found a number of sympathizers, including among Church of England clergymen.

To put this in a slightly different way, the acclamation of religious non-denominationalism among influential Dissenters found its political analogue in the liberalism of the eighteenth century. In the view of these Dissenters, *any* form of authoritarianism—whether taking the form of Catholicism, state-enforced religious belief, or unchecked monarchism—was to be denounced. Feeling themselves "a foreign group in the nation [and] aliens among their fellow countrymen," they became "dedicated to freedom of inquiry and the welfare of mankind . . . disposed to challenge undue or usurped authority" (Schlereth 130). We see the Dissenting disposition displayed in the writings of those such as the Unitarian Richard Price, who wrote in his *Observations on the Nature of Civil Liberty* (1776),[15]

> Let every state, with respect to all its internal concerns, be continued independent of all the rest; and let a general confederacy be formed by the appointment of a SENATE consisting of Representatives from all the different states. Let this SENATE possess the power of managing all the common concerns of the united states, and of judging and deciding between them, as a common Arbiter or Umpire, in all disputes; having, at the same time, under its direction, the common force of the states to support its decisions.—In these circumstances, each separate state would be secure against the interference of foreign power in its private concerns, and, therefore, would possess Liberty; and at the same time it would be secure against all oppression and insult from every neighbouring state.—Thus might the scattered force and abilities of a whole continent be gathered into one point; all litigations settled as they rose; universal peace preserved; and nation prevented from any more lifting up a sword against nation. (7)

Though the most radical of the Dissenters in their political leanings and controversial espousal of Socinianism, the Unitarians were hardly the only Dissenting denomination to see liberalism as corresponding with religious tolerance. The Particular Baptist Robert Robinson deprecated "religious uniformity [to be] an illegitimate brat of the mother of harlots," and compared the various Protestant denominations to "so many little states, each governed by its own laws, and all independent on [sic] one another. Like confederate states they assembled by deputies in one large ecclesiastical body, and deliberated about the common interests of the whole" (qtd. in White, *Early* 7). In this

---

15. My gratitude to Dan White for alerting me to this passage years ago.

sense, freedom of conscience and interdenominational cooperation translated into a set of political values that tended to valorize liberty, rationality, freedom of conscience and expression, as well as individual and national self-determination within a broader scheme of federation.

As I discuss in chapter 1, this political vein of Dissent profoundly influenced the modern missionary movement. For instance, the aforementioned LMS director, David Bogue, exemplified the Dissenting predilection to see "political liberty [as] inseparable from the freedom of conscience" (White, *Early* 20–21). Under the banner of these values, then, early nineteenth-century missionary societies and their supporters banded together to advance shared moral, spiritual, and pragmatic interests. As Penny Carson observes in regard to the 1813 evangelical campaign to allow missionary work among native Indian populations, "Many of the petitions [to Parliament] used the language of 'the rights of man' and came from 'the friends of religious liberty' who demanded 'the liberty to transmit our faith'" ("The British Raj" 67). Drawing from the political discourse of Dissent, the missionary supporter and later missionary Rev. Robert Burns thus framed missionary work as part of the larger Christian project to "secur[e] the essential rights and liberties of mankind" (qtd. in A. Johnston 16). No wonder that the *History of the London Missionary Society* (1899), looking back at this period, could proclaim with such confidence, "The great vice of all missionary institutions, in the eyes of the colonists, was that they enabled the Hottentot to learn that, as a human being, he had rights; they taught him to claim these rights" (qtd. in Rutz, *British* 1).

Later in the nineteenth century, these values would be channeled into missionary support for laissez-faire economics. Not only did global free trade seem the economic corollary of individual liberty; it was also portrayed, with ever increasing frequency, as part of the (nondenominational) providential plan to achieve global Christianity. Thus figures such as Thomas Chalmers, the Scottish evangelical and missionary society supporter, would vociferously argue that "Barriers to Free Trade . . . not only offended the unprivileged, but were elements of friction obscuring God's clockwork providence" (qtd. in Hilton 69), and periodicals such as *The Baptist Reporter and Missionary Intelligencer* would imply commerce to be almost as efficacious as Christianity itself in the task of securing freedom and banishing social evils: "We regard Free Trade as a question of the first importance to mankind, exceeded only by the glorious gospel of the blessed Lord. . . . [W]ar and slavery, the twin curses of the earth, will vanish before the spirit of equitable and friendly commerce" ("What Else Doth Hinder?" [1846] 153, 155). This union between Christian humanism and global commerce would reach its apotheosis in the 1850s with the Great Exhibition and the celebrity of the LMS missionary and explorer David Livingstone, who famously declared, "Those two pioneers of civilization—Christianity and commerce—should ever be inseparable" (165).[16] Such was the ideological foundation of the missionary movement.[17]

In these ways, the missionary societies of the late eighteenth and early nineteenth centuries positioned themselves as "modern." No doubt a degree of self-interest inspired missionary societies to style themselves as rational, as they needed to distance themselves from the uncouth enthusiasm associated with other strands of religious revivalism in order to gain and sustain support from those more aligned with the Church establishment.[18] However, these practical considerations do not diminish the earnestness with which missionary societies saw themselves as participating in a tradition of Protestantism that emphasized individual freedom and thus converged with the egalitarian politics espoused by Enlightenment thought (White, *Early* 19; Stanley, "Christian Missions" 12).

Moreover, as I will go on to show, the values that came to the fore in the modern missionary movement—the faith in the universality of reason, the belief in the equality and independence of all men and thus the inalienability of each man's civil rights, and the striving toward both religious *and* political federalism as a means of preserving individual freedom in an overarching governmental structure—strongly corresponded to attributes of Enlightenment cosmopolitanism. This is the basic groundwork for understanding the key characteristics that govern my own (but by no means unique) use of the phrase "modern missionary movement."

---

16. I discuss the mid-century enthusiasm for free trade and missionary philanthropy a bit more in chapter 1. My work in progress on David Livingstone's *Missionary Travels and Researches in South Africa* (1859) also details this history.

17. As shown in the examples above and in the following chapters, missionary debates reached a broader public in various and disparate ways, including by reviews of missionary narratives in nonevangelical periodicals, Parliamentary debates, satires, and commentary by prominent literary figures, as well as through official missionary publications.

18. In his discussion of Sidmouth's 1811 bill to regulate the licensing of Nonconformist preachers, Rutz notes that there was a growing sense among the Church establishment and its sympathizers that the "new kind of preacher [was] 'less well educated than the older sort of Dissenting minister' and . . . was usually associated with the Methodists or evangelical congregations among the Independents and Baptists" (*British* 32). I discuss the strategies of missionary societies to distance themselves from this "enthusiasm" at greater length in chapter 2.

The "Imperialist Mentality"

In order to explain "cosmopolitanism" as the conceptual framing for a book about missionaries, I first want to give an overview of the intellectual and argumentative threads that unite the body of historical and anthropological research on missionary work. Generally these studies have moved "beyond [the] dichotomy of agents of empire or Christian humanitarians" in their treatment of missionaries, recognizing the inadequacy of such a narrative in capturing the complexity of missionary history (Rutz, *British* 5). Hilary Carey, for one, notes that while the missionaries and British imperialists both considered the "gospel [as] the source of England's power," there also "was an important theological tradition that considered all empires to be tainted with a burden of sin, if not actually evil," which at times put missionaries as well as native and colonial churches at odds with the policies of the British government (6). Similarly, Keane acknowledges that while "colonial power was . . . a necessary condition for the missionary project," we nonetheless "miss something crucial" if we dismiss native claims to Christian belief as "only the effects of colonialism," or ignore the degree to which missionaries "ruled out many possible strategies [for conversion] that they saw as reliant on external pressure" (8). In this manner, anthropologists such as John L. Comaroff and Jean Comaroff and historians including Catherine Hall, Jeffrey Cox, Elizabeth Elbourne, Brian Stanley, and Esme Cleall have charted missionaries' complicated, often conflicting, attitudes toward the British Empire. As Cox writes, "The Empire of Christ could never be identified with the Empire of Britain in the long run, for the Empire of Christ was a multiracial, multinational empire that not only transcended the provisional (if providential) boundaries of the British Empire, but transcended the boundaries of time itself" (*British* 14).

Yet the field of literary studies has yet to grapple fully with the implications of these studies. Indeed, missionary writing has commanded attention among literary scholars mostly insofar as it can be shown to accord with the "imperialist mentality" (Christopher Herbert's term for the postcolonialist dispensation to see all "the mechanisms of imperialist society, political, cultural, psychological [as] work[ing] in concert to reinforce and rationalize domination" [*War* 5]).[19] Consider, for instance, Bruce Robbins's brief mention of

---

19. There are important exceptions. The chapter on missionaries in Vanessa Smith's *Literary Culture and the Pacific* stands out, as does Herbert's discussion of missionary ethnography in *Culture and Anomie*. More recently, a focus on the material networks of exchange established and sustained by missionaries, in chapter 2 of White's *From Little London to Little Bengal* (2013) and Madsen's 2018 NAVSA conference paper, yields new understandings of how objects such as idols and dead bodies were de- or resacralized in the British imagination by virtue of

missionary Christianity in his afterword for a special issue of *Romantic Circles* dedicated to "Secularism, Cosmopolitanism, and Romanticism." Taking issue with Colin Jager's argument that "global Christianity" represents a non-normative cosmopolitanism capable of countering a distinctly Western (and sometimes oppressive) "ideology" of secularism, Robbins specifically points to missionary Christianity as a sort of critical checkmate to Jager's argument: "Christian missionaries, once assumed to be agents of empire, are here made over into spokespersons for the world's grievances against Europe's secular rationality and its supposedly imperial designs" ("Afterword"). Yet Robbins's assertion reveals less the weaknesses of Jager's critique of secularism than it does our tendency to equate missionary work reflexively with "Eurocentric arrogance," in Robbins's words. Missionary Christianity could not *possibly* be cosmopolitan, because *we all know* that missionaries were but bad-faith agents of Western imperialism.

We see a similar set of assumptions at work in Patrick Brantlinger's *Taming Cannibals* (2011), which proposes to "investigate the intricate and often contradictory connections between abolitionism and liberalism on the one hand, and imperialism and racism on the other" (1). In his chapter on missionary writing from the South Sea Islands, he acknowledges, "Missionaries to the South Pacific were . . . often fearless defenders of the indigenous peoples they encountered, even those they held to be cannibals, against nonmissionary colonizers. And some of them wrote detailed, surprisingly sympathetic accounts of the cultures of those they sought to convert" (33). However, Brantlinger ultimately subsumes missionaries' complicated and often ambivalent reactions to cultural alterity into a narrative of missionaries' complicity in the construction of racism and the civilizing mission. For instance, he observes that the LMS missionaries Thomas Williams and Joseph Waterhouse "rarely denigrate the Fijians in terms that we would today identify as racist" (38). But rather than interrogating this rather remarkable absence of racist sentiment, he immediately dismisses the phenomenon, opining, "Perhaps this was because of the theory that many South Sea Islanders were an ancient branch of the Aryan race" (38). Transfiguring a lack of racism into direct evidence for missionary racism, Brantlinger implies that these missionaries were indeed racist in exactly those "terms we would today identify as racist."[20]

---

missionary efforts—readings that complicate assumptions that missionaries were always complicit in the consolidation of imperial power.

20. I'm indebted to Beverly Lyon Clark for reminding me that in the nineteenth century, Fijians were considered culturally Polynesian but physically Melanesian. Thus, if Brantlinger were right, Williams and Waterhouse would be attributing Aryan qualities to people who—in the view of Europeans at the time—would physically resemble, say, black Africans.

To critique such lines of scholarly reasoning is not to say that missionaries did not act, consciously or not, as imperial functionaries, nor is it to allege that missionaries did not hold profoundly racist views. It is to say, however, that there exist other contexts by which literary studies can interpret missionary writing, contexts that highlight rather than diminish the disconnect between missionaries' earnest (and, as I discuss later in this chapter, sometimes even radical) plans to realize cosmopolitan ideals and their simultaneous participation in imperial practice. After all, many missionaries did not feel themselves beholden to the British Empire per se. Rather, the central question that galvanized their work in the early to mid-century was, "Can we participate in a shared faith, on the basis of spiritual equality, in an imperial setting?" (Cox, *Imperial* 16). A "cosmopolitan" rather than an "imperial" framework is fitting, then, because it expresses a tension intrinsic to the missionary endeavor wherein evangelicals' practical cooperation with British imperialism was always potentially compromised by what they felt to be their higher allegiance to the transcendent Kingdom of God. In light of this tension, as well as missionaries' engagement with Enlightenment ideas and rhetoric, it perhaps isn't entirely surprising that missionaries and missionary society directors called themselves "citizens of the world," "cosmopolites," and key actors in the project to realize global human solidarity.

Cosmopolitanism

More surprising instead is the extent to which literary scholars have downplayed the influence of mainstream religion and religious movements on nineteenth-century cosmopolitanism. More or less, these studies seem guided by the understanding that cosmopolitanism was effectively secularized during the Enlightenment, that "cosmopolitanism and secularism are historical fellow-travelers," to use Jager's wry summation of this line of thought ("Introduction"). What *had* been the universalism of primitive Christianity was now in its instantiation as Enlightenment "cosmopolitanism" an ideal of global cooperation founded on nature and reason rather than faith, one established firmly within the "immanent frame" of lived experience and natural law without reference to a transcendent Creator beyond.[21]

---

21. For instance, Kant's "Idea for a Universal History with a Cosmopolitan Purpose" left out references to "God" or a divine creator, relying instead on the "course intended by nature" to sketch out its plan for global peace. Examples such as this undergird Schlereth's understanding of "universalism" versus "cosmopolitanism." For Schlereth, the former is "a distinct theological

To illustrate my meaning, I want to give a brief account of what has been widely called the "cosmopolitan turn" in literary scholarship. Often credited with reviving critical interest in cosmopolitanism is Martha Nussbaum's essay in *For Love of Country?* (1996), which argued that the Enlightenment ideal provides a template for an ethical universalism, one, she contends, that ought to be cultivated to respond to the unprecedentedly globalized problems facing the world today. The revival of "cosmopolitanism" inaugurated by Nussbaum subsequently provoked skeptical reactions, such as Brennan's *At Home in the World: Cosmopolitanism, Now* (1997), a work that denounced the scholarly deployment of "cosmopolitanism" as American cultural imperialism under the guise of an ostensibly universalist ethics. The essays represented in Pheng Cheah and Bruce Robbins's edited volume *Cosmopolitics: Thinking and Feeling Beyond the Nation* (1998) came about as a collective attempt to recuperate the term from its associations with suspect universalisms such as those identified by Brennan. The "new cosmopolitanisms," as they were called, distanced themselves from the elite "view from above" (which, as Robbins notes, often proved only a "reassertion" of the centrality of Western Enlightenment values) in favor of renewed attention to cultural situatedness. These early landmark contributions thus all grappled with the same problem: how, in the words of Kwame Anthony Appiah, to balance "universal concern and respect for legitimate difference" (xv).

Nineteenth-century literary studies, in turn, responded to this question by examining Romantic and Victorian notions of "cosmopolitanism." Galvanizing this effort was Amanda Anderson's call for a "rigorous genealogy of cosmopolitanism," which she posited would contribute "more calibrated analyses of the history of universalism, rendering reductive oppositions between modernity and countermodernity obsolete by bringing into sharp relief modernity's own divided histories" ("Cosmopolitanism" 71). Accounts of "actually existing cosmopolitanisms" subsequently flourished in nineteenth-century studies.[22] Amanda Anderson's own *Powers of Distance: Cosmopolitanism and the Cultivation of Detachment* (2001) perhaps stands as one of the most prominent progenitors and enduring examples of this scholarship. Tracing "the cultivation of detachment as a structure of feeling, as a lived relation" to the "estranging, impersonal practices" of an emergent modernity (*Powers* 178), it provoked

---

doctrine," whereas the latter, "ambivalent . . . toward the authority of the divided church," finds strength instead "in identifying with antiquity's cosmopolites" (xii, xxiii).

22. Robbins defines "actually existing cosmopolitanisms" as those "habits of thought and feeling that have already shaped and been shaped by particular collectivities, that are both socially and geographically situated" ("Introduction" 2).

widespread interest in cosmopolitan discursive formations in the Romantic and Victorian periods.[23]

A number of fascinating studies came out of this flurry of scholarship. In *Romantic Cosmopolitanism* (2009), for instance, Esther Wohlgemut reevaluated the relationship of "cosmopolitanism" to its supposed antithesis, "nationalism." For many Romantic writers, she argued, cosmopolitanism emerged as a hotly contested "non-unified formulation of nationness" that provided a more expansive alternative to Burke's notions of nationality as founded in "unified" formulations of history, blood, and geography (3). Considering "cosmopolitanism" as it appeared in the writings of Kant, Edmund Burke, Madame de Staël, Byron, and others, she demonstrated how the Enlightenment idea—far from being opposed to nationalism—in fact helped articulate the idea of "Britain" in a rapidly globalizing world. Two years later, Agathocleous's contribution, *Urban Realism and the Cosmopolitan Imagination in the Nineteenth Century,* looked to extend the study of nineteenth-century cosmopolitanism in two directions: first, in terms of the historicity of "cosmopolitanism" (as a word "used frequently by Victorians" [*Urban Realism* 2]) and second, as a formal technique. She thus considered "cosmopolitanism" as it appeared in Victorian periodicals, pamphlets, and a recipe book, among others, to demonstrate that cosmopolitan discourses brought into view a profound connection between the "visible" city of international London and the "invisible" larger world. Victorian authors, she contended, capitalized on this relationship, using the technique of "cosmopolitan realism" to slide in perspective from "city to world and back again" as a means of shaping "a new global consciousness" ("Cosmopolitanism" 458).[24]

But instead of historicizing "actually existing cosmopolitanisms" further, scholars have tended to concentrate on the second proposition offered by Agathocleous, that is, to consider "cosmopolitanism" as a formal technique.[25]

---

23. This interest was evinced, for example, in the 2004 NASSR conference on "Romantic Cosmopolitanism," as well as special issues dedicated to the concept in *European Romantic Review* (2005) and *Victorian Literature and Culture* (2010).

24. Goodlad's *The Victorian Geopolitical Aesthetic* (2015) similarly focuses on form in asking "how realist fiction altered in its multiple efforts to craft aesthetic forms receptive to the dynamism of a fast-globalizing world" (2).

25. More specifically, rather than considering cosmopolitanism as a term that circulated within nineteenth-century discursive networks, scholars tend to focus on cosmopolitan *forms* evinced in nineteenth-century literature, drawing their understanding of cosmopolitanism from contemporary rather than historical debates. Thus Keirstead understands Victorian poetry, insofar as it explores universalist thinking and critical self-reflection, as "anticipat[ing] how theorists of cosmopolitanism today . . . have sought to temper the concept's former adherence to universalistic thinking and give it new purchase as a guide for individual and national conduct" (*Victorian Poetry* 4). His explicit aim, then, is "to test the applicability of [new] cos-

One suspects this is a development in part brought about by recent skepticism of the so-called positivist historicism that some feel have dominated nineteenth-century studies for too long. But contributing more significantly to this attention to form (over literary history), I think, have been assertions such as Lauren Goodlad and Julia Wright's that "literary histories of cosmopolitanism . . . may offer a somewhat finite critical project, one compelled to predict the foundering of the ethical aspirations it describes," or Agathocleous's own warning that historical studies on the topic "risk falling into a familiar subversion/containment pattern of argumentation, given the predictability of cosmopolitanism's limitations and failures" (qtd. in Agathocleous, "Cosmopolitanism" 453; 453). Such statements certainly were intended to diagnose a problem with literary histories of cosmopolitanisms, insofar as these studies haven't yielded any ethically feasible means of squaring the aspiration toward human unity with respect for irreducible particularity. Yet they also seem to have discouraged the very line of "genealogical" research called for by Anderson, as literary studies seems to have turned away from the project of historicizing cosmopolitanism, perhaps seeing it as a spent line of inquiry.

As a result, nineteenth-century literary studies has left us with an oddly monolithic understanding of cosmopolitanism's genealogy, a development that seems all the more strange in light of many of these same scholars' assertions that cosmopolitanism is necessarily "plural" in its manifestations. To use Agathocleous's summary, these accounts of cosmopolitanism tend to follow the same narrative. They "start with Kant's Enlightenment ideal of perpetual peace, explore Victorian associations of the term with the globalization of capital . . . , foreground modernist depictions of the cosmopolitan exile, and conclude with the current day, where all its varied historical connotations vie for prominence" ("Cosmopolitanism" 454). The authority of this story has found support in Lauren Goodlad's contention that "from a mid-Victorian perspective, the word 'cosmopolitanism' was more likely to evoke the structures of capitalism and colonial expansion than an ethos of tolerance, world citizenship, or multiculturalism" (*Victorian Geopolitical* 23). This argument, regularly advanced by way of John Stuart Mill's pronouncement that "capital is becoming more and more cosmopolitan" and some of the writings of Karl Marx, has meant that the most prominent studies of cosmopolitanism and nineteenth-century literature have focused on the "clash between Victorian liberalism and imperialism, and the modern postcolonial aftermath of that

---

mopolitan interpretive frameworks to the period" (5). The effort to apply contemporary understandings of cosmopolitanism to instances of internationalism in nineteenth-century literary form is evinced in a host of other essays, too (see, e.g., Albrecht; Bonfiglio; and Kurnick).

clash"—in other words, on mostly the *secular* ideas and institutions involved in globalization rather than the overtly religious ones ("Cosmopolitanism" 456–57; see also Agathocleous, *Urban Realism* 2; Goodlad and Wright).[26]

Even Agathocleous, who brilliantly examines the intersection of Christian philanthropic efforts and cosmopolitan perspectives in the late nineteenth century, somewhat deemphasizes the role of Christian movements in shaping the cosmopolitan imagination of the Romantic and Victorian eras. Here, cosmopolitanism, "alongside nationalism and socialism," is identified as one of "modernity's great sublimations of religion" rather than as a concept significantly mediated by Christian institutions and movements (*Urban Realism* 18).[27] Similarly, Michael Scrivener, who focuses mostly on how second-generation Romantics took up Kantian cosmopolitanism as a means of challenging narrow-minded nationalism, depicts today's "extreme versions of the religious revival, international in scope," as "challeng[ing] the very basis of the Enlightenment [cosmopolitan] project and seek[ing] to undo modernity" (10).

Other studies that do examine cosmopolitan sentiment and religious feeling have excluded British religious movements and institutions as participants in defining or enacting various forms of post-Enlightenment cosmopolitanism.[28] In this vein, Keirstead finds in Browning's "Cleon" and "Karshish" a

---

26. Many of the "new cosmopolitanisms" as explored in disciplines such as anthropology and sociology evince similar concerns, some even positing mutual exclusivity between cosmopolitanism and religion. Take, for instance, the sociologist Anthony Smith's observation that the "timeless global culture" animating some theories of cosmopolitanism is ultimately inadequate and unrealistic when one considers "the masses of peoples divided into their habitual communities of *class, gender, region, religion, and culture*" (24). Here, Smith reveals one of the tacit biases of contemporary cosmopolitan theory in considering religion as a form of localized "community." Or, alternately one can look at Vertovec and Cohen's influential articulation of why "the processes and conditions" of the present "have led to a call to conceive cosmopolitanism afresh": "Secular protests against corporate-led globalization . . . as well as the excesses displayed and atrocities committed by those who evince narrow religious and ethnic identities, have led to the urgent reposing of two basic cosmopolitan questions: Can we ever live peacefully with one another? What do we share, collectively, as human beings?" (1). The implicit suggestion is that cosmopolitanism is in fundamental tension with localized and divisive "religious identities." Religion is regarded not as a site of cosmopolitan thought in its own right, but instead as one of the numerous forms of particularized belonging in need of management by larger and more "rational" cosmopolitan structures (for more on this phenomenon, see Lecourt, *Cultivating* 15–16). Conversely, cosmopolitanism is imagined, as Calhoun observes, "as a sort of escape from culture into a realm of reason where religion has little influence" ("Secularism" 76).

27. Agathocleous's pronouncement regarding religion's "sublimation" in the more "modern" forms of nationalism, socialism, and cosmopolitanism brings to mind Mendieta's important observation that "one of the fundamental myths of modernity was its promise to abolish religion by sublimating it. . . . This myth went by the name of secularization" (46).

28. By "post-Enlightenment," I follow the usage of scholars such as Charles LaPorte to designate that period of time after the Enlightenment rather than referring to postmodernity.

"kind of Christian cosmopolitanism that is not exclusively or dogmatically Christian," while Sebastian Lecourt identifies an important locus of cosmopolitan feeling in the writing of nineteenth-century crisis-of-faith writers (Keirstead, "Cosmopolitan" 8; Lecourt, "Matthew Arnold").[29] But what such arguments imply is that cosmopolitan discourse was not quite the domain of mainstream religion; rather, it belonged to those at the margins of institutionalized religion, those who were questioning the tenets and foundations of their faith rather than embracing its "dogma." Such accounts, I submit, invite us to broaden rather than bridge the divide between cosmopolitanism and institutionalized religion, to see the two as antipoles rather than close associates. Yet the missionary movement—indisputably in the religious mainstream by the mid-century and hardly the site of profound doubt—explicitly participated in defining and enacting various forms of cosmopolitanism.

My argument, then, comes down to this: Due to the general critical presumption that cosmopolitanism has never been, could never be, part of religion "proper," the obvious has remained hidden in plain sight. Always mediating nineteenth-century cosmopolitanism was the inescapable fact of nineteenth-century religious culture. In this sense, this book joins the chorus of those reassessments of religion's impact on nineteenth-century literature in correcting the assumption that the evangelical movement was but a "narrow, limited, and . . . spent force by the mid-1830s," a convulsive and last-ditch effort to counter the receding importance of religious institutions in social and political life (Knight and Mason 121). It also offers, I hope, something more. Bearing in mind Boyd Hilton's observation that "before 1850 . . . religious feeling and biblical terminology so permeated *all* aspects of thought (including atheism), that it is hard to dismiss them as epiphenomenal" (ix), it shows that the genealogy of cosmopolitanism in the post-Enlightenment era must be traced with reference to the history of missionary and evangelical Christianity as much as to the histories of nationalism, capitalism, and imperialism.

Focusing less on the history of missionaries' cross-cultural engagement (a topic on which many excellent works have already been written) to attend instead to the fluid meanings of "cosmopolitanism" vis-à-vis the mission-

---

29. Keirstead makes a similar argument about both Brownings in saying that they "pushed for a broadly ecumenical, nondogmatic form of Christian cosmopolitanism" (*Victorian Poetry* 14). However, he distinguishes Elizabeth Barrett Browning's religiosity from Robert's in briefly noting her "efforts might be more closely aligned . . . with the religious cosmopolitanism that arose in conjunction with Enlightenment rationalism but has since fallen off our historical radar due to the same 'Enlightenment metanarrative which proclaims the birth of modernity in the decline of religion'" (21). Thus what Keirstead mentions in passing, I try to make my primary focus: the remarkable extent to which nineteenth-century religious cosmopolitanism was indebted to and fueled by Enlightenment rationalism.

ary movement, such a genealogy reveals previously unexamined ways that the interplay of Christian responsibility and humanist universalism contributed to various "new cosmopolitanisms" appearing in the second half of the nineteenth century and onward.[30] It complements recent studies on fin-de-siècle "spiritual cosmopolitanisms,"[31] for instance, providing something of a prehistory of shifting cosmopolitan sentiments among missionary societies in the early to mid-nineteenth century. By understanding how missionaries were compelled to recognize the irreducibility of cultural differences in their vision of a "universal humanity," we perhaps might better understand how some later missionaries, such as Charles Freer Andrews of the SPG (as Leela Gandhi discusses), would argue for a break between Christianity and European culture and eventually collaborate with Mohandas Gandhi for the cause of Indian nationalism.

In short, I propose that the example of the missionary movement helps us perceive the extent to which the histories of religion, imperialism, and cosmopolitanism entangled. As such, this book not only testifies to the plurality of cosmopolitan discourses that "actually existed" in the nineteenth century.

---

30. In part, I shied from making these encounters more explicit in this book not only because of the existence of a rich body of historical work on this topic but also because of my complicated feelings regarding my own family history as having been shaped by missionaries. That is, my sense of responsibility to representing these encounters is so profound and, to me, so overwhelming, I felt such an investigation must be left to its own study, which, as I imagine it, would span the mid-nineteenth to the late twentieth centuries. This may read as an excuse for not writing a more comprehensive book, but I explain my personal relationship to my research to account more fully for this book's framing.

31. Belonging to this cluster of studies is Aravamudan's *Guru English*, which argues that the self-consciously globalizing religious discourses of South Asia represent a "commodifiable cosmopolitanism" (that is, a religiosity tooled for global markets), and Gandhi's *Affective Communities*, which identifies an "affective cosmopolitanism" undergirding the cross-cultural bonds of British and South Asian anti-imperial dissidents. Joining such contributions is Agathocleous's recent essay on an "anti-Western 'spiritual cosmopolitanism'" that informs the syncretism of the periodical *East and West* ("The Coming Clash" 663). In these studies, "cosmopolitanism" is made central to understanding late nineteenth-century religion and spirituality, but it is also taken as a somewhat fixed term; "cosmopolitan" functions as the relatively stable adjective to describe the remarkable and often overlooked forms of collaboration, engagement, or dialogue between South Asian and British religious figures that (appear to) challenge stark binarisms of East and West, secular and religious. In other words, the understanding of cosmopolitanism governing these studies is the contemporary one, which identifies a cosmopolitan ethos as the retention of universalist aspirations while nevertheless respecting the particular and embedded (A. Anderson, *Powers* 73). Whatever instability is attached to "cosmopolitanism" in Aravamudan's, Gandhi's, and Agathocleous's accounts mostly originates in the conceptual slipperiness that attends today's theorizations (Agathocleous, "Cosmopolitanism" 453). In contrast, I hope to highlight the conceptual slipperiness of cosmopolitanism as it appeared in the nineteenth century.

It also stands to nuance and complicate the oddly homogenous genealogy ascribed to cosmopolitanism today.

Globalization, Religion, and Postsecular Studies

In sketching a series of cosmopolitan experiments undertaken by missionary societies and missionaries, I participate in the broader effort of postsecular studies to "read religion in rather than out of history" (M. Anderson, *Imagining* 237). This brings me to a secondary thesis of this book: If we fail to see the ways that nineteenth-century cosmopolitanism was negotiated in relation to an increasingly global Christianity, this isn't because the relationship didn't exist. Rather, as outlined above, it is because understandings of "religion" often are circumscribed by and defined in opposition to an often under-interrogated understanding of the "secular." The past quarter-century has witnessed an effort to correct this tendency. Nevertheless, we continue to see the repercussions of the "secularization narrative," which Eduardo Mendieta pithily summarizes as the presumption, "Where superstition and religion were, reason and science shall be" (46). As a number of scholars of secularism and "postsecularity" have noted, the most obvious of these repercussions has been a sort of entrenched assumption that the ruling structures or ideologies of our "modern" moment (i.e., capitalism, tolerance, rationality, universal rights, and, of course, cosmopolitanism) are not, could not be, essentially influenced by or entwined with religion. In such an account, "secularity" is not ideological but descriptive—it merely designates religion's absence. But, as Lori Branch notes, "To begin seeing secularism [as an ideology] would necessarily be also to see religion differently, since religion in modernity has been constituted by the logic of secularism" (96). The impulse in postsecular studies to view "religion" and "secularism" as mutually informing rather than mutually exclusive thus has been characterized by John Caputo and William Scanlon as the "pushing past the constraints of this old, methodologically constricted, less enlightened, strait and narrow Enlightenment, which found it necessary to cast 'reason' and 'religion' in mortal opposition" (2).

Informing my own approach in *Missionary Cosmopolitanism* is the postsecular resistance to the narrative of religion's inevitable decline, as already examined and explored in myriad ways by scholars hailing from history, religious studies, anthropology, sociology, and philosophy, as well as literary studies, including Talal Asad, José Casanova, Webb Keane, Christian Smith, Colin Jager, Regina Mara Schwartz, Charles Taylor, Sebastian Lecourt, and many others. Indeed, in my view, the phenomenon of "missionary cosmopolitanism" suggests not "a *decline* of those practices identified as 'religious,' but rather their *relocation*" (Kauffman 612). On a concrete, tangible level, we can see the "relocation" of these missionary practices today in their movement out of "official" Western state politics and formal church institutions, and into other public and still political entities, including charitable societies, Christian legal and political organizations, schools, hospitals, nongovernmental organizations (NGOs), and organizations such as the World Council of Churches (WCC), the Council for a Parliament of the World's Religions, or the Ecumenical Association of Third World Theologians (EATWOT) (see Hopkins 7–8). On a theoretical level, the persistence of religion in *all* public life the world over suggests that defining religion as the superstitious, parochial antagonist of rational, global, and historically inevitable secularism is something of a dead end. More promising is a reevaluation of religion as a politically and socially powerful "modern" force, which derives much of what makes it compelling from its role as that which simultaneously advances *and* interrogates globalization.[32]

Jacques Derrida's understanding of "religion" is useful here: "Religion today allies itself with tele-technoscience, to which it reacts with all its forces. It *is, on the one hand,* globalization; it produces, weds, exploits the capital and knowledge tele-mediazation . . . But, *on the other hand,* it reacts immediately, *simultaneously* declaring war against that which gives it this new power only at the cost of dislodging it from all its proper places, *in truth from place itself,* from the taking-place of its truth" (*Acts* 82). In other words, religion "is" and provides the basis for globalization. As Mendieta notes, "the rise of the state apparatus, its legal and constitutional norms, its principles of legitimation" that facilitated globalization "would have been unthinkable without the presence of religion in society" (60). The applicability of Mendieta's and Derrida's understandings of religion to nineteenth-century imperialism is obvious to scholars of the period; the language of Christian humanism and humanitarianism authorized and abetted the worst excesses of imperialism.

But "religion" is also the repudiation of much of what constitutes modern globalization, a keen wariness of the dehumanizing (and what Derrida also notes are the *desacralizing*) effects of global financial, technological, and polit-

---

32. In my use of "globalization," I follow Gottlieb in relying on those definitions laid out by Zygmunt Bauman ("Globalization refers to a multidimensional set of social processes that create, multiply, stretch, and intensify worldwide social interdependencies and exchanges while at the same time fostering in people a growing awareness of deepening connections between the local and the distant" [qtd. in Gottlieb 3]). These definitions reflect the fact that globalization is not just a contemporary phenomenon, but rather is rooted in the histories of the "world-changing technological and political revolutions" of the late eighteenth and nineteenth centuries (3–6).

ical structures. Hence his careful parsing of the English word "globalization" from the French term *mondialisation* in "Globalization, Peace, and Cosmopolitanism." Where "globalization" tends only to designate the ahistorical impersonal forces of "tele-technoscience," *mondialisation,* argues Derrida, does the supplementary work of invoking the historical dimensions of the idea of the "world," one that imagines the "*world* as [a] *fraternal* community of human beings, of fellow creatures, sons of God and neighbors to one another" ("Globalization" 374). And this historical understanding of the "world" "begins by designating, and tends to remain, in an Abrahamic tradition" (374–75). Thus the "Judeo-Christian-Islamic" tradition *is* "globalization," but it is also—as the French *mondialisation* suggests—the "bulwark against the largely inhuman 'techno-science' that, [Derrida] fears, appears increasingly to determine the course of contemporary globalization" (Gottlieb 10). Samir Haddad helpfully summarizes the relationship Derrida perceives between "globalization" and "religion":

> World religion needs technology to survive. At the same time, this necessity necessarily undermines their health. Derrida argues that religion, insofar as it aims at the purity of the unscathed, must simultaneously oppose itself to the repetition in technological reproduction. In their necessary mechanization, world religions touch the untouchable, corrupt the pure, and reduce the sacred to the profane. . . . Derrida's claim is that religions must die a little, in truth, *put themselves to death* a little, in order to keep themselves alive. (31)

Akin to Derrida's definition of "religion" as simultaneously inimical and complementary to modern forces of globalization, Mendieta observes that "religion"—as much as it gave rise to and fed these forces—also came to designate "what had been left behind, to bemoan what was lost, and to project on others what they had that we had overcome, or what they retained that might save us (the West)" (60). Taken together, Mendieta and Derrida highlight a constitutive aspect of "religion" that *Missionary Cosmopolitanism* echoes. In its capacity as a system of beliefs and practices comprising a god, faith, a theological anthropology, and revelation (see Hopkins 9), "religion" in the post-Enlightenment period is not what secular globalization, in the forms of global finance or supranational institutions, leaves behind or sublimates. Rather, "religion" is constituted and continuously revitalized by the growth of "secular" globalization ("tele-technoscience"), a growth that it *also* interrogates.

Simply put, "religion"—and specifically in this book, missionary religion in the nineteenth century—is that which repudiates the processes of globalization on which it simultaneously depends *and* advances. Because it often reaches beyond observable, material, verifiable, instrumental phenomena—confronting believers with questions such as, "What is the meaning of life?," "What connects me to others in the world?," "What does it mean to live rightly?," and "What comes after death?"—religion becomes an (often unpredictable) "shifting range of practices and experiences" that are in dialogue with *and* look to get beyond the mere facts of lived existence (Branch 96). Such a definition gets us out of thinking of religion and belief as being destined to pass with the "global" age, helping us instead see why they stubbornly persist: They respond to and help make meaning of the ever-expanding web of global interconnection.

Hence, as this book shows, nineteenth-century missionary Christianity, rather than being only a conservative reaction against secularizing forces of change, proves more complex. It is in lockstep with *and* critiques the rapid growth of world commerce, and it simultaneously endorses (and capitalizes on) the growth of science and the discovery of "natural laws" as much as it resists the total ascendance of scientistic thinking in public governance. Not the "faith"-based substitute for scientific knowledge and certainly not some simple throwback to a pre-"enlightened" time, "religion"—and in this case, "religion" as expressed in the commitments of missionary work—instead should be seen as very much in dialogue with globalization.

We see this sometimes antagonistic and sometimes mutually fortifying relationship, too, on the level of missionary language, as well as missionary commitments. In *Cultivating Belief*, Lecourt takes a cue from Charles Taylor in framing his investigation of the ethnicization of religious belonging in light of a "secularity" taken as a "new social imaginary that includes normative views as to what religion is or does," as the project of articulating "non-religious identities [according to] particular conceptions of what counts as religion" (27). This framing also helps clarify why I insist on the (relative) secularity of discourses of Enlightenment cosmopolitanism as opposed to the (relative) religiosity of discourses of Christian responsibility. The missionary movement, these chapters demonstrate, were not only cognizant of the relative secularity of Enlightenment cosmopolitan discourses; they also sometimes capitalized on this supposed secularity precisely to limn a Christian-philanthropic identity at once resonant with but nevertheless distinct from the Dissenting and enthusiastic revivalist traditions that had been their antecedents, as I discuss especially in chapter 2. In other words, they recognized that the Enlightenment stress on the "autonomous individual," rationality, and political tolerance was not (only) a conceptual or cultural competitor to religion, but (also) an opportunity to articulate new understandings of Christian responsibility and thereby attract new supporters.

In a manner not unlike missionary Christianity, Enlightenment cosmopolitanism also captures this "dialectical relationship between political arrangements and cultural-psychological dispositions" (Scrivener 1; see also Agathocleous, *Urban Realism* 3). No wonder that the language of cosmopolitanism—at once separate from older traditions of Christian universalism in its Enlightenment instantiation but still complementary to Christian missionaries' universalist concerns—becomes for missionary societies a means of capturing this relationship between the individual and the universal, between religion and globalization.

The Structure of the Book

To tell the story of how missionary work brought into view a site wherein cosmopolitan assumptions could be tested, questioned, and reassessed, I examine in the following chapters some of missionary societies' cosmopolitan experiments and the way nineteenth-century literature engaged with these experiments. I consider specifically Charles Dickens's *Bleak House* (1852–53), Robert Southey's *Tale of Paraguay* (1825) and *Sir Thomas More: Colloquies on the Progress and Prospects of Society* (1829), Charlotte Brontë's *Jane Eyre* (1848), and finally, Sydney Owenson's *The Missionary* (1811), which was revised and rereleased as *Luxima, the Prophetess* after the Indian "Mutiny" of 1857 (1859).

Previous readings of these works, when they have attended to missionary themes, generally focus on whether each text appears to agree or disagree with the imperial dimensions of the missionary project.[33] By putting these texts into conversation with the archive of missionary writing, I try to deepen and productively complicate such readings. I consider, then, how these authors looked to discourses of missionary cosmopolitanism to expand or critique existing schemes of moral and Christian responsibility to others abroad (as well as their fellows at home) in the context of nineteenth-century global developments—a project that at times dovetailed with jingoistic imperialism, in the case of Southey, and at other times defied easy identification with either pro- or anti-imperialist sentiments, as in the case of Owenson's revisions. Disparate as they initially appear, then, the texts I analyze all participate in a common critical conversation in which understandings of cosmopolitanism shifted, adjusted, or were readapted in light of the perceived and actual promises or

---

33. See, for instance, Moore's *Dickens and Empire*; Thomas's *Imperialism, Reform and the Making of Englishness in Jane Eyre*; and Wright's *Ireland, India, and Nationalism in Nineteenth-Century Literature*.

failures of missionaries' engagement with the "complex, incoherent web of interconnections."

Chapter 1 focuses on how the first societies and supporters of the missionary movement tried to distance the Enlightenment cosmopolitan idea from its associations with a suspect radicalism, realigning it instead with a relatively apolitical philanthropic orientation. Showing how prominent British conservatives considered the cosmopolitan idea nearly synonymous with Jacobin sympathies and revolutionary intent, I argue that missionary societies invoked cosmopolitanism less to capitalize on its positive connotations than to recuperate and adapt for their own purposes one of the key tenets of cosmopolitanism. Specifically, they wished to revitalize the idea that the fulfillment of each man's moral, spiritual, and intellectual destiny hinged on his broadening his sympathies and responsibilities beyond his immediate family and nation to encompass all humankind. They did so by obliquely addressing conservative suspicions of cosmopolitanism's *political* intent, insisting that the fundamental interests of evangelicals' cosmopolitanism lay not in widespread social reform but instead in Christian charity and the touching of individual hearts. So successful was this reinvention of cosmopolitanism that the missionary instantiation of the cosmopolitan idea became the cornerstone of the mid-century British nationalism on display at the 1851 Great Exhibition.

Bleak House, I argue, helps tell this story in presenting what we might call a "Burkean" history of the cosmopolitan idea. Urging its reader to read Harold Skimpole, the Leigh Hunt-esque cosmopolite, and Mrs. Jellyby, the mission-minded international philanthropist, as analogues of one another despite their seemingly total dissimilarity, *Bleak House* effectively novelizes Victorian historiographical conventions—a formal choice that positions the novel as commentary not only on England's current condition, but on its current condition as crucially informed by its recent past. By reanimating earlier Burkean suspicions of the cosmopolitan idea in the context of the Great Exhibition period, *Bleak House* delivers a scathing critique of the cosmopolitan and religio-philanthropic fervor of the 1850s, denouncing it as little more than a cancerous moral indifference and a sort of aesthetic corruption bound to attenuate domestic stability. As such, Dickens brings to light the dangerous sociopolitical implications of missionary cosmopolitanism, which missionary societies had tried to sublimate into philanthropic feeling.

Chapter 2 represents an offshoot from these arguments, as it seizes and builds on a key issue arising from the discursive history I trace in chapter 1. If chapter 1 details *how* missionaries adopted a distinctly cosmopolitan rhetoric, chapter 2 explores the *why* of missionaries' cosmopolitanism, tracing part of cosmopolitanism's appeal to the desire of missionary societies to distance themselves from what they felt was the taint of working-class religious enthusiasm. As a hybridized language that evoked secular *and* religious associations and ideals, a (de-radicalized) cosmopolitan rhetoric aided missionary societies in their quest to appear reasonable and pragmatic, winning them supporters otherwise wary of Dissent and the evangelical movement more generally. One of the most prominent of these supporters was the poet laureate Robert Southey. Taking a cue from missionaries' cosmopolitanism, I demonstrate that Southey conceptualized his *own* Christianized version of Kantian cosmopolitanism in an effort to make explicit the political agenda he thought missionaries were too timid and shortsighted to make themselves: namely, that colonial oppression was the ticket to global emancipation and, eventually, would lead to world peace. Triangulating among Southey's reviews of missionary periodicals, A *Tale of Paraguay,* and *Sir Thomas More,* I argue that Southey represents one of the strange paths by which cosmopolitanism transformed from an emancipatory Enlightenment idea, one associated with guaranteeing individual freedoms within a scheme for global peace, to a means of legitimizing and abetting the worst excesses of Christian colonial expansion in the nineteenth century.

Chapter 3 turns to the concept of "universal kinship" in relation to marriage, family, and racial thinking in missionary work. I contend that *Jane Eyre* roots itself in a fraught phase of the Protestant missionary movement: the brief period of time prior to the 1820s when some missionary societies, eager to realize the "universal kinship of mankind," not only permitted but encouraged missionaries to enter into interracial marriages. These marriages, however, proved more reciprocal in influence than missionary societies had anticipated. Ultimately they undermined assumptions of British Christians' "natural" superiority over "natives"—assumptions that largely (if not entirely) underwrote missionary work in the first place. Unnerved by the reciprocity and openness these unions appeared to establish between spouses, missionary societies reversed their position on intermarriage and began dissociating conceptions of "universal kinship" from *actual* racial mixing, thus making them key actors in conferring to later instantiations of "universal kinship" what Gauri Viswanathan calls its "sterile," *unsexed* character (195). Drawing on this missionary history, I connect St. John's endogamous choice of a marriage partner to the Bertha-Rochester interracial marriage plot, arguing that *Jane Eyre* foregrounds contradictions between the missionary ideal of a "universal kinship" and the paradoxical insistence of missionary societies on strictly policing marriage according to ever sharper racial and cultural lines.

My fourth and final chapter analyzes Sydney Owenson's revisions to her popular 1811 novel, *The Missionary*. Republished in 1859 in the immediate wake of the 1857 Indian "Mutiny," the new edition of the novel—retitled as *Luxima, the Prophetess*—promised that it had been "greatly alter'd" in response to contemporary events. This chapter places Morgan's reedited novel, rooted in the Romantic era, revised for the mid-Victorian one, and expressive of the post-Mutiny failure of Enlightenment humanism, at the cusp of a crucial transformation in missionary attitudes toward its evangelical mandate. Tracking the differences between *The Missionary* and *Luxima*—the former expressive of Enlightenment conceptions of humanity's fundamental similitude, the latter grappling with the possibility that people of other cultures were radically "other" and unknowable—I argue that Owenson's revisions extract from the furious, confused body of missionary writing a subtle yet significant shift in changing cosmopolitan views and the politics of religion following the "cataclysm" of the 1857 revolutions.

A brief coda extends this last development to the twentieth and twenty-first centuries. In this section, I examine a movement among some missionaries based in India to disassociate Christianity and Western culture. Speculating that the conceptual roots of this geographically and culturally unbounded spirituality can be found in the revised conception of universal humanity that circulated in missionary writing and practice post-1857, I suggest links between my work here and a body of recent studies on religion, cosmopolitanism, and literature. First, I propose that the evolving story of missionary cosmopolitanism perhaps represents something of a prehistory for "spiritual cosmopolitanisms" identified by Gandhi, Aravamudan, and Agathocleous in the late nineteenth-century intercultural dialogues between India and Britain. And, second, I speculate that in these fin-de-siècle missionary efforts to envision an instantiation of Christianity as infinitely accommodating, yet always transcendent, of cultural specificity, we might see something of religion's response—one originating not only among religious practitioners but among religious *proselytizers*—to the reconceptualization of religion that Sebastian Lecourt identifies as taking place among literary liberals and secular social scientists in post-1860 Britain. Contra the conviction of early nineteenth-century missionaries of the fundamental inseparability of Christianity and "civilization," *and* contra late-century liberal efforts to redefine "religion as a matter of racial or ethnic identity," as "embedded in the unconscious inheritances of the past" rather than as freely chosen by an individual (Lecourt 2), some missionaries envisioned a new religious universalism built on the principle that Christianity was essentially independent of culture. Examining reports from the 2010 World Missionary Conference, I propose that this universalism persists now, not only informing some current strands of missionary theology and discourse but also, unexpectedly, positioning missionary work as a rival to the "new cosmopolitanisms" of today.

This is the ground I look to cover. There is much, then, that falls outside my scope, aims, and capacity. For one thing, this is not an authoritative history of missionary work. Many excellent histories of the nineteenth-century missionary movement do exist, including those by Brian Stanley, Andrew Porter, Andrew Walls, Jeffrey Cox, Hilary Carey, Catherine Hall, Elizabeth Elbourne, Susan Thorne, and Esme Cleall, among others. This book attempts something different. To borrow Tomoko Masuzawa's formulation, it draws from historical sources to construct a genealogy of a particular "discursive formation": namely, "missionary cosmopolitanism" as it appeared within missionary writing and practice, and various ways in which it informed and was informed by the broader literary culture with which it was in dialogue (11). In focusing on a discourse that wends its way through a broader British missionary culture, this study was compelled to part ways with some of the methods and framing devices that tend to govern histories of missionary work. To get the larger sense of how missionary cosmopolitanism was formulated and functioned, I found it necessary to step back from overattending to a particular society or geographic region—that is, from the very frames that tend to be the necessary precondition of writing an authoritative history of a missionary society in a particular region. My hope is that in the depth necessarily lost in not delimiting my investigative scope, we might gain something of a broader view of patterns of cosmopolitan thought as evinced in the interplay between nineteenth-century literature and missionary writing.

And unlike many historical accounts, *Missionary Cosmopolitanism* does not attempt to narrate a series of events in any linear or cumulative fashion. Although for the sake of organization and convenience the chapters are organized somewhat chronologically, I do not mean to imply the passing of one cosmopolitan thought experiment among missionaries (i.e., Christian colonialism) with the commencement of another (i.e., universal kinship). Ann Laura Stoler perhaps best articulates the schema I employ here: Where many projects "often prompt a search to impose coherence retrospectively," these chapters, though obviously distinct from each other, nevertheless should be seen as a "dogged pursuit of recurrent themes, a sustained focus on the same archival densities [and] an insistent return to hauntingly similar quotes" (as well as, often, to the exact same quotes) (7). Taken together, they aim to provide not an exhaustive account of change over time but a synthetic depiction of the links between missionary writing and the cosmopolitan visions evinced in nineteenth-century literature.

Neither is *Missionary Cosmopolitanism* a book concentrated on theological issues, though from time to time reference to theological debates crops up in its pages. This makes some amount of historical sense, as the missionary movement arguably "affected every department of scholarship—except theology" (Walls, *Cross-Cultural* 42). As Walls notes, "For missionaries, theology generally remained a 'given'" (42). As my overview of the modern missionary movement discusses, those theological debates that tended to divide the various denominations from one another were largely sidelined in the modern missionary movement. With the immense task of "Christianizing the heathen" before them, most missionary societies set aside theological squabbling in favor of practical and practicable strategies for raising funds, bolstering political and public support, and aiding (often struggling) missionaries and missionary stations abroad.

A final note is required on historical framing and my choice of methodology. *Missionary Cosmopolitanism* spans 1795 to 1860 as, arguably, these years encapsulated an era in which missionary enterprises were characterized by their general unity of purpose as well as by shared optimism in the achievability of global cooperation and perpetual peace. I begin with the decade that witnessed the advent of the modern missionary movement and the founding of the LMS. Though not the wealthiest of the foreign mission societies, the LMS nonetheless was "the largest evangelical institution peddling its spiritual wares in the arena of empire" (McClintock 261), at least in terms of influence over the general structure and practices of missionary work in the early to mid-nineteenth century. I end the bulk of my study with the cataclysm of the so-called 1857 Indian "Mutiny" and its aftermath. Provoking a profound crisis of confidence in the national soul, this event joined a string of other perceived failures (such as that of the missionary David Livingstone's Zambezi expedition from 1858 to 1864) to trouble earlier assumptions held by mission societies regarding the fundamental similitude of all humankind. Together with the ebb of religious zeal in the latter decades of the nineteenth century and the emergence of smaller and more denominationally driven missionary societies, the last years of the 1850s fractured what Stanley calls the "eschatological consensus" originally shared by mission societies in the first decades of their operation (*Bible* 75).[34] Difficult as it is to talk of a holistic missionary society sensibility as I do in the chapters that follow, the project becomes almost

---

34. The fracturing of consensus in missionary work in the 1860s reflected the growing conservatism and partisanship of evangelicalism post-1858. As Bradley notes, "The Second Evangelical Revival, which began around 1858, radically changed the character of the movement and inspired adherents who were more fanatical, more bigoted and more introverted than those who followed Wilberforce and Shaftesbury" (17).

impossible after the 1850s due to the sheer proliferation of societies and resulting intersocietal fractures.

Beginning and ending my study with these landmark years in missionary work has the added benefit of allowing me to situate the novels I examine within both the Romantic and Victorian periods. Doing so permits me to assess the continuities and changes that occurred between the early- to mid-decades of the nineteenth century—continuities and changes, which prove to be central thematic concerns of several of the works examined and which are sometimes occluded in studies governed by a stricter sense of the self-containedness of literary periods. Take, for instance, *Jane Eyre* and *The Missionary*. The former displays a keen awareness that the institution of marriage represented a contested site in missionary work in the early nineteenth century, drawing its inspiration from the renowned, aspiringly celibate missionary Henry Martyn (1781–1812), among others, in its creation of the forbiddingly pious St. John Rivers. The latter was reedited and rereleased in the wake of the 1857 "Mutiny" in an effort to capture both similarities and differences between this uprising and the 1806 Vellore "Mutiny." In their respective articulations of how cosmopolitanism has (or has not) changed over the course of the nineteenth century, the novels, in remarkably self-conscious ways, thematize those unique "features and sensibilities" we tend to assign to the periods we call Romantic or Victorian to interrogate the extent, or existence at all, of their differences (Galperin 362).[35] Therefore, even as my project is unabashedly historicist in its leanings, it also suggests that "placing" literature in history is always vexed, never straightforward.

This last point brings me to methodology. In *Missionary Cosmopolitanism*, I've drawn on a range of primary sources, including novels, sermons, periodicals, and archival documents, to reconstruct shifting meanings of what it meant to be "cosmopolitan" in the early to mid-nineteenth century. In doing so, I've tried to refrain from imposing current theories of cosmopolitanism onto these texts in favor of letting these "cosmopolitanisms"—which frequently were termed as such, in their own historical moments—manifest themselves, no matter their internal contradictions or their conceptual distance from the cosmopolitanisms offered today. As I've worked on these chapters, then, I've kept in the back of my mind Michel Foucault's suggestion:

---

35. Of course, this is to retread familiar arguments. As William Galperin has convincingly shown, "there exists in the literature of the nineteenth century, as in all literature undoubtedly, enough of an element of self-contestation to render its circumscription by period—certainly by the notions Romantic and Victorian—a mere mystification" (363). I hope, then, that another contribution of this book is additional evidence of the ways in which texts self-consciously examined the zeitgeist of their moments to draw troubling analogies or definitively assert the distance between it and others.

"The description of a statement does not consist therefore in rediscovering the unsaid whose place it occupies; nor how one can reduce it to a silent, common text; but on the contrary in discovering what special place it occupies, what ramifications of the system make it possible to map its localization, how it is isolated in the general dispersion of statements" (119). In mapping the discursive field of missionaries' cosmopolitan statements, I try to comprehend their cosmopolitan horizons as they were explicitly claimed in the nineteenth century, hopefully highlighting "something true and visible on the text's surface that symptomatic reading [has] ironically rendered invisible" (Best and Marcus 12). Thus I consider how notions of universal kinship bolstered a sense of responsibility to, as well as fed anxieties about, cultural and racial others, for example, or, at another moment, how these same notions differently inform Owenson's revisions to *The Missionary* when the Indian "Mutiny" makes clear the fundamental irreducibility of different peoples and cultures.

I also want to come clean: I admit that there was a period when I was so deeply immersed in missionary writing and history that I lost sight of the literary component of this project. It was at this time that Sharon Marcus's question, "Why focus on literature at all, and why on the texts I do," hit me with particular force (8). But then I realized that just as my interest in missionaries has always been determined by and filtered through the lens of my mother's encounter with them, so, too, has my approach to missionary writing inevitably been the product of the nineteenth-century novels I love. As I discuss above, given that the archive of missionary publications is head-spinningly vast and in significant part functionally propagandistic (Carey 81), Romantic and Victorian literature has acted as something like a compass and dowsing rod rolled into one. Presented with the quantity of missionary writing, as well as the efforts of missionary societies to impose consistency and coherence on their textual output, literary narratives set me on a path that isn't immediately obvious (I would like to think), clueing me in to obscured veins of inquiry or ideological fractures.[36] I have tried to capture this central function of nineteenth-century literature in each of my chapters.

I also believe that the prominence of each of these texts in its own time testifies to the significance of these veins of thought in the broader British culture. Hence my answer to why *these* texts: Though works such as *A Tale*

---

36. Southey's *Tale of Paraguay* is no novel, obviously. Yet in *Tale of Paraguay*, Southey explores the social ramifications of his theories of Christian colonialism, finding in the long poem format a means of making concrete his abstract vision of a colonial cosmopolitanism. His use of narrative thus resembles the ways in which Brontë and Dickens used their narratives to test the viability of cosmopolitan sensibilities within a scheme of social relations (though Southey does this in worse faith, as we'll see).

of Paraguay, Sir Thomas More, and *The Missionary* don't enjoy the same canonicity as *Jane Eyre* and *Bleak House,* they have in common the fact of being widely read in their own time, making them stakeholders and participants in the cosmopolitan debates they stage, thematize, and, most of all, personalize. For, as I've written with Joshua King elsewhere, a focus on literature tends to "counterbalance" the tendency of "historians and scholars of religious studies to emphasize institutional, denominational, and disciplinary factors in the construction of religion" by instead "prioritiz[ing] individual religious expression, genre formation, and the singularity of articulations of faith and doubt in literary works" (King and Werner 5). If the literary tends to foreground certain fractures or contradictions that attended missionary efforts, this tendency perhaps inheres in the way that fictional narratives concretize otherwise abstract ideas in depicting individual characters' actions and motivations, as well as the tangible effect of such actions on others.

In sum, *Missionary Cosmopolitanism* seeks to complicate the often underexamined binaries that govern understandings of religion, imperialism, and cosmopolitanism in literary scholarship. Examining a network of rich evidence from the past, it demonstrates how evangelical revivalism could take up Enlightenment ideas; how missionaries associated themselves with progressive, even radical, sentiments; and how nineteenth-century literature seized on missionary cosmopolitanism to explore how imperialism complicated and compromised Christianity's cosmopolitan ideals.

CHAPTER 1

The Cosmopolitan Idea in Early Nineteenth-Century Missionary Societies

> Benevolence to the whole species, and want of feeling for every individual with whom the professors come in contact, form the character of the new philosophy.... Their hero of vanity ... melts with tenderness for those only who touch him by the remotest relation, and then, without one natural pang, casts away, as a sort of offal and excrement, the spawn of his disgustful amours, and sends his children to the hospital of foundlings.
>
> —Edmund Burke, *Letter 35*

FOR MUCH of the eighteenth century, cosmopolitanism, a philosophy that espoused the virtues of being a "stranger nowhere" or "at home every place" (McMurran 28), suggested more a cultural ethos than an overt political program.[1] Though the "citizen of the world" eschewed narrow nationalist prejudices in favor of a supposedly more aloof and balanced view of mankind as a whole, his appeal lay less in the political activism that the ethos implied than in the cultural capital he wielded. The "cosmopolite" was commonly associated with a hallowed tradition of Greek thought and frequently was styled a "humanitarian or impartial judge," who "embod[ied] wisdom and benevolence" (30). He dwelled in *salons* and coffeehouses, where he propounded the relative value of other countries' virtues, arts, and manufactures versus his own, or, like Addison's Mr. Spectator, reflected on what it meant to inhabit an increasingly global society. In other words, he fashioned himself as belonging to an "elite class (the world's *petite troupe des philosophes*) that transcended national boundaries" (Schlereth 1).

---

1. Though it did not enjoy the widespread currency it has today, "cosmopolitanism" in fact was a term used in the eighteenth century. McMurran notes that a search for cosmopolitanism in Eighteenth Century Collections Online (ECCO) yields eleven results, while a search for "cosmopolism" yields twenty-three (36n53). The terms much more frequently used were "'cosmopolite,' which brings up over three hundred hits, and 'citizen of the world,' which recovers over 1600" (28).

But as the epigraph to this chapter suggests, these connotations shifted in the late eighteenth century. In the revolutionary atmosphere of these last decades, cosmopolitanism came to be associated with more overt political intentions. Thus in his 1791 takedown of Jean-Jacques Rousseau and (what Burke took to be) the main pillars of Rousseau's philosophy, Burke not only looked to expose the hypocrisy of the French humanist; he also attributed Rousseau's infamous abandonment of his children to a "new philosophy," which he believed had seized the popular political imagination. Burke was hardly alone in his suspicions. As revolutionary unrest spread across continental Europe, British conservatives assigned seditious political motives to would-be "cosmopolites." Soon, "Burkean type hostility towards cosmopolitanism" became widespread (Wohlgemut 34), a dynamic partially fueled by paranoiac reactions against Kant's essays on international federation and the "cosmopolitan idea." Discarded children were not simply indicative of a personal moral failing on Rousseau's part, then. For some prominent conservatives, they were also symptomatic of a broader political conspiracy that was urging cosmopolites to break ties with family and nation for the sake of global revolution.

I emphasize these negative political connotations to underscore the remarkable renaissance of the cosmopolitan ideal in the mid-nineteenth century. As Britain became confident in its status as *the* global superpower, it increasingly celebrated its "cosmopolitan" character as a cornerstone of its national self-identity. It was in this vein that an 1851 article published in *The Economist* praised the Great Exhibition of the Works of Industry of All Nations as unique and unprecedented in its international scope, while deriding earlier industrial exhibitions held in Paris (1844, 1849) and Bordeaux (1847) for being "anti-cosmopolitan." "Our own Exhibition," the author announced, "is cosmopolitan, in contradistinction to theirs which were national and political or anti-cosmopolitan. [Thus] the Great Exhibition falls in with that general progress towards peace, towards common and reciprocal enjoyments, towards planing down national differences, and perhaps obliterating national distinctions, which has for some years been very marked in Europe" ("Some Moral Aspects" 532). From being considered a suspect philosophy at odds with British nationalism and associated with the revolutionary sentiments of continental Europe, cosmopolitanism became one of the foremost attributes of Britain, one that distinguished it from "anti-cosmopolitan" France.

These snippets from Burke and *The Economist* help me to segue into the main arguments of this chapter. First, where cosmopolitanism had been regarded as unpatriotic, contemptible, and almost irredeemably "Continental" in the 1790s, it came to celebrated as one of the key structuring ideas of the Great Exhibition and British national identity. And, second, this sea change in the public understanding and acceptance was due to a profound shift in the global responsibility and political stance implied in cosmopolitanism—a shift in no small part fueled by missionaries' controversial adoption of unmistakably cosmopolitan language at the turn of the century.

Although the specific words missionary societies used to describe their views and work explicitly marked them as cosmopolitan (i.e., "cosmopolitan," "citizen of the world," and "cosmopolite"), the actual *meaning* of "cosmopolitan" in the missionary sense of the term did not cleanly graft onto eighteenth-century concepts of the idea. Missionary usages of cosmopolitan language instead evoked *and* departed from these understandings. While missionary societies and their supporters aligned themselves with those Enlightenment humanist ideals that attended late eighteenth-century "cosmopolitanism" (i.e., freedom, self-determination, tolerance), thereby attracting the suspicions of conservatives who labeled missionary supporters "noisy cosmopolites" who looked to undermine national order, their use of cosmopolitan language also amounted to a sort of rhetorical feint. For even as missionary societies seemed to allude to politicized understandings of Enlightenment cosmopolitanism, they also denied that *their* cosmopolitanism implied a political agenda. Such claims were somewhat disingenuous, of course; missionary societies and the evangelicals who supported them emerged as potent political forces in the early nineteenth century, and the Enlightenment ideals of inalienable freedoms and rights (the corollaries of their "cosmopolitan" views) informed their popular agitation for the abolition of slavery, among other hot-button causes.[2] But in their language and writing, missionaries and their supporters worked to dissociate cosmopolitanism from its ostensibly radical politics, insisting that a cosmopolitan orientation was never at odds with patriotic feeling nor aligned with any definite political interests beyond that general benevolent interest in the fate of mankind as was required by Christian piety.

In other words, we find among early nineteenth-century missionary societies the same propensities for making use of "available semiotic resources" while "recontextual[izing]" them that Webb Keane identifies among Dutch Calvinist missionaries working in Sumba, Indonesia (257). Eighteenth-century cosmopolitanism, as I discuss below, was less a unified concept than a "language ideology"—"a cultural system of ideas about social and linguistic

---

2. Not that all missionaries supported emancipation, however. Infamously, Rev. James Curtin, the Anglican missionary who baptized Mary Prince, argued against antislavery.

relationships, together with their loading of moral and political interests," in Judith Irvine's definition (qtd. in Keane 16). Distasteful as figures such as Voltaire, Rousseau, and Kant no doubt were to evangelical missionary supporters, they nevertheless seemed drawn to the larger ecology of cosmopolitan language, intuiting that such language could signal their commitment to universal brotherhood and human rights within the framework of foreign missionary work.[3]

Thus the popular understanding of cosmopolitanism morphed over the course of the early nineteenth century: As missionary societies and mission-minded evangelicals recast cosmopolitanism as a sort of abstract humanism effected by Christian morality, the cosmopolitan ideal began to shed the more revolutionary connotations it had carried at the turn of the century. By 1818, one evangelical periodical would remark the extent to which the "cosmopolitan," thanks to foreign missions, had come to signify a "Christian enlargement of sentiment," in contrast to the moral "indifference" that had marked the earlier iteration of "cosmopolitan liberality" ("Art. II" 330). By the 1850s, a self-congratulatory and distinctly Christianized understanding of cosmopolitanism had become paradoxically a nationalist discourse.

This, then, is the story this chapter looks to tell. The exultant cosmopolitan spirit of the mid-century had a likely antecedent in the cosmopolitanism that animated the first flush of the modern missionary movement. Moreover, if this mid-century cosmopolitan spirit was patriotic rather than antinationalist, philanthropic rather than political, this was because its contours had been defined by the myriad sins with which "cosmopolitanism" had been saddled in the late eighteenth and early nineteenth centuries, sins from which missionary societies felt compelled to defend themselves. It was precisely on the grounds of their "cosmopolitan" sympathies, after all, that missionary societies were accused of redirecting energy needed at home to suspect foreign causes, attenuating ties to family and nation, and inculcating a spirit of immorality and sedition in the name of a false egalitarianism. In other words, cosmopolitanism came to be associated with a "Christian expansion of benevolence" not because it was a given that the "cosmopolitan" stance was inherently desirable, moral, or virtuous. Instead, the philanthropic and jingoistic cosmopolitanism underwriting the Great Exhibition was forged in an earlier period of rhetorical conflict and controversy, when missionary societies and their supporters

---

3. In this capacity, the modern missionary movement represents one case study among many in the dynamic observed by Keane, in which liberalism's "notions of freedom and its value have sources, or at least strong parallels, in certain aspects of the Protestant tradition" (38n2).

insisted on describing themselves as "cosmopolitan" despite provoking conservative antagonism for doing so.

Of course, there are other stories of cosmopolitanism's shifting meanings to be told, but *Bleak House* (1852–53), I suggest, alludes precisely to *this* historiography of cosmopolitanism. In a Burkean vein, Dickens's expansive novel recalls the morally "indifferent" roots of the cosmopolitan idea to deliver a scathing indictment of its mid-century instantiation. In its two "cosmopolitan" characters, Harold Skimpole and Mrs. Jellyby, the novel satirizes—so as to delineate the obvious differences between—early nineteenth-century cosmopolitanism, on the one hand, and mid-nineteenth-century cosmopolitanism, on the other (i.e., the idealized coffeehouse cosmopolite who espouses a dangerous doctrine of "common brotherhood," and the "telescopic philanthropist" who pleads for British action to alleviate suffering abroad). But *Bleak House* also does something more than this. In staging these seemingly distant cosmopolitan philosophies, it also exposes their fundamental similarities.

More specifically, I contend that while *Bleak House* testifies to the degree that missionary usages of "cosmopolitanism" had (in fact) changed popular understandings of the idea, it simultaneously emphasizes that the faults some conservatives had originally perceived in early nineteenth-century cosmopolitanism subtly, cunningly, perniciously persist in the cosmopolitan idealism of the Great Exhibition. Thus the novel reiterates conservative suspicions of cosmopolitanism but newly applies those suspicions to the mid-century moment: To be cosmopolitan, even in the Christian philanthropic sense of the word, still entails the abandonment of one's children and domestic duties, still contributes to fomenting chaos and unrest in one's home community.

To be clear, the main thrust of this chapter is to provide a discursive history of "missionary cosmopolitanism" in the early nineteenth century. Rather than providing a comprehensive account of the ways *Bleak House* challenges, promotes, or rewrites Victorian internationalism,[4] I concentrate on what I take to be the novel's keenly historic sense of cosmopolitanism: its savvy recovery of early nineteenth-century conservative fears of missionaries' (supposedly) depoliticized, re-Christianized cosmopolitanism in order to critique the "cosmopolitan" fervor surrounding the Great Exhibition. To trace this history, I structure my arguments as follows. First, I describe eighteenth-century cosmopolitanism to give some grounding by which we can track later permutations of the idea. Then, I examine early-century controversies surrounding

---

4. For interpretations of the novel along these lines, see Buzard and Agathocleous, *Urban Realism*.

the missionary use of cosmopolitan language, showing how the missionary movement deemphasized the political implications of the cosmopolitan view to stress instead its consonance with Christian virtue and philanthropic feeling. With this history in hand, I turn to *Bleak House*. Considering what I take to be its historiographical interest in cosmopolitanism, I suggest the novel denounces the mid-century upsurge of "cosmopolitan-philanthropic-commercial hymns of peace" (to use Marx's sardonic characterization of Great Exhibition fervor) on the grounds that it represents nothing but the *same* suspect and morally dissolute cosmopolitanism of the late eighteenth century—only now bathed in the sheen of humanitarian benevolence ("Letter to Frederic Engels").

Eighteenth-Century Cosmopolitanism

The preponderance of scholarship focusing on Kantian cosmopolitanism might lead one to believe that his understanding of the idea originated and dominated *all* eighteenth-century usages (see McMurran 22, 35n16). Yet, as Helen McMurran and Thomas Schlereth point out, this wasn't the case. For most of the eighteenth-century, there was a "paucity of discourse elaborating the cosmopolitan ideal as a theory" in the manner of Kantian cosmopolitanism (McMurran 22), making the ideal "more symbolic and theoretical than actual and practical" (Schlereth xii). But despite lacking firm political or practical grounding, "cosmopolitanism" (and the constellation of terms with which it was associated) nevertheless exercised significant cultural pull. Part of cosmopolitanism's cultural capital derived from what was perceived to be its classical lineage, which dated back to "the shadowy personage of Diogenes" (McMurran 30). Drawing from this antique past, the self-styled, eighteenth-century "citizens of the world" were unfettered by blind nationalism, marked by an aura of urbanity and polish, and ran the spectrum in terms of their attachment to their fellow man. Thus some cosmopolites, such as Addison and Jefferson, saw cosmopolitanism as entailing allegiance—and therefore attachment—to a broad "universal brotherhood" regardless of nationality; others, such as Fougeret de Montbron, asserted that they possessed "no allegiances because they hate[d] every country they visit[ed]" (Stanton 635). But no matter the degree (or existence at all) of fellow feeling he bore for mankind, the cosmopolite's implied invocation of Diogenes and, by extension, the Stoic philosophers who developed Diogenes's sentiments, lent a rarefied air to his cosmopolitan orientation. Though there was no "distinct or systematic idea of the cosmopolitan," the reference to the classical tradition of thought imbued the "citizen of the world" with intellectual and cultural profundity (McMurran 30).[5]

Such referencing also signaled the ethical underpinnings of cosmopolitanism as composing the humanistic effort to reconcile "individualism . . . and an abstract faith in the humanity of the mass" (Schlereth 14). In looking to what was considered to be a classical, *pre*-Christian philosophy, Enlightenment writers perceived in cosmopolitanism "a moral code that would not be imposed by a specific religion nor be dependent upon its coercive authority and dogmatic metaphysics" (56). Insofar as cosmopolitanism signaled the aspiration to shift "ethical responsibility from the hierarchy of the church to the conscience of the individual," the philosophical ideal grafted onto the ruling predilections of the Enlightenment moment (56). Thus the eighteenth-century cosmopolitan idea had two characteristics of particular interest to this chapter: (1) its political vagueness, and (2) its effort to imagine a moral universalism without recourse to the authority of any one religious institution.

In the later decades of the eighteenth century, however, the urbane or frivolous figure of the cosmopolite (depending on one's view) became more politically charged. "As the cosmopolite gained a foothold," notes McMurran, Enlightenment thinkers "attended more critically to the belief in the virtues and even the possibility of being 'stranger nowhere' or 'one who adopts no homeland'" (30). Kant's two essays on cosmopolitanism helped crystallize the transformation of the idea from implying a *cultural* position—that is, a "highly subjective state of mind that sought to grasp the unity of mankind, without, however, attempting to solve the relations of the part to the whole" (Schlereth xii–xiii)—to concrete political scheme. To use Pauline Kleingeld's formulation, "Kant add[ed] to his moral cosmopolitanism a cosmopolitan political theory" (510).

I want to focus on these essays for a moment, as they eventually proved influential to nineteenth-century understandings of cosmopolitanism.[6] In "Idea for a Universal History with a Cosmopolitan Purpose" (1784) and its post-Revolutionary follow-up, "Perpetual Peace: A Philosophical Sketch" (1795), Kant maps a plan in which worldwide order is accomplished by international federation driven inexorably by human nature, which he characterizes as fundamentally social yet self-interested and competitive. This "social unsociability" intrinsic to human nature makes two broader developments inevitable. First, it drives men to establish a constitutional republic that possesses not only "the greatest freedom . . . but the most precise specification

---

5. It should be added that this is why skeptics regarded the cosmopolite of this time as somewhat below serious consideration (McMurran 22).

6. See Agathocleous, *Urban Realism* 32; Agathocleous and Rudy 392; and Wohlgemut 34.

and preservation of the limits of this freedom in order that it can co-exist with the freedom of others" ("Idea for a Universal History" 45). Within this social arrangement, each man becomes a rational, moral citizen; his "primitive natural capacity for moral discrimination" evolves into "definite practical principles" and a "*pathologically* enforced social union is transformed into a *moral* whole" (44–45). Second, it prompts nations—imagined as the individual writ large—to enter into society with each other, an agreement that guarantees the freedoms of each nation without grossly impinging on the freedoms of any other. The essays therefore point to a "larger three-fold political structure in which the freedom of the individual is contingent on the state, and the freedom of the state on international purpose" (Wohlgemut 19). The "cosmopolitan purpose" in accordance with this structure is realized by the final establishment of "cosmopolitan law" in addition to that of constitutional and international law—in other words, a third realm of public law founded on individuals possessing rights not only as citizens of particular states but as common occupiers of the same finite globe (Kant, "Perpetual Peace" 105–8). I discuss Kant in greater depth in chapter 2, noting how he argues for a teleological history without reference to God or a higher power—a key characteristic of Enlightenment cosmopolitanism in general.

For the purposes of this chapter, though, I wish to emphasize the degree to which Kantian cosmopolitanism breaks from the more ambiguous understanding of cosmopolitanism that dominated the earlier decades of the century. Whereas previous manifestations of the cosmopolite suggested that his importance lay primarily in his work as a cultural critic or member of the intelligentsia, Kant's essays are *explicitly* politicized. As such, they participate in a larger discursive shift in which cosmopolitanism went from designating a sort of airy cultural aloofness to a moral idea that mandated, or at least seemed to mandate, definite political action. In the charged climate of the late 1700s, which was reeling from major revolutions in the American colonies, Haiti, and France, as well as witnessing political unrest across the rest of the European continent, one can imagine how some conservatives received *this* politicized iteration of cosmopolitanism. Far from being an unequivocally praiseworthy idea, cosmopolitanism was regarded by a significant segment of British conservatives as irredeemably connected to loose morality and revolutionary sympathies. Predisposed to distrust *any* agitation for republicanism, let alone those efforts that trumpeted fealty to the "universal brotherhood of mankind" over one's nation and family, they saw confirmation of their worst suspicions in the politically loaded "cosmopolitan idea." Any claim to "world citizenship" implied potentially seditious aims, and the coffeehouse cosmopolite of an earlier period became a potentially treacherous political agent.

Cosmopolitan Controversies

The late eighteenth-century hostility toward cosmopolitanism was evinced in a number of popular and conspiracy-minded works. One of the most striking examples of this phenomenon was Abbé Augustin Barruel's *Memoirs Illustrating the History of Jacobinism* (1797), a best seller that endeavored to prove how a coalition of Enlightenment thinkers, Freemasons, and Illuminati had catalyzed the French Revolution as part of a larger plot to overthrow European Christianity and aristocracy. A key prong of this conspiracy, it argued, was the "Cosmopolitan Empire announced by Professor Kant" (Barruel 528). Under the "pretence of perpetual peace," Barruel asserted, Kant enjoined each man to "betray his country, his laws, and his fellow-citizens" (528). Implausible as Barruel's claims might seem to readers today, his memoirs found a number of influential admirers, among them Edmund Burke. Praising *Memoirs* as a "wonderful narrative" in a 1797 letter to Barruel, Burke remarked, "I forgot to say, that I have known myself, personally, five of your principal conspirators; and I can undertake to say from my own certain knowledge, that as far back as the year 1773, they were busy in the plot you have so well described, and in the manner, and on the principle you have so truly represented" ("Edmund Burke to Abbé Barruel" 319–20).

As the letter from Burke suggests, Barruel was hardly alone in entertaining outlandish conspiracy theories centered on the clandestine political motives of the cosmopolitan agenda. In *Proofs of a Conspiracy* (1797), the Scottish physicist John Robison adopted a similarly frenzied tone. Echoing Barruel's claim that the chimera of "Cosmo-political good" was working to extenuate the "atrocities of France" and, ultimately, to abolish "all the feelings which link men together in society," Robison warned, "The ties of father, husband, brother, friend—all are abandoned for an emotion which we must strive to excite,—universal philanthropy" (361).

Conservative periodicals and satirical works motivated by nationalist sentiments reiterated the general thrust of such conspiracy theories, albeit in a (slightly) less agitated form. An essay appearing in the *Anti-Jacobin Review* in 1799, for instance, declared that the "CITIZEN OF THE WORLD ... will not scruple a moment to act just as his immediate interest dictates, without any regard to national honour or individual honesty.... If [a man] calls himself a CITIZEN OF THE WORLD, I always set him down as a TRAITOR" ("A Citizen" 593). Writing in a similar vein, Mary Anne Burges, sister of the politician Sir James Bland Burges, published a nationalist adaptation of Bunyan's *The Pilgrim's Progress* entitled *The Progress of the Pilgrim Good-Intent, in Jacobinical Times* (1800). In the satirical work, she described a glib "Mr. Cosmopolitan," who outwardly lives by the philosophy, "Are we not equally citizens of that great city the world?" (160). Mr. Cosmopolitan's supposed detachment from all nations, however, belies his *true* sympathies with France. Ultimately he takes up residence among the treacherous and immoral Frenchmen, finding himself most comfortable in their society. If the "idealized cosmopolite" of the coffeehouse was treated with "skepticism and even flippancy" in the mid-eighteenth century, he had morphed into a far more dangerous figure by the 1790s (McMurran 22).

Given this context, it's perhaps surprising how frequently proponents of the modern missionary movement insisted that they were "cosmopolites" and urged fellow Christians to embrace a more cosmopolitan perspective. Moreover, such language appears across the publications of the different missionary societies. For instance, in an 1806 essay depicting the life of a "good pastor," the LMS-affiliated *Evangelical Magazine* states that because he takes "the whole world" as the object of his preaching, the good pastor is "a cosmopolite," no matter how small his congregation ("The Good Pastor" 13). But it wasn't enough for a pastor to be a cosmopolite; he also needed to impart this view to his congregation. Thus the appendix to Rev. William Whitehead's *Letter to the Rev. Daniel Wilson* (1818) reprints the following recommendation issued by the CMS: "*Clerical members* [are] to give occasional lectures from that celebrated *text book,* the Missionary Register, and thus to assist the favorite scheme of enlarging the *at present confined affections* and charity of the poor, to feelings and benevolences more *cosmopolitan*" (41). The exhortation to be "more cosmopolitan" is also implied in the title, *The Missionary's Portable Christmas Box, and Cosmopolitan's Seasonable New Year's Gift* (1825), a work written by the missionary surgeon and Indologist John Borthwick Gilchrist. As suggested in an advertisement for the book that ran in *The Asiatic Journal and Monthly Miscellany,* the work of the "cosmopolitan" missionary ran contrary to the agendas of "selfish Rulers, arrogant Monopolists, and plausible Crafts in the World" ("New Publications" 269).[7] Collectively, these usages of "cosmopolitan" demonstrate the various positive connotations that Dissenting and Anglican-leaning missionary societies attached to the term between 1800 and 1830. To be "cosmopolitan" was to be "good," as well as to possess laudable "feelings and benevolences" for those beyond one's immediate community. But, as the last example suggests, some lingering flavor of the Enlightenment emphasis on individual liberation was also retained in the missionary invocation of the "cosmopolitan."

---

7. I've tried to recover a copy of this book, but there appear to be no copies in existence today. My reading thus is constrained to this advertisement in *The Asiatic Journal.*

Hence a broader, recurring pattern in this period, in which missionary invocations of cosmopolitanism would recall Enlightenment connotations of the term just enough to align the missionary movement with eighteenth-century "cosmopolitan" idealism (i.e., its emphasis on freedom and aloofness from a narrow parochial nationalism) but with a crucial difference: Missionaries' cosmopolitanism implied universal responsibility born of Christian belief rather than from an explicit political agenda. Take, for instance, a sermon given by the LMS director Rev. Samuel Greatheed to commemorate the founding of the society in 1795. Here, Greatheed strenuously argued against hierarchizing one's affections, loyalties, and responsibilities:

> Is it not evident that the affection required by the law of God is not a mere emotion of natural feelings, produced by accidental circumstances, and dependent upon different degrees of constitutional sensibility?—It is also plainly distinct from that partial attachment, which is produced by the amiable and excellent qualities of some, in mind or person; or a similarity of disposition, habits, or sentiments in others. If you are biased by prejudices of a national or sectarian partiality . . . attend to our Lord's reply. (94–95)

On the one hand, Greatheed's argument is polemical and startling. Nationalist feelings are "prejudices," amounting to a "*mere emotion* of natural feelings, produced by accidental circumstances," in contradistinction to what he implies is the more rational cosmopolitan view. But the argument is also tempered: A cosmopolitan view is an "affection" required by God's law, an individual responsibility born of faith rather than a comprehensive political scheme.

A similar message would be reiterated by Rev. Bogue in a circular that appeared in an 1804 issue of the *Missionary Magazine*. In terms that Burke no doubt would deplore, Bogue associated the "peculiar attention" to oneself and one's family with "the selfishness of depraved nature":

> Improve your humility and diligence with various dispensations of providence. Those which relate immediately to yourselves and to your families will naturally attract peculiar attention. But as every christian [sic] is a citizen of the world; and from the selfishness of depraved nature, his heart expands in universal benevolence; and from being arrested solely by the conduct of those around him, he extends his views to the acts of the great Ruler of the universe, you will likewise fix your eyes on the dispensations of God towards the community, of which you form a part, and also towards all the nations of the earth. ("A Circular Letter" 2–3)

The sequence of affiliations and attachments Bogue outlines—from being "arrested solely by the conduct of those around him," to considering "the community, of which you form a part," to, finally, encompassing in one's benevolence "all the nations of the earth"—bears striking resemblance to the "*cosmopolitain our cosmopolite*" of Diderot's *Encyclopédie*, which included Montesquieu's articulation of cosmopolitan sympathies: "I prefer my family to myself, my country to my family, but the human race to my country" (qtd. in Schlereth 47). Moreover, it uses those phrases denounced by the *Anti-Jacobin Review* as rhetorical cover for popular agitation (i.e., "citizen of the world" and "universal benevolence") while insinuating that the prioritization of home and country amounts to nothing but "the selfishness of depraved nature."

But Bogue also transfigures this suspect language of cosmopolitan humanism into an apolitical program of Christian responsibility. If one becomes cosmopolitan, he suggests, this is because the cosmopolitan outlook is the inevitable corollary of being a good Christian. After all, one should be attentive to the workings of God and His providence in the world that is His creation and dominion. Indeed, Bogue implies, to be inattentive to anything *less* than the entire world is to fail to appreciate "the acts of the great Ruler of the universe." At stake is religious understanding, not earthly politics. In this sense, Bogue's "citizen of the world"—even as it alludes to the social and political values of Enlightenment cosmopolitanism—*also* asserts enough difference from these values so as to plead ignorance that such associations were meant at all.

Given such ambivalent usages of "cosmopolitanism" by the burgeoning missionary movement, there is considerable temptation to ascribe to them no significant intention. That is, we might be inclined to say that missionaries' "cosmopolitan" feelings were merely shorthand for some vaguely conceived condescension and pity for "perishing heathens" abroad, a sentiment entirely distinct from the suspect cosmopolitanism of Kant and his ilk. Certainly no one could read political—let alone revolutionary—intent into such sentiments.

And yet British conservatives *did* perceive revolutionary undercurrents in the discourse of missionary cosmopolitanism. Muted and faint as they might seem today, the links between the politicized cosmopolitanism of the Enlightenment and missionaries' exhortations of "universal benevolence" were thunderously obvious to some conservatives. Far from seeing missionaries as politically neutral actors (or as enthusiastic, naïve maniacs operating at society's margins, as Sydney Smith might have it), they insisted that missionaries' cosmopolitan sentiments were indelible proof of republican sympathies and confirmation of their essential indifference to local community and country.

That missionary societies used cosmopolitan terms to describe the aims of global evangelicalism nearly drove them to distraction.

This isn't to say that conservative suspicions were unfounded. As Jeffrey N. Cox observes, some of the loudest self-proclaimed "cosmopolites" of the early nineteenth century were the Romantic writers belonging to and associated with the Cockney School, including Byron, Leigh Hunt, Keats, and Shelley, who were accused of disseminating the same "radical thought that lay behind the French Revolution," in effect fashioning themselves as "another Voltaire or Rousseau" (as Robert Southey characterized Hunt) (Cox, "Cockney Cosmopolitanism" 249). The shared use of cosmopolitan language by Romantic radicals and missionary leaders thus appeared to signal some underlying political agreement between these two groups despite their blatant dissimilarities (and, often, mutual antipathy). Indeed, several conservatives noted that certain leaders of the missionary movement had even publicly celebrated the advent of the French Revolution when turmoil first broke out (Rutz, *British* 33).[8] Bogue, for instance, seemed to endorse Jacobinic methods and sentiments when he pronounced of the French Revolution in a 1791 sermon, "This generation shall not pass away before the expiring groans of arbitrary power are heard through every country in Europe" (qtd. in Carson, "The British Raj" 61). Little wonder that Bogue and other evangelicals of similar persuasions were kept under surveillance by domestic authorities into the early 1800s (Rutz, *British* 33).[9]

Periodicals such as the *Anti-Jacobin Review* urged readers to maintain this keen vigilance. In their eyes, the cosmopolitan language associated with missionary societies and their supporters was unquestionably code for some far-reaching conspiracy to upset the status quo. Hence the near hysterical response of the *Anti-Jacobin Review* (1800) to the publication of *A Sermon, Occasioned by the Death of the Rev. Joseph Towers, LL. D.* (1799). Composed of a sermon by the Presbyterian Rev. James Lindsay and an oration by the Unitarian Rev. Thomas Jervis, *A Sermon* celebrated Towers for the "considerable" role he played in the "original institution of the [Missionary] society" (Lindsay

---

8. In the eyes of these figures, the French Revolution portended the "apparent collapse of papal 'tyranny'" (Rutz, British 33).

9. For reasons I outline in my introduction, Dissenting evangelicals were more "inclined to adopt the terminology and campaigning methods of radical politics" than their Anglican counterparts (Carson, "The British Raj" 67). As Carson notes in her study of the 1813 campaign for "religious liberty" in India (i.e., the campaign to end the prohibition on missionary work among native populations), the Anglican Evangelicals "adopted a lower profile" and expressed more wariness than Dissenters in resorting to the "political vocabulary of the Enlightenment" (67). Here we see one of the splits between Dissenting missionary societies and the CMS—a split that brings into fuller relief the remarkableness of their close cooperation.

41).¹⁰ Lauded as a "citizen of the world," Towers was remembered for possessing a "benevolence . . . not confined to persons of any particular party or persuasion, of any specific colour or complexion, of any region or country of the globe" (54). Such descriptions enraged the *Anti-Jacobin Review*. Rev. Towers, the anonymous reviewer ranted, must have been a "noisy cosmopolite," who "deplor[ed] what he thought arose in the various systems of human policy" ("Art. X" 304). Thus it was inarguable, the reviewer continued, that he "wished to overturn these systems [while] worshipping with undissembled devotion a phantom which he called freedom!" ("Art. X" 304). What Rev. Lindsay and Rev. Jervis framed as Towers's all-encompassing human charity born of profound piety, the *Anti-Jacobin Review* interpreted as hatred of the status quo.

It's tempting to see the *Anti-Jacobin* as taking issue with Towers's Unitarianism rather than with his cosmopolitanism and support for the Missionary Society. Yet when the Missionary Society published a tract recommending the widespread distribution of tracts (evincing that evangelical tendency for textual proliferation satirized in Wilkie Collins's Miss Clack), the *Anti-Jacobin Review* renewed its attacks specifically on missionary cosmopolitanism. The "*Missionary Society*," spat the *Anti-Jacobin* (1802), was, in fact, "a heterogenous composition of sectaries of various descriptions, which seem to be united in nothing, but their hatred of establishments, and their zeal in the propagation of their dangerous tenets" ("An Address" 433). They had "lately sent some of its members to the French Republic," the periodical charged, and they had also "established extensive correspondence in that country" (433). All evidence thus pointed to a dismaying, incontrovertible truth: Missionaries and their supporters were "united *in one body* to promote *throughout the*

---

10. Originally the pastor for the Presbyterian congregation in Southwood Lane, Highgate, Towers went on to join the Newington Green Unitarian Church, where he served as coadjuster to Richard Price. Lindsay may also have been Unitarian (or at least shared Towers's nontrinitarianism), but his religious leanings are somewhat harder to pin down. According to a footnote in Alexander Bain's biography of James Mill (1882), when Lindsay was ordained and put in charge of the Monkwell Street Chapel, his "ordainers . . . were all of the Arian section of the English Presbyterian Church," and eventually Lindsay succeeded Price as the afternoon preacher at the Newington Green meetinghouse—events that strongly suggest Lindsay's strong Unitarian leanings (120n). But these religious commitments only make these figures' connection to the LMS founder and Anglican Evangelical Rev. Thomas Haweis all the more surprising. In his sermon, Lindsay *explicitly notes* the cooperation between Towers and Haweis, stating that Towers "had a considerable share and connexion" with Haweis "in the original institution of the [Missionary] society" (41). That Haweis—and not, say, Bogue—is named is startling. Haweis attempted to steer the LMS toward a more "Methodistic and monarchical" outlook, in contrast to Bogue, who harbored more "Dissenting and republican sympathies" (Gunson 64). Such strange networks of cooperation not only indicate the commitment to interdenominationalism within the modern missionary movement but also suggest that the LMS's more conservative factions were (relatively) quite liberal in their leanings.

world . . . the most abominable arrogance, presumption, and falsehood, that ever revolutionary pride engendered, or reforming malice proclaimed" (435). The Missionary Society therefore posed a larger and more immediate threat to England than even "the papists" (433).

Such suspicion was not restricted to the *Anti-Jacobin Review*. In 1799, a clergyman of the General Assembly of the Church of Scotland "made explicit the association of missionary activity with political radicalism," claiming, "They are *affiliated*, they have a *common object*. . . . They look for *assistance from foreign countries*, in the very language of many of the seditious societies" (Carson, "The British Raj" 59; qtd. in Carson, "The British Raj" 59–60). This line of critique continued into the 1810s. A satirical piece on "Benevolent Institutions" in an 1812 issue of *The Scourge; or, Monthly Expositor of Imposture and Folly* (the periodical that launched George Cruikshank's career) satirized the missionaries' cosmopolitan views not only as absurdly "romantic" but also as unpatriotic; so devoted were missionaries to a misguided conception of universal brotherhood, the satire implied, that they even preferred foreign autocracy over domestic democracy. Wearing the guise of a "member of the Missionary Society, a director to the Bible Society, one of the committee for Promoting Christianity in the East, and a coadjustor with the Rev. John Owen in many laudable undertakings," the satire mocked missionary societies for insisting that Christians were as responsible to the needs of the globe as to their own families or nation ("Benevolent Institutions" 132). "In order to render a plan of benevolence acceptable to the public at large, or to the religious part of it in particular," the "member" remarks, "it is absolutely necessary that it should be directed to the benefit of distant nations." He continues, "To administer to the wants of the poor of our own country is a common, and vulgar practice: exalted minds own no distinction between their native soil and the dominions of a barbarian monarch, unless it be to the advantage of the latter. We are all brethren in the flesh; and why should one of our brethren be dearer than another?" (132–33). An 1816 pamphlet on "the Dangerous Tendency of Bible Societies" made more explicit the dangers of missionary cosmopolitanism in a tone that recalled the *Anti-Jacobin Review*. Missionary societies, it argued, were "indiscreet and inauspicious union[s]" whose every member "is a kind of christian [sic] citizen of the world" (*Additional Thoughts* 22). Such cosmopolitan sentiments, it warned, would surely "destroy all respect for the clerical order" and "endanger the Church of England" (*Additional Thoughts* 19).

It was to counter or preempt such charges, one imagines, that some advocates of missionary work couched their claims of harboring "cosmopolitan" sympathies with assurances of their deep local attachments. For instance, in

An Apology for the Missionary Society (1799), John Wilks briefly references the revolutionary zeal and political turmoil of the European continent: "At this period . . . direful horrors stalk through Europe [and] a dark and portentous cloud overspreads the political horizon of our native country" (1). Having implicitly established his stance against the continental threats that menace the domestic "political horizon," Wilks goes on to explain why the LMS in such troubled political times is "intitled to animated applause":

> The person who attends to domestic arrangements, and the performance of relative duties, in an excellent member of society. He, however, who feels interested for the welfare, not of his friends and children only, but also of his fellow citizens and his country, claims a prouder distinction. But, the individual, who, not inattentive to the former objects, is, at the same time, anxious for the general felicity; who . . . would emulate the orb of day, and diffuse to the inhabitants of every clime information and enjoyment; evinces the existence of excellent principles—of sentiments divine. (8)

Even as he anticipates the sequence of attachments that Bogue would outline in 1802, Wilks also adds a clause (i.e., "the individual, who, *not inattentive to former objects*, is, at the same time, anxious for the general felicity"), which emphasizes that existing loyalties are not compromised by cosmopolitan concerns. In alluding to the "direful horrors stalking through Europe"—acknowledging, that is, that political upheavals on the continent *are* horrors rather than the "expiring groans of arbitrary power"—as well as in obliquely confronting the Burkean insistence that attention abroad means neglect at home, Wilks anticipates and preemptively assuages conservative suspicions.

That conservatives so readily assigned political motives to the cosmopolitan idealism of missionary societies perhaps also explains the insistence of the LMS on its "fundamental law." The "fundamental law of the Society," Bogue emphasized in a 1795 sermon, was that missionaries "shall not in the smallest degree interfere with the political concerns of the countries in which they labour, nor have any thing to say or do with the affairs of the civil government. And whoever shall transgress this rule, will be immediately dismissed with shame" ("Objections" 183). While one can think of several reasons for this staunch adoption of political neutrality in the mission field—for instance, to address the East India Company's apprehension that a missionary presence in India would antagonize the "natives" and upset colonial control, or to reiterate the Dissenting commitment to the separation of church and state—the law also responds to conservative distrust of missionary societies. If missionaries are cosmopolitan, the law suggests, *their* cosmopolitanism does not entail meddling "with the affairs of civil government." Thus while the LMS recently might have "sent some of its members to the French Republic," as the *Anti-Jacobin Review* had furiously observed, it certainly had not done so for "political concerns."[11]

Of course, this isn't to say that mission-minded evangelicals weren't participating in politics. Evangelicals "had no sympathy with those who hid themselves away in the hermitage or the cloister," tending instead toward an active public life (Bradley 30). But missionary society supporters also tended to argue that whatever politics they practiced sprang from the imperatives of their faith. Invocations of the rights of man and the equivalence regularly drawn between religious liberty and civil liberty (for instance, in petitions to Parliament for the expansion of missionary work in India [Carson, "The British Raj" 67]) were motivated by evangelicals' profound sense of responsibility to spread the "good word." In their view, the guarantor of civil rights was genuine Christian belief; thus the universal recognition and implementation of these rights primarily depended on Christianity's expansion. This attitude finds clear expression in *A Practical View of Christianity* (1797), the best-selling work by the politician and philanthropist William Wilberforce. "True Christianity," pronounced Wilberforce, is "peculiarly and powerfully adapted to promote the preservation and healthfulness of political communities," for "Christianity in every way sets herself in direct hostility to selfishness, the mortal distemper of political communities" (224, 226). In this manner, Wilberforce perceived social ills to have their roots in a "moral distemper" proceeding from irreligion and mere "professed" religion. The implications of this reorientation of Enlightenment political values is significant; while missionary societies shared with Enlightenment thinkers a common commitment

---

11. This is not to downplay the profound religious commitments of missionary societies and missionaries, which often effectively checked any political ambitions they otherwise might have entertained. While the objective of realizing the "Kingdom of God" on earth—that is, "a vision of unitary Christian polities governed by a partnership of church and state dedicated to the overthrow of 'heathen idolatry'"—motivated the creation of missionary societies, the actual worldwide establishment of a particularly Christian polity was an enormously vexed issue for these societies (Stanley, "Christian Missions" 15). Always in tension with their dreams of a global Christendom was the "separatist vision of a church set apart from the structures of an apostate world, seeking to renew society by the evangelism of individuals rather than by imposed structural change" (15). In this sense, the emphasis the Dissenting tradition placed on political freedoms, religious tolerance, and the right to self-determination required that the "Kingdom of God" be achieved without positive or negative coercion, whether through military might, social benefit, or political means. Hence the LMS director Rev. John Hey's sermon, in which he reminded congregants that missionary efforts "aim not at the acquisition of territory; or the accumulation of wealth; we do not aspire after dominion over the persons [or] the property, the consciences and liberties of men; no, we wish to promote the temporal and everlasting happiness of our fellow creatures" (133).

to "democratic notions" (Carson, "The British Raj" 61), evangelical leaders emphasized that political change foremost hinged on the transformation of individual hearts rather than, say, the implementation and enforcement of a social contract.[12]

On the one hand, then, "the distinctively evangelical belief that known wrong could not be tolerated was hitched to the Enlightenment ideal that government should aim at the happiness of the people" (Carson, "The British Raj" 57). On the other hand, the potential revolutionariness of the Enlightenment ideal to realize the "happiness of the people" was moderated by the growing evangelical belief that such societal happiness obtained less from *institutional* change than *individual* salvation. Here, then, we see the subtle split between eighteenth-century radical Dissent and the modern missionary movement despite their shared values (and leaders). Certainly, benevolence, sympathy, charity, and other virtues deriving from "true" Christianity *might* lead to political action (as in the case of missionary support for the cause of abolition). But, as the "Fundamental Law" of the LMS suggests, it was not foregone (or even expressly desirable) that missionary societies and their supporters would involve themselves in explicit "political concerns."

In this insistence that a "cosmopolitan" perspective arose naturally from Christianity, together with repeated claims of possessing mostly philanthropic rather than political interests, missionary societies helped rid the cosmopolitan ideal of those qualities that made it most threatening to a conservative faction. To be "cosmopolitan," they asserted, was to practice and feel "universal benevolence," but not at the expense of nationalist feeling and local attachment. It also meant endorsing political and commercial federation as a desirable and equitable system of ensuring global peace, but only insofar as such international systems did not impede or overpower any individual's or nation's "freedom of conscience." Most of all, missionary societies and their sympathizers implied that cosmopolitanism designated—indeed, depended

---

12. To be clear, I do not mean to imply that Enlightenment thinkers' conception of rights was secular. As Dan Edelstein observes, "With very few exceptions, natural right was perceived as deriving from God, the 'divine legislator.' . . . If a few authors, such as Diderot and d'Holbach, removed God from the equation, they ended up resacralizing nature" (558). Instead I only mean to note a difference in the emphases between these two groups regarding the preconditions for healthy political communities. Where the Enlightenment tradition tended to emphasize the formation of a contract (whether tacit or explicit) between the government and people (551, 555), evangelicals stressed instead individual transformation through faith. Neither precondition mutually excludes the other, of course, but the privileging of the latter over the former by British evangelicals has repercussions in terms of how the missionary movement would eventually be viewed by the broader public.

on—adherence to Protestant Christianity and what were considered to be its attendant virtues.

By the mid-nineteenth century, cosmopolitan sentiment was *so* yoked to piety and charitable feeling that the term "cosmopolitan" signaled "enlightened and Christian humanist convictions" as much as it did "the impersonal structures of capitalism and imperialism" (Young 15; Goodlad, *Victorian Geopolitical* 12).[13] It was precisely in this philanthropic spirit that the MP and staunch missionary supporter Charles Hindley would use Terence's famous words, "Homo sum, humani nihil a me alienum puto," on the occasion of 1849 Peace Congress in Paris (Young 24; qtd. in Oldham 265). "There is a language which is unheard, but which speaks in every mind with an eloquence more powerful than the language which falls upon the ear," Hindley explained. "At this moment every heart feels the power of our principles—the principles of universal charity. I do not feel that I am English or French; I know and I feel that I am a man" (qtd. in Oldham 265).[14] At an earlier period, such a pronouncement of cosmopolitan sympathies ("I do not feel that I am English or French") might have invited suspicion. No longer. In the prevailing atmosphere of British Christian mania for international philanthropy and the immediate context of the Peace Congress, Hindley's words were taken to indicate an overflowing of his Christian "charity" rather than a lack of national loyalty.

Thus the missionary movement contributed to redefining the quintessential *anti*cosmopolite. No longer was he the upstanding British patriot, as Burke would have it. Rather, the anticosmopolite had become either the continental European, blinkered by his parochial interests and narrow-minded nationalism, or the ignorant "heathen," pitiably unaware of how "the great Ruler of the universe" united his fate with that of mankind.

---

13. More specifically, it's likely that missionary humanism provided the *personality* that animated such "impersonal structures" of commercial exchange. We see the conjoining of missionary humanism and global capitalism in figures such as the missionary-explorer David Livingstone, who appealed to British sympathies precisely to advance an agenda of aggressive commercial expansion in Africa. As mentioned above, I investigate this union in a future piece on Livingstone.

14. The 1849 Peace Congress inspired the 1851 Peace Congress in London, which ran concurrent with the Great Exhibition. The influence of the modern missionary movement can be perceived in the 1849 Congress, too. In his overview of the 1849 Congress, for instance, Oldham marked Hindley's earlier attendance at "missionary meetings at Staleybridge" and praised the MP for exercising a "liberality as discriminating and unsectarian, as that of any public character whom I have ever known" (264).

Bleak House and the Recent History of the Cosmopolitan Idea

As briefly mentioned in the introduction to this chapter, the *British Review* and the *London Critical Journal* registered the extent that the modern missionary movement helped disseminate a second understanding of cosmopolitanism among the British Christian public, one that competed with many conservatives' suspicious understanding of the Enlightenment ideal. Reviewing Lord Byron's *Beppo, A Venetian Story* in an 1818 issue, the *British Review* remarked,

> We are not among those who rejoice in the cosmopolitan liberality, which as of late years become a marked feature in the system of British philosophy. If it arose from a Christian enlargement of sentiment, like that which animates our societies for carrying to foreign parts the blessings of God's Holy Word, it would at least have commanded our respect; but as, to speak the truth, we impute it rather to a growing indifference of moral worth, than to any Christian expansion of benevolence, we cannot hold it in any high estimation. ("Art. II" 330)

Even as it discredits the rise of "cosmopolitan liberality" associated with Byron and his associates,[15] the *Review* nevertheless makes an exception for the cosmopolitan largess "which animates our societies for carrying to foreign parts the blessings of God's Holy Word." Thus dueling understandings of the "cosmopolitan": One is associated with suspect republicanism and a general "indifference of moral worth"; the other indicates a "Christian expansion of benevolence." In laying out these opposed understandings of "cosmopolitan liberality," the *Review*, I believe, captures a moment of transition in which the Christianized cosmopolitanism of foreign missionary societies was coming to prominence even as cosmopolitan radicalism (associated first with Enlightenment *philosophes* and later with Byron and his Cockney School sympathizers) was fading out of view.

In the early nineteenth century, Byron and his allies appeared largely to adopt the controversial antinationalist cosmopolitanism of figures such as Fougeret de Montbron. As Cox observes, Byron offered "almost a slogan" for the Cockney School "when he opened *Childe Harold's Pilgrimage* with a quotation from [Montbron's] *Le Cosmopolite*: 'L'univers est une espèce de livre, dont on n'a lu que la première page quand on n'a vu que son pays. . . . Je

---

15. Byron even cheekily reprimanded the *Quarterly Review* publisher John Murray for critiquing Sydney Owenson's radicalism when "there is such a fine field of us, Jacobin Gentlemen, for you to work upon" (202).

haïssais ma patrie'" ("Cockney Cosmopolitanism" 252). One can imagine how some conservatives—already convinced that cosmopolitan feeling enervated "the ties of father, husband, brother, friend"—received Byron's declarations of hating his homeland.

But such unpatriotic "cosmopolitan liberality" can hardly be detected in the rhetoric surrounding the Great Exhibition of 1851. Instead, the "cosmopolitan" character of the Great Exhibition took its cue from the evangelical conviction that missionary Christianity, world peace, and a globally ascendant Britain were necessarily entwined (Young 17–56; Agathocleous, *Urban Realism* 40–42). Consider Prince Albert's speech for the Third Jubilee of the SPG. Speaking as one of the lead organizers of the Great Exhibition, Prince Albert credited evangelical Christianity with providing the impetus for and influencing the expression of mid-century economic expansion. "We are celebrating a festival of the civilization of mankind, to which all quarters of the globe have contributed their productions, and are sending their people, for the first time recognizing their advancement as a common good, their interests as identical, their mission on earth the same," he announced. "And this civilization rests on Christianity, could only be raised on Christianity, can only be sustained by Christianity" (Albert, "Speech" 134). Similarly, the prize-winning essay of a nationwide competition to promote the Great Exhibition praised the Exhibition for "bring[ing] glory to God" by erecting a sort of "Tower of Babel," only this time done right ("This marvellous edifice shall prove to our race, a kind of compensation for the Tower of Babel, and become the means of promoting the brotherly union, the peace and prosperity of mankind!" [Whish 8]). It also tied the Christian dimensions of the Great Exhibition to the SPCK. "With respect to any practical efforts we can make to turn this grand event to good purpose," announced John Charles Whish, "almost every plan which can be thought of in connection with religion, has long ago been proposed by the Society for Promoting Christian Knowledge, and we can do little more than amplify their suggestions" (70). When Marx (as mentioned above) characterized England in an 1852 letter to Engels as overrun with "cosmopolitan-philanthropic-commercial hymns of peace," he captured the particularly Christian dimension of the Great Exhibition's cosmopolitanism, which, as Whish and Albert observe, had its precursor in missionary benevolence.

Praise was directed toward the SPG and SPCK on these occasions, but evidence suggests that such accolades widely were taken to extend to missionary work in general. Certainly missionary societies, the SPG and SPCK included, cultivated a public appearance of being fundamentally united in spirit and efforts (though behind the scenes they were often divided). In 1852, for instance, "the [CMS and SPG] formed a committee in order to make representation to government when the renewal of the East India Company charter came up for debate," a move meant to signal the fundamental concord between the Anglican societies (Shenk 55). Moreover, agreement and close cooperation among the societies seemed institutionally enshrined by the establishment of the London Secretaries' Association in 1819 (an association dedicated to promoting an interdenominational "union of heart" and whose members included the BMS, CMS, LMS, Wesleyan Methodist Missionary Society, SPG, and SPCK, among others), as well as the Evangelical Alliance in 1846 (Ritson 5).[16] Public speeches from Church figures, such as the one given in an 1856 speech by the bishop of Lincoln, John Jackson, further drove home that the SPG complemented, rather than competed against, its Anglican sister society: "The Bishop of Calcutta told me, with his characteristic warmth, that the Missionaries of the PROPAGATION SOCIETY—angels he once called them— were working along with the Clergymen of the CHURCH MISSIONARY SOCIETY with the most perfect harmony. In fact, our Church would not be fulfilling her mission if either of these two Societies were to be given up" (19). Such rhetoric reinforced the message emblematized in organizations and edifices such as the London Secretaries' Association and Exeter Hall. Insofar as they took the worldwide "brotherhood of mankind" as their common concern, foreign missionary societies were unified in purpose and principle. The result of midcentury British triumphalism combined with the (publicly) unified efforts of the missionary movement, then, was an understanding of cosmopolitanism that was fundamentally at odds with Montbron's *cosmopolite*. The latter signaled the asocial "moral indifference" of Romantic "cosmopolitan liberality"; the former, by contrast, meant a spirit of enterprising, patriotic, and Christian "universal charity," finally and brilliantly crystallized in the Great Exhibition's Crystal Palace.

Bleak House interrogates these competing cosmopolitanisms by way of its two self-proclaimed "cosmopolites," the Leigh Hunt–inspired Harold Skimpole and the philanthropic, "modern" Mrs. Jellyby. Skimpole asserts, of course, that he couldn't be further from possessing Mrs. Jellyby's "strong will" and "immense power of business detail" (*Bleak House* [*BH*] 67). Yet, weirdly, the novel again and again insists on the characters' core similarities despite their apparently divergent "cosmopolitan sympathies" (*BH* 67). It is in this capacity, I suggest, that *Bleak House* recalls the early nineteenth century and Burkean denouncements of cosmopolitanism in order to remind readers that cosmopolitanism prompted by a "Christian enlargement of sentiment" nevertheless

---

16. Although, as Porter notes, the SPG generally refused to attend the monthly meetings of the Secretaries' Association (*Religion* 158).

fatally retains that "indifference of moral worth," which originally made the cosmopolitan idea so controversial.

Dickens wasn't alone in seeing ties between the asocial and amoral "cosmopolitan liberality" of some early nineteenth-century Romantics and evangelical cosmopolitanism. As Sebastian Lecourt observes, Matthew Arnold's *Culture and Anarchy* (1869) also linked "Biblical fundamentalism" and the "radical left-wing idealism of the French Revolution" insofar as both evinced an "addiction to an abstract system" (Lecourt, "Matthew Arnold" 470; qtd. in Lecourt 470). But Dickens made his case against the spirit of mid-century "universal benevolence" with particular clarity and force. In *Bleak House,* he highlighted how enthusiasm for the "civilization of mankind" roused by the missionary movement could *never* be rid of dangerous moral indifference to those close at home—arguing, in effect, that Christian morality *needed* to be divided from the cosmopolitan orientation espoused and assumed by Exeter Hall evangelicals. By putting Romantic *and* mid-century cosmopolitanisms into human forms, Dickens evoked a half-century genealogy of cosmopolitanism intended to underscore the inherent selfishness of those supposedly devoted to the brotherhood of mankind. True Christianity, he argued, attended to the "evils on its doorstep" rather than "extend[ing] [its] views . . . towards all the nations of the earth" (Pope 98).

Taken alone, Mrs. Jellyby represents an unmistakable condemnation of foreign missionary work. So withering and memorable was the character that even ten years after *Bleak House*'s publication, "Borrioboola-Gha" was still "the worldling's nickname for foreign missions" (qtd. in Pope 142–43). Though Caroline Chisholm (the Australia-based philanthropist whose work had only a tenuous connection to evangelicalism and missionary efforts) provided the model for Mrs. Jellyby's domestic habits, the ill-fated and ill-conceived Borrioboola-Gha mission was directly inspired by the catastrophic 1841 Niger Expedition. Spearheaded and supported by some of the luminaries of the missionary movement, the Niger Expedition hoped that the introduction of commerce and Christianity to the Lokoja area would stem the slave trade, improve local agriculture, and awaken the natives "to a proper sense of their own degradation," in the words of the prominent evangelical abolitionist Thomas Fowell Buxton (qtd. in Moore 68). It's worth mentioning that this sparkling vision of global trade and Christian expansion working hand in hand to promote civilization and peace not only anticipated the lofty ambitions of the Great Exhibition; an 1840 meeting convened at Exeter Hall to rally support for the expedition also helped convince a certain young missionary-in-training that international commerce was key to Christianity's global triumph (Jeal 22). When David Livingstone eventually became a celebrity in his own right in

1857, his message that "those two pioneers of civilization—Christianity and commerce—should ever be inseparable" reinvigorated excitement for the civilizing mission, giving second life to Buxton's ideas (165).

In his review of *Narrative of the Niger Expedition* (1848), Dickens blasted such missionary initiatives. In a sustained invective against "African Civilisation, Church of England Missionary, and all other Missionary, Societies," he argued that the movement suffered from a dangerous lack of "common sense" ("Review" 533, 531). From the opening claim that "it might be laid down as a good general rule of social and political guidance, that whatever Exeter Hall champions, is the thing by no means to be done," Dickens went on to criticize a model of Christian charity that sought to expand "the circle of enlightenment" by "convulsive effort, or far-off aim" (531, 533). Britons instead should attend to the urgent task of establishing Christianity and civilization at home, for, if world enlightenment were ever to be accomplished, it would be due to "natural" and "progressive changes of the globe" rather than direct missionary intervention (533).

Mrs. Jellyby embodies this line of critique. Staunchly devoted to the Borrioboola-Gha "mission" and harboring a "serene contempt" for others' "limited spheres of action," she takes missionary cosmopolitanism to its extreme (*BH* 602). In an echo of Greatheed's and Bogue's admonitions that Christians shed "the mere emotion of natural feelings" and the "selfishness of depraved nature" in favor of "universal benevolence," Mrs. Jellyby declares her own sympathies to lie neither with family nor nation but instead "with the destinies of the human race" (296)—a declaration that amounts to an admission that she has no sympathy at all (least of all for her eldest daughter Caddy, whom she makes a "slave" to her philanthropic work [167]).

But *Bleak House* does more than criticize the dubious value of ill-planned philanthropic missions or the (paradoxical) myopia of the universal view. In an effort to quash fully the notion that cosmopolitanism could *ever* be a Christian virtue, the novel denies that cosmopolitanism prompted by a "Christian expansion of benevolence" differs fundamentally from the radical Romantic cosmopolitanism arising from its seeming antithesis, "indifference of moral worth." To drive home this message, the novel repeatedly draws parallels between Mrs. Jellyby and Skimpole, its two self-professed cosmopolites. Just as Mrs. Jellyby asserts that "the Brotherhood of Humanity" motivates her mission, so, too, does Skimpole profess a belief in mankind's "brotherhood." In both cases, the sentiment initially works to obscure how little either character cares for the well-being of those immediately affected by their actions (*BH* 41). Mrs. Jellyby's concern for the "destinies of the human race" provides public cover for her mistreatment of and profound indifference to those closest to her, and Skimpole similarly invokes "common brotherhood" in order to justify his refusal to return a pair of armchairs loaned to him by a local baker: "We are all children of one great mother," he says when asked for the armchairs. "I entreat you, by our common brotherhood, not to interpose between me and a subject so sublime" (521).

Moreover, the characters' supposed admiration of "the human family" comes at the direct expense of their actual families (*BH* 67). "I always wondered," Esther Summerson reflects, "whether [Skimpole] ever thought of Mrs. Skimpole and the children, and in what point of view they presented themselves to his cosmopolitan mind. So far as I could understand, they rarely presented themselves at all" (227). Esther may as well be describing Mrs. Jellyby, whose obsession with the far-off Boorioboolans begets her utter indifference to her spouse and children. Thus the neglected Jellyby children, who "tumbl[e] downstairs," invite comparison to Skimpole's own neglected children, who have "tumble[d] up somehow or other" (167, 64), as both families fulfill Burke's warning that the "new philosophy" of cosmopolitanism dissolves natural family ties. Despite Jarndyce's insistence that Jellyby and Skimpole are "opposites," there's no mistaking the resemblance between her telescopic philanthropy and his "cosmopolitan mind" (183). That each uses cosmopolitan language to dismiss and minimize harmful behavior suggests that the ardent philanthropist and the idle bohemian may not satirize entirely different objects. Instead, the novel suggests, they orbit the same moral failing, a failing that originates in their deliberately cultivated indifference to the "obligations of home" (61). Small wonder that Skimpole admits that he can "sympathise with the objects" of Mrs. Jellyby's ardor (67).

Of course, Skimpole's "sympathy" for Africa at first glance implies a quite different moral orientation than Mrs. Jellyby's philanthropy. In the manner of the coffeehouse cosmopolite, the world for Skimpole is an opportunity for poetic reflection. For him, slavery is a matter of "aesthetic contemplation" rather than a social wrong in need of redress (Agathocleous, *Urban Realism* 109). In this capacity, Skimpole's passive aestheticism starkly contrasts the philanthropic activity of the Niger Expedition evangelicals and the abolitionists of the "Jellyby" camp.

But underlying this apparent difference is a shared sensibility: Missionary cosmopolitanism, the novel suggests, is *also* motivated by aesthetic susceptibility rather than genuine moral conviction. Such is the implication, at least, when the narrator remarks of the starving, illiterate Jo breakfasting on the doorstep of the SPG, "He has no idea, poor wretch, of the spiritual destitution of a coral reef in the Pacific, or what it costs to look up the precious souls among the cocoa-nuts and bread-fruit" (*BH* 199). The missionary concern for the spiritual (i.e., "spiritual destitution" and "souls") is juxtaposed with descriptions of the exotic materiality of the South Sea Islands (recalling the glancing mention of Captain Cook when Ada and Esther, earlier in the novel, first explore their sitting room in Bleak House [63]). It seems no mistake that of all missionary outposts, the novel chooses to allude specifically to the ones in the South Sea Islands. Tahiti was chosen as the inaugural site of missionary work by the LMS in 1795 because its founders had "read Cook" and therefore determined the "only anticipated difficulties" of the area were "such as may arise from the fascination of beauty, and the seduction of appetite" (qtd. in Edmond 98). Thus *Bleak House* mentions the site of foreign missionary work most associated with sensual pleasure to make a devastating accusation. If missionary societies and their circle of domestic supporters turn their backs on domestic problems, it's not because international iniquities are more pressing. Rather, the novel suggests, "telescopic philanthropists" have been seduced by the exoticism and glamor of far-off places. Their action and Skimpole's "inaction" stem from the same perverse spirit of cosmopolitan aestheticism (Agathocleous, *Urban Realism* 35).

Fascinatingly, the various outward differences between the cosmopolitan characters—the one's activity versus the other's passivity; the one's philanthropic interest in "the Brotherhood of Humanity" versus the other's (supposed) artistic interest in this "common brotherhood"—are pinned to sensibilities and fashions associated with distinct time periods. Mrs. Jellyby is unambiguously "modern," not only embodying the faddish "cosmopolitan-philanthropic-commercial hymns of peace" that Marx saw surrounding the Great Exhibition but also anticipating the "modern woman" of the late nineteenth century in her zeal for public work.[17] Thus in a play called "A Woman's Luncheon," published anonymously in an 1895 issue of *The Atlantic,* the various women characters remark on Mrs. Jellyby's continued relevance in the late nineteenth century. "When Dickens wrote *Bleak House*," notes one character, "Mrs. Jellyby was considered an amusing caricature. . . . It seems rather odd

---

17. It is also worth mentioning an 1887 essay on "British Missions and Missionaries in Africa," which appeared in the periodical *The Nineteenth Century*. Authored by the explorer and linguist Harry Johnston, the essay generally lauds missionaries and missionary work. Yet it strongly condemns "the palmy days of Exeter Hall, when eminent philanthropists led unreasoning mobs of weak-brained men and silly women to rave about the emancipation of the negro" (716). Johnston continues, "Then, no doubt, the canting, ignorant, fulsome type of missionary might be met with. . . . Read the contemporary pamphlets of philanthropic societies, the sectarian journals, and religious gift-books for the young, and you will see that Dickens wrote no caricature in his description of Mrs. Jellyby's associates and the mission of Borrioboola-Gha" (716). Notable in the essay is Johnston's conviction that Mrs. Jellyby is no eccentric "caricature" but instead represents the type of Christian philanthropist who prevailed from the 1840s to the 1860s.

that she is at last being brought to the front as the typical modern woman" (200–201; see McParland 135).

But if Mrs. Jellyby is "in advance of her day" ("A Woman's Luncheon" 201), Skimpole is unmistakably a throwback to past decades. Indeed, one of the most notable aspects of his character is its anachronism—a fact often remarked by critics but never quite put into conversation with his "cosmopolitan mind." Modeled on Leigh Hunt,[18] an "anachronistic survival in the Victorian world" whom Mary Russell Mitford would scornfully dismiss as belonging to "days happily past" in her 1852 *Recollections of a Literary Life* (Parrinder 121; Mitford 29), Skimpole nonetheless appears in this most contemporary of novels, a work intended to offset the self-congratulatory nationalism of Great Exhibition fervor (Buzard 110).[19] If *Bleak House* represents an almost surgical delineation of modern British culture's failure to provide its members a sense of meaningful cohesion (contra "the vision of Britain on offer in the Great Exhibition"), to what ends does this luminary of the Cockney School appear here? How does *he* respond to the "false internationalism" of the Great Exhibition? The answer, at least in part, lies in two interrelated phenomena: the conventions of Victorian historiography, and the remarkable parallel the novel draws between Skimpole's "truly cosmopolitan" aestheticism and the "cosmopolitan-philanthropic-commercial hymns of peace" that were the motive force of the Great Exhibition.

As Neil McCaw observes, the past for the Victorians was never (quite) past; when Carlyle pronounced, "We do nothing but enact history," he captured the broader "sense of being in the simultaneous presence of past and present," which was "the foundation of the so-called Victorian 'mirror of history'" and the heart of its historiographical work (McCaw 3). "Reject[ing] static schemas, epic narratives, and the stability of earlier typologies of change," Victorian historicism preferred "comparing and analyzing local patterns *between* individuals, artifacts, epochs, and social systems" (Griffiths, *Age* 3). Comparativist historiography thus stood in contrast to its precedents, "the liberal progressive thesis of Whig history, and the stadial histories of the Scottish Enlightenment" (Griffiths, "Comparative History" 813). Devaluing these totalizing, "systems building" modes of historical analysis, Victorian authors turned to specific problems of the historical past in order to explain and give definite

---

18. Dickens insisted in a September 25, 1853, letter that Skimpole "is the most exact portrait that was ever painted in words!" (qtd. in Brewer 11).

19. Heady similarly argues that *Bleak House* responds to a distinctly contemporary ethos embodied in the Crystal Palace. She reads the novel as "a critique of Crystal Palace progressivism," and she remarks Boasberg's observation that "*Bleak House* . . . could be read as a parody of 'Crystal Palace'" (313).

shape to issues besetting the present moment (McCaw 3; see also Griffiths, *Age*). Analogy became the prevailing tendency of this historiographical work, as a rhetorical device and ontological lens that privileged the "local" and the "individual" (Griffiths, *Age* 3).

Bleak House employs this "mirror of history" by way of "a series of temporally ambiguous images that show the past in conversation with the present" (Heady 317). Although it famously opens with a near hallucinatory vision of a Megalosaurus wandering the streets of modern London, the novel gives most of its historical airtime to the more recent past of the late eighteenth and early nineteenth centuries. A number of characters, Heady observes, embody particular types associated with these decades: Hortense is "a furious French revolutionary"; Turveydrop, a "Regency gentleman who specializes in 'deportment'"; Jo "references . . . eighteenth-century discourses on Romantic childhood"; and Skimpole emerges an embodiment of "Regency panache" and "the proto-modern hero" (317). But this past isn't merely embodied in characters that (like the Megalosaurus) wander the streets of London, out of their proper time and bumping haphazardly into more "contemporary" characters. As though anticipating the strategies that Griffiths argues are fully developed in *A Tale of Two Cities* (for instance, its encouragement of comparativist reading in its assemblages of characters and events, or the "moral allegory" staged in the encounters of characters belonging to two distinct thought systems ["Comparative History" 826–27, 828]), *Bleak House* "novelizes" Victorian historiographical conventions, urging the reader to read Skimpole's and Mrs. Jellyby's respective "cosmopolitanisms" as temporally and socially distinct but functionally and morally analogous.

Hence *Bleak House* introduces Skimpole by way of his oddly hyperbolic praise of Mrs. Jellyby, in which he catalogs his own qualities in comparison with the (supposedly) sterling qualities of Mrs. Jellyby:

> We have been mentioning Mrs. Jellyby. There is a bright-eyed woman, of a strong will and immense power of business-detail, who throws herself into objects with surprising ardor. I don't regret that *I* have not a strong will and an immense power of business-detail, to throw myself into objects with surprising ardor. (*BH* 67)

This comparison is so odd—so seemingly unnecessary in light of the distance between the characters' respective social circles and so seemingly superfluous in advancing the plot—that rather than definitively establishing their difference, it alerts the reader to the characters' potential similarities. The invitation to examine Skimpole and Mrs. Jellyby side by side is underscored by the parallel sentence structure Skimpole adopts in this moment. Despite the content of his claim (i.e., he couldn't resemble Mrs. Jellyby less), the form his claim takes—repeating the same words and phrases—suggests some essential correspondence between Mrs. Jellyby and Skimpole that belies their outward dissimilarities.

This correspondence, I propose, originates in the unflattering understanding of cosmopolitanism that circulated in the early nineteenth century: the radical "cosmopolitan liberality" of Byron and his ilk, which the *British Review* derisively contrasted with the "Christian enlargement of sentiment, like that which animates our societies for carrying to foreign parts the blessings of God's Holy Word." That Skimpole, a minor character, is accorded such an outsized capacity for destruction (i.e., he causes Jo's death, leads Richard Carstone to his doom, and brings grief to nearly all the main characters of *Bleak House*, in addition to irreparably "stunting" the growth of his own daughters [Buzard 143]) suggests that the Romantic "cosmopolitan mind" is not a "past" problem, as Mitford might have it, but an urgent and current one. Rooting Skimpole's poetic and artistic cosmopolitan sympathies in the *early* nineteenth century while making him still so much in "sympathy" with the fashionable objects of Mrs. Jellyby's "mission," *Bleak House* argues by way of these analogous characters that the worst traits of "cosmopolitan liberality"—its deleterious effects on family ties, perverse susceptibility to the aesthetically piquant, and total abnegation of domestic responsibility—persist in present-day "telescopic philanthropy." Thus the novel suggests continuity rather than a clean break between the amoral "cosmopolitan liberality" associated with the Cockney School and the "cosmopolitan-philanthropic-commercial hymns of peace" of the 1850s. The latter still resemble—because they still harbor the failings of—the former.

In this manner, *Bleak House* acknowledges the outward unlikeness between the Romantic "cosmopolitan liberality" despised by Burkean conservatives and the "universal benevolence" urged by missionary societies and their supporters, even as it challenges the notion that the two cosmopolitanisms fundamentally differ. Dickens, of course, famously disliked missionaries, characterizing them as "perfect nuisances [who] leave every place worse than they found it" (*Letters* 282). But the foundation for his dislike is composed of something more than irritation at their self-importance and needless busybody-ness. Missionary societies had legitimated, even elevated in moral standing, the "'rootless cosmopolitan,' devoid of attachments and loyalties" (Agathocleous, *Urban Realism* 34). In their largely successful efforts to make the cosmopolitan idea of "universal brotherhood" accord with Protestant morality and nationalist feeling, missionary societies had equated Christian feeling with the rejection of what they had termed the "selfish" "partial attachments" to one's family and nation.

In Skimpole and Mrs. Jellyby, then, Dickens reanimates drowned-out Burkean suspicions of missionary cosmopolitanism and brings these suspicions to bear on the cosmo-philanthropic mania of the 1850s. In doing so, he asserts that the "citizen of the world," who endlessly "extends his views to all the nations of the earth," can never be the locus of genuine Christian benevolence. Instead, Christian feeling finds its truest form in restricting its attentions to a small "circle of duty [that] gradually and naturally expand[s] itself," as Esther Summerson puts it (*BH* 96)—that is, in precisely that hierarchy of affection privileging "friends and children [and] country," which the missionary movement disdained as but symptomatic of man's "depraved nature."

Thus we see how understandings of cosmopolitanism shifted in the nineteenth century due to the influence of the modern missionary movement. But how did the missionary movement gain this sort of cultural influence in the first place? I turn now to one story (of many potential stories) of how the modern missionary movement went from marginal to mainstream, winning an unexpected and powerful supporter in the process: Robert Southey.

CHAPTER 2

Robert Southey and the Case for Christian Colonialism

THE "NOISY COSMOPOLITES" of the missionary movement launched an involved public relations campaign—one composed of travelogues, missionary narratives, periodicals, and public lectures—that eventually precipitated a shift in their public reputation. From being considered "little detachments of maniacs," missionaries and their societies came to enjoy widespread admiration. Reflecting on this period of transition, John Eimeo Ellis, the son of the famous LMS missionary William Ellis, wrote in his biography of his father (1873), "The appearance of [William Ellis's] *Polynesian Researches* [1829] . . . was greatly applauded by the contemporary press in a spirit very different from the reception which missionary records heretofore too often met" (134). He continued,

> It tended, in no small degree, to raise the character of the missionary to the heathen, and the claims of his work in public estimation. It is scarcely too much to say, that its publication effected a revolution in the general sentiments of all but the most determined enemies of religious enlightenment. (134)

Ellis went on to single out the poet laureate Robert Southey as exemplifying this "revolution in the general sentiments": "The commendation [*Polynesian Researches*] received from some of the foremost Reviews of the period may be inferred from the terms in which Southey speaks of it in the *Quarterly Review*. 'A more interesting work than this,' says that able critic, 'we have never perused'" (134). John Ellis's remarks are an apt entry point for this chapter. Tracing the curious historical circumstances that brought together the missionary movement and the poet laureate, I show in the following pages how the cosmopolitan discourses of the former influenced the late works of the latter.

At first glance, Southey might seem an odd figure to include in this book. Generally he is remembered as "the associate of Coleridge and Wordsworth . . . rather than as the bard he strove to be," a reputation born at least in part from his failure to exhibit that introspective Romantic "consciousness" for which his peers were known (Berhardt-Kabisch 9). Recently, however, scholars such as Tim Fulford, Lynda Pratt, Carol Bolton, and Daniel White have sparked renewed interest in Southey's writings. As studies in Romanticism have shifted toward "debates about the content, formation and politics of the Romantic canon" (Pratt xix), Southey's works have received increased interest precisely to the extent that they so determinedly look outward to contemporary political and social issues. To borrow White's critical assessment (drawn from De Quincey's comments on the poet laureate), Southey is "objective" in a manner that distinguishes him from the canonical Romantic poets. His writings "too much reflect the mind, as spreading itself out upon externall things—too little exhibit the mind, as introverting itself upon its own thoughts and feelings" (White, *From Little London* 85; De Quincey qtd. in White, *From Little London* 85).

Southey voraciously consumed periodicals, histories, and books, and relative to Coleridge and Wordsworth, he appears to have considered himself less a creator of original works than a synthesizer of various sociopolitical ideas and histories, as well as a translator of sorts who rendered secondhand knowledge from (and about) different countries, cultures, religions, and social groups accessible to learned readers in Britain. It is difficult to overstate Southey's importance as a social commentator. By the 1820s, he had become "the most powerful literary supporter of the Tories" (Lowther qtd. in Speck 207), and he was particularly "pre-eminent among his peers for his direct and consistent engagement with colonial issues" (Bolton 2). His public presence was such that it is nearly impossible to discuss early nineteenth-century social history without some mention of him. He pops up, for instance, in Raymond Williams's *Culture and Society: 1790–1950* (1958) as "an influential if unacknowledged figure" in the development of Owenite Christian Socialism (22), Catherine Gallagher cites him as particularly responsible for fostering the distaste for political economy among the literati (7–15), and he regularly makes cameos in Victorian scholarship as Charlotte Brontë's most infamous correspondent. No matter the topic, Southey had an opinion.

He had particular interest in the missionary movement, which he maintained over the course of his long career. Most critics have tended to take his support for missionary societies as comprising little more than his broader interest in "the expansion of empire" and his desire "to export British institutions and values across the world" (Bolton 6). Certainly this is true. But Southey's embrace of missionary societies is far less straightforward than this narrative suggests. In many of his early works, the poet launched fierce criticisms of evangelical Dissent, which, in his best-selling *Sir Thomas More* (1829), he placed in the same dangerous political camp as Roman Catholicism and atheism: "If a breach be made in our sanctuary, it will be by the combined forces of Popery, Dissent, and Unbelief, fighting under a political flag" (1:345). Such remarks compel us to wonder how Southey could have ever become one of the foremost supporters of Dissenting missionary societies. What arguments and historical forces drew the poet to the cause of expanding evangelical values abroad when he was so suspicious of those values at home?

The answer to this question, I suggest, lies in missionaries' success in communicating their evangelical agenda using the language of Enlightenment ideas. As mentioned in the introduction and chapter 1, the use of such language was by no means purely or even primarily strategic; instead, the missionary movement represents an episode in a centuries-long history of interaction between Protestantism and democratic politics. However, we would be naïve to think that missionary societies didn't materially benefit from their rhetoric of "reasonable" religion. For even as the missionary leavening of cosmopolitanism with Christian humanism helped make cosmopolitanism more palatable to suspicious conservatives, so, too, did the missionary valorization of toleration, reason, and pragmatism (rather than fundamentalism, revelation and emotionality, and blind idealism) mitigate the impression that the movement was motivated by religious enthusiasm. The domestication of cosmopolitanism and Dissent, in other words, happened in concert. Thus in the previous chapter, I discussed how missionaries domesticated the cosmopolitan idea insofar as they treated it as a "language ideology" rather than a strictly defined political ideal. In this chapter, I focus instead on the strategic considerations behind the missionary adoption of Enlightenment language—the ways that such language could "domesticate" evangelical Dissent, so to speak—as well as the broader consequences of such considerations.

By claiming that they promoted not only strictly religious but relatively "secular" humanistic values—including political self-representation, inalienable rights, tolerance, freedom of conscience, and the necessity of scientific progress—missionary societies distanced themselves from enthusiasm, and thereby fashioned themselves as moral, pragmatic, and eminently reasonable representatives of British Christianity.[1] The goal of the missionary movement, they argued, was not to export religious fanaticism, as some critics feared. Instead, it was to pave the way for "progress" and "civilization" based on a rational Christian morality. It was in this manner that missionaries secularized their evangelical agenda, rendering their efforts more attractive and acceptable to polite society.

This language appealed to nationalists and imperialists such as Southey, who, despite advocating for imperial expansion, nonetheless considered himself a champion of emancipatory Enlightenment ideas. Indeed, as I will show, Southey's reviews of missionary publications—in particular *Periodical Accounts Relative to the Baptist Society* (1802, 1809) and *Transactions of the Missionary Society* (1803, 1804, 1809)—demonstrate that Southey found in these writings a means of smoothing out an ideological conundrum that profoundly troubled missionary work, and, to a lesser extent, Southey's own schemes for British Christian colonization. This was, namely, that the spread of supposedly liberatory Christian humanism seemed very much to depend on manifestly oppressive, domineering forms of power over foreign lands and peoples.

The conceptual framework with which missionaries and then Southey ultimately reconciled the contradictions between the lofty ideals of Christian evangelicalism and its far more unsavory manifestation in practice turned out to be cosmopolitanism, specifically Immanuel Kant's "cosmo-political" idea (which Southey praised profusely in *Sir Thomas More*, and which I discuss in chapter 1). In his essay "Idea for a Universal History with a Cosmopolitan Purpose," Kant proposed a "Plan of Nature" in which each individual, no matter his individual actions and intentions, would inexorably help realize "perfect Civil Union" and "the establishment of a Cosmopolitan State" (qtd. in De Quincey 439, 441). The mid-step to realizing this cosmopolitan existence was the establishment of societies in which "freedom under laws is united with the greatest possible degree of irresistible power" (434). The emphasis that Kant placed on individual freedom accorded with and conveniently enabled Southey's own moral justification for Christian colonial expansion. That this

---

1. This is not to claim that "religious" and "secular humanistic" values are mutually exclusive; as already discussed, "religion" has played and continues to play a key role in the construction of "secular" modernity. Instead (as explored at more length below), I understand the missionary advocacy of certain values as *relatively* "secular" insofar as missionary societies seemed to have distinguished such values (and the discourses that deployed and defined such values) as distinct from those associated with "enthusiasm."

freedom was to be attained by the (perhaps paradoxical) exercise of "irresistible power" helped excuse what the poet laureate believed would be short-term iniquities of colonialism.

The remainder of this chapter unfolds in three parts. The first provides the historical backdrop, recounting how missionary societies tended to use a more "secular" speech, relative to evangelical revivalists, to make themselves "respectable" in the eyes of (and thus deserving of donations from) a moneyed middle class. These efforts had the added effect of reinforcing the notion that Enlightenment values were fundamentally aligned with evangelical ones, which gave increased credence to religiously informed discourses in the public sphere. In the second part, I turn to consider how this rhetoric affected Southey. Examining his reviews of the missionary periodicals noted above, I illustrate how he derived his conception of a supposedly "moral" Christian colonialism largely from missionary work. The last section of this chapter then demonstrates how Southey's "Christianized" version of Kantian cosmopolitanism represented his most sustained rhetorical and schematic effort to demonstrate that colonial oppression could achieve global emancipation. Specifically, it argues that *A Tale of Paraguay* (1825) and *Sir Thomas More* should be read as counterparts to one another: *Paraguay* sketches out a scheme of Christian colonialism that finds its conceptual framing (or, its "proper position," as Southey terms it) in *More* (2:407). Together, the works reveal how his engagement with missionary writing and advocacy for colonialism found their unlikely synthesis in his peculiar understanding of Kantian cosmopolitanism. Southey thus represents one of the strange paths by which "cosmopolitanism" morphed from a relatively secular Enlightenment ideal, associated with guaranteeing individual freedoms as much as with attaining global peace, to a means of legitimizing Christian colonial expansion.

"Rational and Elevated Devotion"

Before we can understand how Southey ultimately came to sympathize with evangelical missionary societies—so much so that he would consider the aforementioned missionary, William Ellis, a "hero"—we must first understand the rhetorical strategies that these societies adopted in the early 1800s to appeal to the British public (Storey 322). This shift in discursive tactics and thus public reputation is highlighted by the remarks of John Eimeo Ellis quoted above. Through an efficient public relations campaign (Elbourne 14), missionary societies cultivated a public image mostly free from those negative stereotypes that generally attended evangelicalism in the eighteenth and early nineteenth centuries. Fashioning themselves as rational and disciplined, they took part in what historian Ben Wilson identifies as a broader movement among nineteenth-century evangelicals, such as William Wilberforce, to make their religiosity "attractive to the upper and middling classes" (xxv).[2]

I identify this rhetorical self-fashioning as "secularizing" in order to register the extent to which it was indebted to the ethos of the eighteenth-century Enlightenment *philosophes*. As Craig Calhoun, Mark Juergensmeyer, and Jonathan VanAntwerpen note, these *philosophes* were "secular" insofar as they could not imagine "social progress . . . without liberation from previous social and political institutions and the religious ties that had justified them" (7).[3] Of course, such a position did not entail the abolishment of religion. Rather, these *philosophes* sought an iteration of "religion" that would not lead to a repeat of "the preceding century's Wars of Religion" (7). They emphasized "a 'reasonable' religion," one "potentially limited and controllable," and which in large part they negatively defined by invoking its supposed, uncontainable, and uncontrollable opposite, "excessive 'enthusiasm'" (7).

Missionary societies sought to make use of this same binary. Through their periodicals and narratives, the societies rebutted criticisms leveled at them by periodicals such as the *Anti-Jacobin Review*, *The British Critic*, and *The Satirist, or Monthly Meteor*, asserting their disdain for and distance from those forms of religious revivalism that could be labeled unreasonable or "enthusiastic." Cultivating what Sivasundaram calls "cogent links between the Enlightenment and evangelicalism," missionary societies argued that a "relationship with God" proceeded not from "intuitions and passions" but rather from "a process of step-by-step reasoning" (37).

The emphasis the societies placed on the reasonableness of missionaries' religion in part was a reaction to the perception among the conservative moneyed classes that evangelical Dissent was "vulgar and appallingly fanatical" (Wilson xxv). From the mass conversions to Methodism that took place from 1738 onward, the religious revivalism of the eighteenth century was regularly linked with the "lower orders" (xxv). Forms of worship that were popular among the religious revivalists—including the lay sermon, group prayer, itinerant preaching, and prophetic speech—were common subjects of ridicule. The *Quarterly Review* (1823), for instance, insisted that Methodism "strikes,

---

2. See also White, *From Little London* 58. White usefully reminds us that the BMS was especially associated with the Calvinist Particular Baptists, who were predominantly from the working classes. This association made respectability more difficult for the BMS to achieve compared to, say, the CMS.

3. For more on Enlightenment thoughts' convergences with the commitments of British Protestantism, see my introduction.

inflames [and] makes the effect of obstructed bile, and the state of animal spirits, the test of religion" (Milman qtd. in Canuel 23). Moreover, the *Monthly Review* (1808) pronounced evangelical preaching to be a *"mania"* that had taken hold of the "illiterate" and the "deluded vulgar" ("Art. VIII" 181, 180). Perhaps one of the most devastating attacks on evangelical forms of worship came from the Cambridge scholar and controversialist Gilbert Wakefield. In his *Enquiry into the Expediency and Propriety of Public or Social Worship* (1792), Wakefield declared that the "mode of *prayer* among *dissenters*" struck him as "unedifying and intolerably irrational" (3). The practice of group prayer "where the congregation is *gaping* for the *ejaculations* of their orator," he continued, was also reminiscent of an image produced by a "facetious painter of antiquity, who represented Homer copiously discharging from his mouth, and the poets of succeeding times licking up his v[omi]t" (37).[4] Consequently, evangelical Dissenters who aspired to polite society were regularly forced to fend off charges of parochialism, fanaticism, and ill-breeding.

One means of countering such impressions, as the essayist and Baptist minister John Foster argued, was for evangelicals to avoid "the accustomed diction of evangelical religion" (144).[5] In an essay addressing "the Causes by which Evangelical Religion has been rendered unacceptable to Persons of Cultivated Taste" (1805), Foster recommended the abandonment of language "exclusively appropriated to christian [sic] doctrine," because, he argued, such a "dialect" becomes "totally unserviceable for any other subject" (146). "It is a kind of popery of language, vilifying everything not marked with the signs of the holy church, and forbidding any one to minister to religion except in consecrated speech" (146–47). Suggesting that evangelicals take their rhetorical cues instead from "Addison or Pope" (151), Foster sought to distance evangelicalism from both reified religious speech as well as the "enthusiastic," "inspired" religious speech linked with the "uncultivated" classes. As we will see, missionary societies seemed to take Foster's recommendations to heart.

Associated as they were with this spirit of religious revival, the BMS and LMS became frequent targets of ridicule and derision by conservative and Church writers.[6] As the previous chapter details, these missionary societies

---

4. Interestingly, Wakefield became a Dissenter later in life.
5. Kirstie Blair notes that Foster in this case mostly identifies evangelicalism "with dissent rather than Anglicanism" (145).
6. While less controversial than the Dissenting societies, the CMS came under attack from conservative Church figures, too. In his *History of the Church Missionary Society* (1899), Stock recounts that "the Archdeacon of Bath, Mr. Thomas, rose unexpectedly and protested, in the name of the Bishop of Bath and Wells, against the invasion of the Diocese by an unauthorized society, which amounted, he said, to a factious interference with S. P. G." (147). The subsequent pamphlet war between the archdeacon and Daniel Wilson of the CMS, Stock crows,

were blasted for their "hatred of establishments, and their zeal in the propagation of dangerous tenets" ("An Address" 431). Elsewhere they were condemned for their *"visionary schemes of fanaticism"* and accused of being "missionary jugglers, who prefer Scotland, and endeavour to sow discord" ("To the Editor" 368; Bisset qtd. in "Review: *Modern Literature*" 50). Travelogue writers, such as the Danish Jørgen Jørgensen, also contributed to the poor reputation of missionaries. In a work bearing the pointed subtitle *Reasons for the Ill Success Which Attends Christian Missionaries* (1811), Jørgensen wrote that the first South Sea missionaries came from the "dregs of the people." "It is easy to observe that they are men of no education," he quipped, "nor have ever conversed with any but the lowest classes of society" (qtd. in Gunson 31). Such negative portrayals undercut the ability of missionary societies to fund-raise effectively. Even more injuriously, they bolstered the arguments of the East India Company, which, to the irritation of evangelicals, opposed the presence of missionaries in India. To argue against the insertion of what was called the "pious clause" in the 1813 renewal of its charter, the East India Company capitalized on the image of missionaries as little more than lower-class "enthusiasts," claiming that their maniacal religiosity only exacerbated native dissatisfaction and undermined British dominion in India.[7]

These stereotypes, admittedly, were not unearned. In their early days, missionary societies tended to value demonstrations of "sincerity" in their missionaries over social and educational attainments. As Gunson notes, there existed an initial belief among some directors of the LMS that the ideal missionary was an uneducated one. "A plain man,—with a good natural understanding,—well read in the Bible,—full of faith, and of the Holy Ghost,—though he comes from the forge or the shop," the LMS director Thomas Haweis argued in 1798, "would . . . as a missionary to the heathen, be infinitely preferable to all the learning of the schools" (qtd. in Gunson 37). Even those directors who preferred some education in the society's missionaries assumed that less "developed" cultures could do with less-educated missionaries. Thus the South Sea Islands and southern Africa were fields suited "for artisans and the less intelligent or less scholarly," while "the more scholarly, gifted and 'respectable' missionaries were sent to India and the Orient"

"profited" both the CMS and SPG by increasing the contributions of the one while "waking" the evangelical sympathies of the other (147).

7. The CMS's alignment with the Church helped them have a much more positive relationship with the East India Company. Carson provides an overview of the CMS's more conciliatory stance toward the East India Company as opposed to the "disappoint[ment] and apprehens[ion]" of the Dissenting societies (*East India Company* 130–31).

(Gunson 96–97).[8] Of course, such rationalizations conveniently accounted for the fact that the LMS could hardly find anyone *but* lower-class "enthusiasts" to volunteer for what amounted to (in the words of an ex-secretary of the LMS) "voluntary banishment" (Fox 71).

Still, the recruitment of "pious tinkers" for its first mission to the South Sea Islands proved a misstep for the LMS. As their deeds and diaries started to attract the attention of nonreligious periodicals in Britain, these missionaries became objects of pity and ridicule rather than admiration.[9] Their narratives reveal much petty infighting among the brethren. Among the sources of tension, as I discuss in chapter 3, was the determination of some of these missionaries to marry Polynesian women—an issue that split the unity of the South Seas mission, and which, consequently, was explored in pages upon pages of *Transactions of the Missionary Society*. Back in England, critics of missionaries seized on these debates as proof positive of missionary idiocy. The intermarrying missionaries were satirized as licentious religious hypocrites, who had succumbed to the seductions of island "Jezebels" ("Memoirs of a Missionary" 284), and the missionaries who condemned this behavior were cast as stiff-necked and uncompromising. And then there was the problem of these missionaries' *language*. While no doubt intended to convey the strength they derived from their faith, the missionaries' writings at times seemed to privilege melodramatic displays of self-imposed suffering over common sense, pragmatism, and even decency. In a 1798 letter authored collectively by "the Missionaries on the Island of Otaheite, or King George's Island" to "the Directors of the Missionary Society; who, under the great Prince of all Missionaries, for the preaching of his gospel in all parts of the World, were instrumental in

---

8. What directors such as Haweis didn't fully appreciate was that part of missionary work's attraction was the social mobility it promised. Though these directors enjoined the first missionaries to ignore the insults of "secret infidel[s]" and "lukewarm professor[s]," missionaries expressed a desire to be recognized as figures of authority and respectability in their new roles as messengers of God (Burder 70). One missionary, for instance, complained to LMS directors about being sent out "in special clothing which robbed [new missionaries] of the status to which they aspired." "You have actually denied us the things which are necessary for maintaining respectability," the missionary continued. "What has greater tendancy [sic] to refine, and make a person engaging in their manners (a thing so necessary to a missionary) than polite company?" (qtd. in Gunson 38). This rebuke to LMS directors back in London illustrates missionaries' yearning to be "respectable" even when bound for the South Sea Islands for an indefinite period of time.

9. Dispatched in the HMS *Duff* in 1796, the thirty missionaries of the LMS's first mission abroad mostly settled in "Taheiti" (Tahiti) and "Tongataboo" (Tongatapu), with two staying on the small island of "St Christina" (Tahuata). Here and elsewhere I refer to place names as used by missionaries and other nineteenth-century commentators for the sake of clarity.

commissioning us to go forth and teach the Heathens in these Seas" (as the letter began), the missionaries pronounced,

> Experience has taught us, the more we are encumbered about worldly things the less concern we have for the conversion of the heathen; and the more we are detached from secular employments, the more, we trust, our minds will be attached to the propagation of the gospel of Jesus Christ. Otaheite affords food and raiment, suitable to its climate, and sufficient to answer the great end of Providence, in granting us these blessings; viz. to cover our nakedness, and to sustain for a while our earthly perishing tabernacles, and having those things, we hope the Lord will teach us to be content. ("Otaheitean Journals" 40–41)

Of course, thanks to Captain Cook's eye-popping accounts of nearly naked islanders, British readers could well envision how much "raiment" was "suitable to the climate." One imagines not a few of them found humorous the image of missionaries' "earthly perishing tabernacles" barely concealed by whatever clothing they had managed to scrape together.[10] Little wonder, then, that the diaries of the LMS's and BMS's first missionaries ended up providing rich fodder for outlets such as *The Satirist, or, Monthly Meteor,* which ran a three-part essay entitled "Memoirs of a Missionary" dedicated to mocking the South Sea missionaries.[11] Even Southey, who hoped to "vindicate" the first missionaries of the BMS, admitted he could not be "blind to what is . . . ludicrous in their phraseology" ("Art. XVII" 225).

The twin determinations of the LMS and BMS to attract middle-class subscribers and debunk what had become an entrenched stereotype that missionary work appealed mostly to "weak and uncultivated minds" prompted them to recast themselves as rational and thoroughly "respectable." To do so, they contrasted themselves against rabid evangelical "enthusiasm." *The Evangelical Magazine and Missionary Chronicle,* for instance, denounced "Modern Visionaries" in an 1805 essay, arguing that they were all "actors in [a] religious farce" led by the self-styled prophetess Joanna Southcott:

---

10. As though aware of the absurdity of the missionaries' language, William Ellis edited this letter when it was reprinted for his *History of the London Missionary Society.* Humorously, he entirely excluded the phrase "to cover our nakedness, and to sustain for a while our earthly perishing tabernacles" (124).

11. A fictionalized account told from the point of view of a lustful thief who joins the first missionary voyage to Tahiti, "Memoirs" ridicules the overblown piety expressed in the diaries of the real missionaries.

> [I] cannot but regret any persons should swallow such palpable absurdities and impositions, which are opposite both to the letter and spirit of divine revelation. Weighed in this righteous balance, the visions and revelations of these misguided enthusiasts are lighter than vanity—what one apostle would call *cunningly devised fables*; and what another would not scruple to name *strong delusions*. ("Modern Visionaries" 41)

The "immediate inspiration" and literal "revelations and visions" so admired by the acolytes of these false prophets, the *Evangelical Magazine* continued, were but "irregulari[ties] of their own imagination" (40, 41).

By contrast, the faith of missionaries and missionary supporters was portrayed as eminently disciplined and rational. Thus the death of a Perth missionary supporter, Catherine Lawrie, became an opportunity for the LMS to counter accusations that its supporters were nothing but "enthusiasts." "Ah, my friend," sighed the periodical, "enthusiasm will be found to assume a very different form. It is wild, vehement, and extravagant, intimately associated with ignorance and self conceit." Lawrie, by contrast, lived a "life of the most rational and elevated devotion—of deep humility—and distinguished superiority to the world" ("Death" 401). A letter written to the *British Critic* took a similar rhetorical tack to counter the negative portrayal of India-based missionaries in the periodical. Answering the *British Critic*'s assertion that "all the wild and discordant effect of *unauthorized missions* . . . can be productive of little permanent good," a supporter of the CMS pointed not to the spiritual but the pragmatic, practical benefits of missionary societies. The "deliberate and long practised plans of Missionary Societies," wrote the supporter, have contributed "towards the translating and printing of the Scriptures and other books in several Eastern languages; and also to the establishment and encouragement of charity schools, and the erection of churches in that quarter of the world" ("To the Editor" 368, 369). In this manner, missionary societies and their supporters increasingly steered clear of the "biblical phraseology" and the evangelical *"peculiarity of language"* despised by Foster (167, 141).

Figures such as William Carey of the BMS and Johannes van der Kemp of the LMS played important roles in this shift in missionary rhetoric. Indeed, the relative success of these missionaries in public esteem appeared to alert their societies to the significant social capital to be gleaned from *respectable* missionaries, as opposed to the "dregs" who had largely composed the first missionaries dispatched to the South Sea Islands.[12] Carey, for instance, became

---

12. The LMS was deeply invested in protecting its public image and heavily edited the journals, letters, and accounts of their missionaries before printing them (Johnston 33).

"one of the premier botanists and natural historians of the early nineteenth century" and displayed a "remarkabl[e] open-minded[ness]" to the writings and arguments of the Orientalists of the Asiatic Society (which, in fact, he joined in 1806) (White, *From Little London* 62, 63; Thomas 46–47). Moreover, his press in Serampore was founded on the belief, in the words of one of his missionary colleagues, that it was "the duty of a missionary to obtain as complete a knowledge as possible of the language and religious institutions, the literature, and the philosophy of the people among whom he laboured, and to leave a record of his acquisitions" ([1859], qtd. in Alban, Woods, and Daigle-Williamson 95). In this manner, missionary researches would go "hand-in-hand with the communication of secular and divine truth" (95).

In South Africa, Van der Kemp, who in his pre-missionary days had been a "deist and a rationalist author," helped to create the style of the naturalist and "ethnographic" missionary report that would later be emulated by some of the most renowned LMS missionaries, including William Ellis, John Williams, and, at a much later date, David Livingstone (Walls, "Eighteenth-Century" 39). These reports would help establish the missionary presence in scientific and social circles. Consider this snippet of Van der Kemp's writing published in *Transactions of the Missionary Society* (1804):

> *Fossile Productions.*—I had no time for investigation, and no instruments to enquire into the nature of the objects that might have presented themselves to my view. I heard say that nitre is to be found in Caffreland, and also brimstone, I never have met them. . . . Between the Debe and the Quakobe I found, about two feet under the ground, a stratum of round grains of the size of small peas, of a brownish red colour, which seemed to be an iron ore.
>
> *Vegetables.*—The most common tree is the large thorn tree, from which the gum-arabic exudes. Its inner rind serves the Caffrees for food, and the outer, which is of a bright red colour, to prepare the skins of animals for clothing. I recollect to have seen only three kinds of wood known in Europe, the willow, and the black and red ebony. (qtd. in "South African Mission" 459)

The account—focused as much on the practical utility of missionaries' "scientific" discoveries as on the work of proselytizing itself—continues for pages in this manner. The epistemological authority of such reports is buoyed further by Van der Kemp's regular allusions to his personal educational attainments—attainments that, in turn, are emphasized by the LMS in its prefatory material to much of Van der Kemp's writing, as well as in its various publications celebrating the missionary (the society, for instance, hardly ever failed to mention that Van der Kemp was a doctor, and its official *Memoir of the Rev. J. T. Van Der Kemp* opened by stressing the late missionary's "respectable" family lineage [3]).[13]

Consciously or not, later missionaries in their writings would evoke this bent toward science and philosophy. John Williams's *Narrative of Missionary Enterprises in the South Sea Islands* (1837) took its tone from Van der Kemp, blending thrilling personal anecdotes with proto-ethnographic descriptions of "native" culture and scientific theories for natural phenomena. This is the spirit, certainly, that animates the passage that opens my introduction, the pronouncement from the American edition of *Missionary Enterprises* (which itself borrows directly from Alexander Pope's "An Essay on Man: Epistle II"): "'The proper study of mankind is man.' . . . Especially should Christians, at this day, be familiar with the condition, and changes, and prospects, of every people, among whom missionary labours have been commenced. They should be at home on missionary ground. The Christian is the only true cosmopolite" (xi). Significantly, "cosmopolite" as used here seems to connote not just Christian universalism, but also missionary Christianity's key role in the growth of scientific knowledge.

By adopting the language of natural theology, proto-ethnography, and cosmopolitanism in this manner, missionaries distinguished their Christianity as "rational," painting a flattering portrait of their own faith as uniquely "enlightened" when compared to superstitious "heathen" belief systems (Sivasundaram 5). Moreover, they successfully capitalized on the emerging print market, catering to a diverse readership that was not necessarily invested in denominational concerns or even religion at all. The combination of first-person adventure with "authoritative" scholarship was irresistible to British readers, who wished to be entertained *and* educated.[14] *Missionary Enterprises*, for one, was a transatlantic best seller, which went into several editions. Interest in the narrative only increased after Williams's "martyrdom," when the missionary was killed and reportedly cannibalized by Eromangans in 1839.

---

13. Van der Kemp's embrace of science and metaphysics did not preclude belief in divine revelation. Like other evangelicals, Van der Kemp experienced a profound moment of being "saved," an experience that he emphasized was *not dependent* on his powers of reason. "I concluded . . . it was entirely out of the reach of my reason to discover the true road to virtue and happiness" (qtd. in Southey, "Art. II" [1804] 624). Moreover, chapter 3 discusses how Van der Kemp's interracial marriage to a thirteen-year-old Malagasi girl shortly before his death undermined the missionary's public image.

14. Mary Wilson Carpenter remarks that the popular genre of "the Family Bible" had similar aims as a result of publishers' efforts to market these Bibles to the mass reading public (122).

In addition to touting their scientific bona fides, missionary texts stressed with increasing frequency the liberalizing spirit of missionary work. By spreading Christian values, these narratives insisted, missionaries promoted laissez-faire economics, representative government, and religious tolerance. Thus *Polynesian Researches,* the narrative so beloved by Southey, asserted that the introduction of Christianity in the region had not only "opened a new channel for commercial enterprise" but had also prompted the creation "for the first time [of] what might be termed a representative government . . . rendering the Tahitian a limited, instead of an absolute monarchy" (Ellis 2:452). Ellis added, "Every friend of liberty and the natural rights of men, and to the order and good government of society, must rejoice" (2:129). In this manner, the philosophical currents of the Enlightenment were portrayed not as antithetical to the spirit of evangelical religion but as part of the natural return that could be expected with the establishment of Christianity worldwide; Christian precepts "furnished 'a complete moral machinery' for carrying forward all the great processes which lie at the root of civilization" (Stanley "Commerce" 71). As such, missionary societies contended that the value of Christianity lay not only in the *spiritual* salvation it offered to each individual but in the comprehensive *social* and *political* program such spiritual salvation birthed. "True Christianity," as Wilberforce had envisaged, indeed seemed "peculiarly and powerfully adapted to promote the preservation and healthfulness of political communities."

Therefore while the missionary societies of the modern missionary movement tended to welcome members from nearly all denominations of Protestantism, their writing suggests that over time they moved toward restricting and marginalizing religious voices that appeared too "enthusiastic." To gain real prominence as a missionary, it seemed, one could be of any denomination so long as one generally practiced and preached a rational and moderate Christianity, one characterized by an attentiveness to scientific progress, attunement to social ills, and support for those liberal values promulgated during the Enlightenment, including tolerance, civil rights, and individual liberty. To a degree, missionary societies thus present a compelling case study for Jürgen Habermas's assertion that the modern secular state demands a "filter through which only 'translated,' i.e., secular, contributions may pass from the confused din of voices in the public sphere into the formal agendas of state institutions" ("Secularism's Crisis" 28). By fashioning themselves not as reactionaries against but rather as the rightful inheritors and key practitioners of Enlightenment liberal principles, missionary societies found common ground among themselves despite their denominational differences and helped launch the evangelical movement more broadly into a position of influence.

By 1828, then, the *Missionary Register* could celebrate the extent to which missionary societies had changed their public image, proclaiming that the world "ceases to regard Missions as the mere product of fanaticism" ("Necessity" 272). By the mid-century, they were seen as "useful part of the middle-class drive to civilize the unruly and the unrespectable within and without Britain," enjoying a reputation of political prominence and social respectability that was far removed from the "vulgar" religious revivalism with which they had initially been associated (Elbourne 26). They embodied an evangelical piety gone relatively mainstream, a success in no small part due to the manner in which they married religious expression to an Enlightenment-inflected humanism and an agenda for social change. Southey, as I will show below, proved himself a keen supporter of this humanist emphasis in missionary work *and* one of its foremost challengers in his advocacy for aggressive Christian colonialism.

Robert Southey and the Missionary Movement

Considering *Sir Thomas More*'s "anti-Enlightenment, anti-reform, and pro-restoration" sympathies, its explicit praise of Kant's cosmopolitan plan is nothing less than "surprising" (Wohlgemut 145). Some critics have tried to make sense of this seeming disjunction between Southey's peevish conservatism and his endorsement of what the conservative (and conspiratorial) Abbé Barruel thirty years earlier had sneeringly called the Jacobinical "Cosmopolitan Empire announced by Professor Kant." Daniel Sanjiv Roberts, for instance, argues that Southey's incorporation of Kant's "optimistic, revolutionary and secularist vision" into "orthodoxy and conservatism" neatly encapsulates the poet's own political evolution from youthful radicalism to middle-aged dogmatism (46). The poet's appropriation of Kantian cosmopolitanism, that is, shoehorns the radical ideals of his college days into the conservative, nationalist politics of *Sir Thomas More*. Southey's nationalistic "cosmopolitanism" was not simply pulled out of thin air, though.[15] Rather, there is reason to believe that it was indebted to missionaries' earlier appropriation of Enlightenment "cosmopolitanism" to signify not a secularized and detached antinationalist view but a Christian "expansion of benevolence" (as detailed in chapter 1). These efforts to wrest cosmopolitanism from its association with Continental

---

15. It certainly had some discursive precedent, for instance, in Coleridge's declaration in *The Friend* that "Cosmopolitanism [is] at once the Nursling and the Nurse of patriotic affection! . . . It is rooted in the soil of the nation: nourished and nourishing the national soil" (qtd. in Wohlgemut 2–3).

radicals and revolutionaries and make it congruent with Christian nationalism paved the way for Southey's own appropriation of Kantian cosmopolitanism in *Sir Thomas More*.

That missionary writing exercised immense influence over Southey's thought is undeniable. In the opening decades of the nineteenth century, he engaged with missionary writing, as well as with missionaries themselves. As I'll discuss, Southey's reviews of missionary reports and periodicals in the *Annual* and *Quarterly* reviews suggest that he saw in these works potential reconciliation between his dedication to the Enlightenment ideals of religious tolerance and freedom of conscience, on the one hand, and on the other, his advocacy for the use of "colonization and . . . force" to achieve these ideals ("Art. LXIV" 200). To understand Southey's "surprising" deployment of Kantian cosmopolitanism in *Sir Thomas More*, then, I propose that we can look to these early reviews to find, perhaps, an early instantiation of this line of thought.

To the extent that it came to stress not its zeal but rather its social and political usefulness, the missionary endeavor appealed to Southey. Although a supporter of the Church of England, he was mostly unconcerned about theological and doctrinal differences; his fierce loyalty to the Church was instead based on the "moral and social benefits" he believed it offered (S. Andrews xi). As long as Dissenters were "moderate" and above petty sectarianism, Southey could appreciate them as potential allies of the Church in "resist[ing] atheism and enthusiasm" (Craig 85). Thus it was precisely insofar as the missionary societies succeeded in *secularizing* their evangelicalism—stressing not theology and creed, but humanist interests, social order, and fair governance in foreign places—that they managed to convince establishmentarians such as Southey to back their cause.

No doubt he was also attracted to the missionary movement's implicit support of strong, centralized government. As chapter 1 discusses, missionary societies, while claiming to advance Enlightenment ideals such as liberty, toleration, and cosmopolitanism, disavowed the notion that these ideals carried any political intent or revolutionary sentiment. "So far from making men enemies to the state," they insisted, missionary work "promote[d] the order and interests of the people, and secure[d] the stability of the prince's throne" (Clayton 43). Such sentiments accorded with those understandings of "toleration" and "religious freedom" articulated by rational Dissenters such as Joseph Priestley. As Canuel observes, the "pleas for tolerance" from these Dissenters "continually linked the advocacy for freedom with an advocacy for government to act as a 'guardian' that could secure 'distributive justice' and supply a protection from 'physical evils'" (33). Missionary societies similarly looked to the government at once to protect their "freedom of religion" abroad and in turn asserted that they helped British governmental interests in inculcating a Christian morality that mitigated "native" unrest. Thus, this "religious freedom" not only supported government authority but, in fact, its implementation and maintenance demanded even more extensive government policing and control. In this way, the "respectable" Christianity adopted by missionary societies contributed to rechanneling the expression of Enlightenment idealism away from political agitation. In laying out the parameters of this Christian faith, societies helped define and naturalize a social position in which one could be a proponent of liberatory Enlightenment principles, such as freedom and tolerance, without signaling political reform or social revolt.

Southey's journalism for the *Annual Review* and the *Quarterly Review* accentuates this refrain in missionary rhetoric.[16] In his reviews, he praises the LMS and the BMS insofar as they exhibit rationality, tolerance, educational attainments, and practical charity, and he tends to deemphasize missionary failures and (what he considered to be) their ridiculous religious scruples. His first reviews of LMS and BMS publications thus advance two main arguments, which later find more urgent expression in the 1809 reviews due to increasingly heated public debates over British colonialism: first, the general praiseworthiness of the missionary endeavor (some individual missionaries notwithstanding), and second, the depravity of non-European races, which he characterized as living in a state of fear, servility, and oppression under the tyranny of their rulers and customs.

This is not to say that Southey had no misgivings regarding the overzealousness and ignorance of the Dissenting missionaries. His first review of *Periodical Accounts* (1802), for instance, lambasted BMS missionaries' biblical literalism, stating, "It is mortifying to observe their abject prostration of intellect to the dogmas of a miserable and mischievous superstition" ("Art. LXXI" 216). Yet unlike his more conservative counterparts, Southey elsewhere

---

16. Southey confirmed his authorship of these anonymous reviews in an 1806 letter: "If you have seen or should see the Annual Review, you may like to know that I have borne a great part in it thus far, and I may refer you for the state of my opinions to the Reviewals of the Periodical Accounts of the Baptist Mission, vol. i., of Malthus's Essay on Population, Miles's History of the Methodists, and the Transactions of the Missionary Society, vol. ii and iii" (Southey, *Life* 3:21–22). In fact, he included some material from volume 1 of *Transactions* in his 1804 review (specifically related to Van der Kemp's mission), despite claiming that only volumes 2 and 3 were addressed. Southey began contributing to the *Quarterly Review* in 1809. In his first year writing for the journal, he penned brand-new reviews of these same BMS and LMS publications—a decision that demonstrates his prolonged preoccupation with the missionary movement. Bolton confirms that Southey wrote the 1809 review of the LMS's *Transactions*; Stuart Andrews establishes Southey's authorship of the 1809 review of the BMS's *Periodical Accounts*.

worked to soften these disparagements, applauding the "abilities of these missionaries" in their capacity as educators and translators and singling out Carey in particular as an "extraordinary man, who unites cool prudence and persevering talents to the zeal of an apostle" (208). His reviews of the LMS's *Transactions* (1803, 1804) strike a similar rhetorical balance. Thus while he denounces the South Sea missionaries as "poor miserable Methodists, without either common talents or common courage . . . utterly destitute of all plan and all forethought," he nevertheless (and improbably) ends his analyses on a positive note ("Art. LXIV" 198). Despite their infighting and ignorance, the missionaries are "honest zealous men"; "we have only to regret, that their zeal has not been accompanied with more knowledge, or directed with more wisdom" ("Art. LXIV" 200).

Unsurprisingly, his most enthusiastic approval was reserved for the LMS's South Africa mission. This mission "has been far more wisely conducted," because its "agent has been Dr. Vanderkemp, a Dutchman of most extraordinary abilities and character" ("Art. LXIV" 200). As though to support his claim that there is nothing "enthusiastic or declamatory" at the heart of missionary work when the right men are sent, Southey details Van der Kemp's impressive educational background (in terms the LMS no doubt appreciated): "He went to Edinburgh, where he graduated in medicine, and published a Latin work on cosmology, entitled Parminedes [before] practising at Middleburgh with great repute" ("Art. LXXI" 208; "Art. II" [1804] 624). Despite Van der Kemp's insistence that his conversion was nothing less than miraculous, caused by "Lord Jesus himself," who "attacked [him] like a warrior, and fell [him] to the ground by the force of his arm," Southey insists, "This particular affection in no degree changed or weakened [Van der Kemp's] general powers of mind" ("Art. LXIV" 200). He finally pronounces, "We cannot speak too highly of this indefatigable man" ("Art. LXIV" 200).[17] In this manner, Southey mostly reiterated missionary societies' rhetoric regarding the distance they had placed between "enthusiasm" and their own respectable endeavors.

The emphasis on missionaries' educational attainments and "cool prudence" also helped Southey make his second point: namely, that there was a sharp distinction between the "civilized" Christianity of the British and the "savagery" of "heathen" nations. In the early nineteenth century, as Tim Fulford, Debbie Lee, and Peter J. Kitson note, there existed "no fully crystallised

---

17. After Van der Kemp's death, Southey wrote the following to his friend and fellow poet James Montgomery: "So we have lost Vanderkemp. I am far from sympathizing with the Directors of the Missionary Society in all their opinions & feelings,—but I feel the whole heroism of such a man as much as they can do,—& would to God that statesmen could see the importance of such men as clearly as I do" (March 26, 1812).

stereotype about the peoples who were subjected to empire" (26). Missionary texts provided supposedly objective, firsthand information regarding these peoples, which in turn was used by writers and politicos such as Southey to convince the public that there were pressing humanitarian reasons for Britain to expand its colonial reach. For instance, in an effort to rewrite Captain Cook's depiction of islanders living in a state of untouched, blessed innocence, Southey drew on missionary accounts to highlight "native" practices no doubt meant to shock the British reader, such as ritualized murder, polygamy, and cannibalism (Bolton 121–25). "These are the customs . . . of these islanders who have been held up as the exemplars of savage innocence and savage happiness!" he exclaims in his review of the LMS's *Transactions* ("Art. LXIV" 199). In this sense, Southey had a vested interest in insisting that the missionaries were something more than "poor miserable Methodists." Indeed, the more that missionary narratives were given authority to speak on "native" customs and beliefs, the more evidence Southey had to argue that non-Europeans—far from living in some prelapsarian state—were backwards, immoral, self-destructive, and ignorant.[18]

The general immorality and ignorance of "natives," Southey believed, were in no small part exacerbated by tyrannical social customs and oppression at the hands of despotic rulers. No matter whether they were from Africa, India, or the South Sea Islands, all "savages," in Southey's view, were subject to such ills. Thus the "king of Caffrees" is an "arbitrary monarch: he kills, robs his subjects, changes laws, rights, &c. according to his pleasure, and his people bear this with a filial submission" (a situation, Southey continues, that is exacerbated and exploited by the Dutch government in South Africa) ("Art. II" [1804] 628, 631). The "Hindoos," meanwhile, are subjugated to the caste system and prone to "lying, deceit, and servility"—"the vices" typical "of an enslaved people, the inevitable effects of oppression" ("Art. LXXI" 211). Finally, the "Otaheiteans" are a "degenerated race," "ignorant" and responsive only to power and fear ("Art. LXXI" 211; "Art. LXIV" 199, 198); if they are "unconvertible," Southey decides, it is because "their own priests contrive

---

18. It's remarkable how supposedly "imbecilic" and "ignorant" missionaries nevertheless were regarded as trustworthy authorities when it came to their knowledge about the "natives." Southey's reviews display some awareness of precisely this disjunction, peppered as they are with extraneous assertions of missionary credibility: "The character which they give of the Hindoos is less favourable than the usual accounts, and probably more accurate," he writes of the Baptist missionaries. "Of [the Hindoos'] moral qualities they may be considered as adequate and impartial judges" ("Art. LXXI" 211). Certainly some confirmation bias is at work here; Southey takes as "accurate" those parts of missionary texts with which he agreed, while dismissing anything with which he disagreed.

to terrify them more effectually than the missionaries have done" ("Art. II" [1804] 622).

Conceiving of non-Europeans only as fearful, unhappy, and oppressed, it is therefore unsurprising that Southey saw missionaries as a means of "native" emancipation. He thus lauded General David Dundas's support for the LMS mission to South Africa, approvingly noting that the general recognized a pressing need to "ameliorate the spiritual and temporal condition of those unhappy people, whom, upon every principle of humanity and justice, government is bound to protect" ("Art. II" [1804] 629–30). He applauded, too, Van der Kemp's stand against the Dutch government's prohibition on teaching reading and writing to the "Hottentots" on the grounds that to honor such a prohibition is "contrary to the apparent interest of Christ's kingdom, and . . . unworthy of the rights of a free people" ("Art. II" [1804] 631). In India, he celebrated that "by taking the exercise of authority into our own hands, we preserve [the Hindoos] from the cruel extortion and oppression to which they had always heretofore been exposed" ("Art. XVII" 211). And, in regard to the South Sea islanders, he argued, "The only atonement which can be made to this wretched people, for the injury we have done them, and the disease we have communicated, is to communicate also our religion, our morals, and our knowledge" ("Art. LXIV" 200). For Southey, spiritual matters were important but necessarily subordinate to the pressing duty to rectify social and political wrongs. Hence his recommendation that missionaries should "dwell upon the great and obvious temporal advantages of Christianity" ("Art. LXXI" 217).

When Southey revisited the original and newer issues of *Periodical Accounts* and *Transactions* for the *Quarterly Review* in 1809, he dwelled further on the supposed depravity of non-Europeans while painting an even more forgiving portrait of the missionaries. Gone were the severest critiques of the South Sea missionaries as "poor miserable Methodists" given to needless squabbling. Instead he characterized their internecine fighting as "deliberation" on important "points" of operation, which had the happy result of the mission running "smoothly for about four months after these points were settled" ("Art. II" [1809] 48). Moreover, he similarly downplayed what he previously had called the "miserable and mischievous superstition" of the Baptist missionaries in India. In fact, his 1809 review now alleged that this depiction of the missionaries was fundamentally unjust. "Nothing can be more unfair than the manner in which the scoffers and alarmists have represented the missionaries," he complained. "The anti-missionaries cull out from their journals and letters all that is ridiculous, sectarian, and trifling; call them fools, madmen, tinkers, Calvinists, and schismatics; and keep out of sight their love of man, and their zeal for God, their self-devotement, their indefatigable industry, and their unequalled learning" ("Art. XVII" 225).

In part, Southey's softened tone toward the missionaries can be attributed to the increasingly heated debates surrounding the East India Company's prohibition of missionary proselytization in India. However, close examination of the 1809 reviews suggests an additional dynamic at work: As missionary reports and letters became more "scientific," measured, and practical in tone, Southey seems to have felt all the more "vindicated" (as he put it) in his original support of the missionaries ("Art. XVII" 225). He commended, for instance, the sound pragmatism of missionaries' recommendation that the LMS send to the islands not "a body of missionaries with a director," but instead "such mechanics as would be able to turn the natural productions of the island to profit" ("Art. II" [1809] 55). "Great good . . . may yet be done," Southey decided, "if the views of the directors in England become as rational as those of the missionaries are grown" (55)—a recommendation that equated "rationality" with attention to production, commerce, and "profit."

Despite his effusive praise of the BMS and the LMS, however, there were notable fault lines between Southey's vision of a global Christianity and missionary societies' own plans. Where Southey argued that Christianity's "temporal advantages" were to be imposed by "colonization and by force,"[19] missionary societies, by contrast, generally opposed overt colonization and coercion for theological, moral, and practical reasons ("Art. LXIV" 200). As Hilary Carey notes, missionary societies were influenced by a "theological tradition that considered all empires to be tainted with a burden of sin, if not actually evil. Christ had said, 'My kingdom is not of this world' (John 18:36), and this was generally taken to mean that Christians, especially professional Christians, such as missionaries, should stay out of politics" (6). Thus while missionary societies certainly looked to influence politics, they hoped to do

---

19. Southey avoided the subject of Christian colonization in India, even stating in his 1809 piece on the BMS that "adherents" to British governance were to be made "not by colonization; colonization is forbidden by the Company, and it is forbidden also by the higher authority of Nature. Of all whom we send out to India, not one in ten returns" ("Art. XVII" 211). Yet Southey's letters suggest that this paragraph was added merely to avoid conflict with the East India Company. In an 1804 letter to his nephew, Southey states, "The best mode of promoting the civilization of *Hindostan* would be by permitting Europeans to colonize there. [But] if you prove this you will lose the prize, inasmuch as to prove it would be to convict the East India Company of impolicy. The first question therefore must be answered by resolving it into the second & showing . . . the best way of promoting the civilization of the *Hindoos* is by converting them" (December 4, 1804). Southey probably took his own advice in crafting his 1809 review.

so—naïvely or disingenuously, perhaps—without becoming obviously politically entangled in the question of British colonization.[20]

In this sense, the societies claimed to have an aversion to mixing overt political force with proselytizing. In part, this was a result of their desire to differentiate themselves from the Portuguese and Spanish Catholic missionaries of earlier centuries (who they believed had made converts often by violent means).[21] To use Andrew Walls's characterization of the modern missionary movement as it conceived itself vis-à-vis those missionary efforts of the past, "The original conception of the expansion of Christendom involved laying down terms for other people; its development in the missionary movement involved preparedness to live on terms set by other people" (*Cross-Cultural* 40). More importantly, however, missionaries' hesitation to enforce belief by way of coercive power was born from Dissenters' own advocacy for free conscience at home. For them, the "locus of Christian commitment had moved from the state church to the voluntary society of 'true,' converted believers" (Stanley, "Christian Missions" 13; see also Sivasundaram 31). Therefore, if

---

20. The extent to which missionaries were implicated in British colonization is a matter of debate (for a concise summary, see Sivasundaram 29–31). However, most agree that in these early days, missionary societies tended to stop short of arguing for direct British control over foreign territories. Even Thorne, who argues that Congregational missionaries constituted "the advance column of imperialism's cultural assault on indigenous subjectivities," acknowledges that there were prominent missionaries who "opposed imperialism in principle" (9). Of course, this early hesitation to endorse colonialism would not always characterize missionary work (see Carey 33).

21. Missionary societies were sensitive on this point. The LMS especially took steps to distance their work from political or social coercion. As chapter 1 discusses, political noninterference was made a "fundamental law of [the] society." Moreover, Ellis insisted that when a convert consulted the missionaries on any question "connected with any civil proceedings, or the internal government of the island . . . the matter was always referred to the king and chiefs" (*Polynesian Researches* 152). But the pledge to refrain from active politicking turned out to be mostly lip service, as missionaries threw their support behind an 1808 revolution in Tahiti and formulated laws (ostensibly written by chiefs) that they ushered into implementation (Gunson 281–85). Nevertheless, missionaries downplayed their influence on "native" politics. This was not only because such a stance corresponded with the Dissenting belief that "private acts of religious commitment could be divorced from issues of communal identity and public allegiance" (Stanley, "Christian Missions" 13). It was also to rebut charges that missionaries had fashioned themselves into mini-despots of island kingdoms, essentially replacing one form of tyranny with another. To use the words of the traveler and writer Otto von Kotzebue, LMS missionaries exercised "unbounded" power over "the minds of the Tahitians." "The Tahitians, accustomed to a blind reverence for the Missionaries," alleged Kotzebue, "consult them in all their undertakings, and by means of the Constitution have so confirmed their power, both as priests and rulers, that it would be difficult for governor, judge, or member of parliament, to retain their offices after having incurred their displeasure" (von Kotzebue 1:163). Such accusations had enough of a public impact to provoke concern from Wilberforce, who, in a private letter to Ellis, noted that Kotzebue's travelogue was probably "injurious to the missionary cause" (June 4, 1832).

"heathen" societies were to be transformed, it would be "by means of procuring genuine individual conversions" that would in turn prompt social change from the bottom up ("Christian Missions" 13). As the missionary John Williams wrote, clarifying the position of the South Sea missionaries, "I would not . . . be supposed to advocate the assumption of political authority by the Missionary, but, on the contrary, that he should interfere as little as possible" (140).[22]

These considerations, taken together with the unavoidable fact that missionary success depended on the hospitality and goodwill of native populations, restrained societies in the early nineteenth century from fully endorsing colonialism. "We are afraid of colonizing, lest it should prove in time, destructive to the liberty, or lives and property of the natives," pronounced the South Sea missionaries. "Some of the islanders themselves have expressed a suspicion, that if a large body of foreigners should come and settle among them, they would be turned out of their possessions, and driven to the mountains" (qtd. in Southey, "Art. II" [1809] 55). The political and cultural benefits of Christianity would only be realized by changing individual hearts, the missionaries believed. Social good followed individual spiritual salvation.

Southey had little patience with such concerns. Rebutting the missionaries, he insisted, "It is only by colonization that these countries can be civilized, and . . . it is our interest and the interest of the whole commercial world that they should be civilized" ("Art. II" [1809] 55). Where missionaries looked to convince each individual to embrace Christianity of his or her own free will, Southey wished to bypass this inconvenient step and impose new social and political mores wholesale. Colonization, he asserted, would give missionaries unilateral power to enforce humanitarian measures—a development that could only work to the aggregate good, even if in the short term it confirmed native fears of a missionary-led takeover. "A hundred Englishmen, with a fort, and a sloop, would be lords of the island," Southey speculated. "They might then authoritatively prohibit infanticide and human sacrifices, and the natives would not venture to offend them" ("Art. II" [1804] 623). In his scheme, then, it was not so far a step to see the natives *themselves* as a central hindrance to the ideal Christian societies he hoped to cultivate:

> In a few generations the colonizers would become the majority. Captain Cook computed the natives at 200,000, probably very much over-rating

---

22. In the early nineteenth century, the CMS also tended to oppose perpetual British rule over indigenous societies (Robert 14). However, "as the British presence moved from informal to formal empire," "pressures grew to shift the goal of missions . . . to a more permanent 'trustee' model of missions" (14).

their numbers. They are reduced to less than half the number at which Mr. W. Wilson calculated them in 1797. There are not 8000 left, probably not more than five. The depopulation continues by the prevalence of that dreadful disease which is the just punishment of their loathsome sensuality. . . . The better and more teachable natives would connect themselves with their more civilized neighbours, and their children be exalted into the higher race; the more obstinate would be cut off by spirituous liquors, their own vices and their own ferocity. This is the order of nature: beast gives place to man; savages to civilized man. (622–23)

The "natives," in Southey's formulation, are to be saved from their own tyrannical rulers and traditions only to die or, for the "better" ones, be assimilated into "the higher race." Southey's plan for Christian colonization thus reduces to two stark recommendations: first, that missionaries "authoritatively" enforce their own rules and codes of conduct on natives, using force if necessary, and second, that they pursue an agenda of what fundamentally amounts to racial extermination. The use of fear and force together with their sheer strength in numbers, Southey anticipated, would permit colonizing missionaries to institute a stable, free, moral, and happy society where currently there existed only "sufferings" and "utter depravity" ("Art. II" [1809] 47, 45). Here, then, was a clear tension in Southey's thought. The justification he gave for British expansion—that is, the emancipation of hapless natives from "the great fear" instilled in them by their despotic ruler and traditions via the "institutions of Christianity," which "produce the greatest possible quantity of virtue and happiness" ("Art. XVII" 216; "Art. II" [1809] 42)—simply did not match the means by which this goal was to be attained, through fear, missionary despotism, and, ultimately, genocide.

Of course, it is no radical insight that humanitarian ideals were invoked to justify imperialism. Still, the logic by which (in Stanley's words) "Christian, liberal and democratic values" are aligned with colonialism in Southey's work is especially peculiar and deserves closer examination (*Bible* 49). To further trace the development of this logic, then, I turn from Southey's journalism to two of his later works, *Sir Thomas More* and *Tale of Paraguay*. In these texts, it becomes evident that the moral disconnect of advocating colonization as a means of achieving "free," Christian societies was not wholly lost on Southey. Indeed, as I'll argue, *A Tale of Paraguay* and *Sir Thomas More* represent two attempts to respond to and ultimately minimize this disconnect. The texts themselves take the form of two very different "secularized" providential narratives: Christian colonization, first, as a "hidden plan of Nature" and second, as a "vaccination" for a disease. The narratives are noteworthy, for while

Southey was always influenced by a certain amount of providential thinking, in *More* and *Paraguay* he supplements his faith in Providence with an air of Enlightenment scientism. It is in this sense that he secularizes his providentialism to justify aggressive colonial expansion—a conceptual turn that culminates in his declaration, in *Sir Thomas More,* that his "opinion" regarding world progress is best captured in Kant's deliberately *non*religious "Universal History on a Cosmo-Political plan."

In other words, Southey appears to draw on two discourses in an effort to legitimate his plan of Christian colonialism. First, he looks to the writing of missionaries, who, in an effort to avoid the appearance of lower-class "enthusiasm" to broaden their base of support, adopted some of the rhetoric and humanist sensibilities of Enlightenment thinkers. And, next, in *Sir Thomas More,* Southey discovers that the secularized providentialism he wishes to articulate has a name, as well as a more rigorous conceptual framing: the "cosmo-political" plan of Kant. One could say that Southey ultimately tries to appropriate missionary cosmopolitanism to suit his own nationalist ends.

A Tale of Paraguay

A Tale of Paraguay draws on the process of "vaccination" and the "hidden plan of Nature" as metaphors, or complementary "naturalizing principles" (to use Mary Douglas's term), in its effort to convince missionaries and the broader British public that they should conceive of missionary work not in terms of changing individual hearts but transforming entire "institutions" by colonization (52–53). Contrary to those early nineteenth-century missionaries who had argued against colonization and the use of institutional force in missionary work, Southey wanted to show that the use of force and an expected degree of resulting native suffering were actually providential and emancipatory *processes,* which, moreover, were observable in nature. Thus the poem repeatedly asserts that there can exist ideological agreement between native freedom and native capitulation to British colonization. Contrary to its own intentions, however, the poem ends up displaying the immense difficulty of reconciling these two visions. Ultimately, it suggests that only in the death of natives can the colonial imperatives—to free and to rule—be brought into agreement.

First, it may be helpful to provide some background information on the poem. The source material for *A Tale of Paraguay* was the Jesuit missionary Martin Dobrizhoffer's *Historia de Aponibus* (1784). Southey's imagination was captured by the missionary's account of a native family, a mother, son, and daughter, whom he discovers "living in complete isolation in the forest, after war and smallpox had decimated and dispersed their tribal group" (the father having already died) (Fulford). In Dobrizhoffer's history, the mother and her grown children embody a state of prelapsarian innocence. He brings them to live in a Jesuit Reduction, and all three are baptized as Christians. However, their residence at the Reductions is short-lived. A few weeks after their arrival, mother, daughter, and son all contract a horrific, consumptive disease and die.

Thus the story seems to confirm missionary apprehensions regarding colonization as a strategy for proselytization, as the most obvious takeaway is that colonization (to return to the phrase of the LMS missionaries) is "destructive to the liberty, or lives and property of the natives." In taking up Dobrizhoffer's narrative for his subject in *Tale of Paraguay*, then, Southey sets up for himself an exceedingly difficult challenge. If he is to justify the emancipatory potential of colonization, his poem's *language* must work against his poem's *plot*. In other words, *A Tale of Paraguay* seeks to use the poet's rhetorical tools to challenge the story's obvious message.

This Southey pursued in a number of ways. For instance, smallpox is transformed from "a disease of colonial guilt," in Fulford's phrase, into a form of divine deliverance from corrupt society. From his prolific reading on the subject, Southey knew "how devastating smallpox had become in South America after its introduction by the colonists" (Fulford). Eager to make the case for Christian colonization, however, Southey refused to accept that the introduction of smallpox to South America should be held as a mark against colonization. Hence, he makes smallpox play a key function in the poem. As Alan Bewell argues, it "rid[s] the three Guaraní of all that links them to native culture," so that when Dobrizhoffer encounters them in the forest, they have "already undergone a process of cultural unmaking" (111, 110). What must be stressed, however, is the extent to which Southey insists that the devastating outbreak amounts to an unqualified good for the Guaraní family. By virtue of smallpox, mother, daughter, and son are "deliver'd from [the] yoke" of "heathen paths," freed of the "force of impious custom" that pits itself "Against [Nature's] law" (*Paraguay* 42). The extinction of a "feeble nation of Guarani race" (25) is portrayed not only as inevitable (in its violation of "unerring Nature's order" [42]). In a manner reminiscent of Southey's journalism, which continuously casts non-Western societies as oppressive, unhappy, and fearful, smallpox also becomes a manifestation of divine deliverance from the tyranny of "heathen" society. In these few short lines, the death of an entire society is transmuted into liberation for a deserving few.

In this sense, Southey's goal was to overturn the Rousseauian notion of the "noble savage" and make the case for absolute European control over "savage" societies. His Guaraní family therefore needed to be reintegrated into a society firmly under Western Christian direction. One imagines that Southey saw the Jesuit Reductions as an ideal representation of this society. As Bewell notes, the Reductions "were a favourite topic among eighteenth-century philosophes, one that brought out the contradictions between Enlightenment values and the realities of colonialism" (98). This was because, on the one hand, the Reductions upheld individual freedom in protecting indigenous people from the "exploitative enslavement practices of the Spanish *encomienda* system" (98). The Guaraní peoples were free, that is, insofar as they were not slaves. On the other hand, as Bewell reminds us, the protection offered by the Reductions greatly compromised positive freedoms, including those of mobility and belief. "The term '*Reduction*,'" he notes, "refered to the 'concentration' of people dispersed over large areas, but it also meant 'reducing' native peoples to European ideas of civilized, Christian behaviour, even at the cost of their civil freedom" (98). For Southey, then, the Jesuit Reduction thus holds out the tantalizing possibility of a society that protects, by severely limiting, "native" freedom.

Yet the poem displays some awareness that this sort of negative freedom—that is, the freedom from being enslaved—would likely not satisfy the British reader. In order to reassure the reader that life in the Reduction does not simply amount to re-"yoking" the sympathetic native family, Southey argues that we should "deem not their lives of happiness devoid . . . Sufficient scope was given. Each had assign'd / His proper part, which yet left free the will" (*Paraguay* 113). This curious assertion that life in the Reduction "left free the will" comes on the heels of the reader learning that Dobrizhoffer is something like God to the native converts. In him, they "Reposed alike their conscience and their cares; / . . . for their good he holds them thus in thrall, / Their Father and their Friend, Priest, Ruler, all in all" (113). There is something incongruous in Southey's declaration that "free will" is somehow preserved in this "thralldom." As though anticipating missionary objections to the colonial scheme, Southey tacks on assurance that "free will" is somehow maintained despite the loss of civil and spatial freedoms.

To square this circle, Southey invokes providential design, and for him, nothing better exemplifies the workings of providence in this regard than vaccination. "Jenner! For ever shall thy honour'd name / Among the children of mankind be blest," are its exclamatory first words (*Paraguay* 23). At first glance, this encomium to Jenner seems out of place, least of all because of its anachronism. However, as Fulford argues, the appearance of Edward Jenner's vaccination makes sense in light of Southey's advocacy for aggressive British colonialism: Vaccination, Southey felt, was one of the many unequivocal goods that Britain had to offer the world. If European settlers were to blame for devastating outbreaks of smallpox in the Americas, they also held the cure to those outbreaks. Thus Jenner is summoned in the poem to show that "paternalist colonisation need no longer be implicated in colonial guilt, to reassure readers that the 'art' of Europe can now prevent the infection that Europeans spread" (Fulford).

But there is something even darker underlying Southey's interest in how people are made "sick to make them well" (as he understood the vaccination process) (Fulford and Lee 142). His 1809 essay on the BMS missionaries, which likened the expansion of Christianity in India to a "vaccine," for instance uses "disease" as a synonym for "vaccination," a confusion that suggests that the disease and its preventative amount to same thing. In reference to the missionaries, he writes,

> Their progress will be continually accelerating; the difficulty is at first, as in introducing vaccination into a distant land; when the matter has once taken, one subject supplies infection for all around him, and the disease takes root in the country. The husband converts the wife, the son converts the parent, the friend his friend, and every fresh proselyte becomes a missionary in his own neighborhood. Thus their sphere of influence and of action widens, and the eventual issue of a struggle between truth and falsehood, is not to be doubted by those who believe in the former. ("Art. XVII" 225)

Of course, vaccinations were derived from infectious material, introducing a small portion of the original disease (or a related one, in the case of Jenner's cowpox) in order to render immunity to the more severe form of the disease. But Southey's confusion between "vaccination" and "disease" goes beyond this. Jenner's vaccine, for instance, differed from earlier forms of inoculation in that it did not give people a communicable form of pox. However, Southey's imagined "vaccination" in a "distant land" is highly contagious, certainly more akin to actual smallpox than its vaccine. The collapse between "vaccination" and "disease," then, raises a troubling possibility: Southey, perhaps, did not really perceive the difference between the "cure unto diseases" and the disease itself. Twenty years later, the poet laureate's peculiar understanding of vaccination as being interchangeable with disease manifests itself again in *Sir Thomas More*, when he approvingly quotes Lord Brooke's poem: "Whereby disease grows cure unto diseases . . . A wisdom proper to humanity" (2:244).

The confusion between disease and cure may appear relatively benign in the above contexts, but it becomes far more insidious in the context of the poet's advocacy of aggressive colonial expansion. For Southey, who regularly looked for the rational underpinnings of Christian belief, vaccination neatly illustrated how greater good could emerge from suffering.[23] The natural process of inoculation seemed to justify active colonial and missionary interference in foreign societies, for, whatever its ill effects, the "collateral good is yet greater" (to use Southey's phrase in his defense of the colonization of Australia) (*Sir Thomas More* [*STM*] 2:287).

A Tale of Paraguay, I propose, takes this confusion between disease and cure to troubling extremes in its suggestion that native deaths caused by colonial disease are not necessarily a tragedy. Instead, the poem urges the reader to see death itself as something like a vaccine: that is, as a preventative against something more terrible (such as, in Southey's view, "oppressive," sinful societies), as well an unlikely harbinger of better, more moral times (and people) to come. This is the logic that underlies his troubling eagerness for the "depopulation" of the South Sea islanders by virtue of the "prevalence of that dreadful disease" first introduced by European sailors ("Art. II" [1804]). For not only does he regard disease to be a "just punishment" for the islanders' sinful behavior; according to the logic of vaccination and inoculation, "pestilence" also is "the means of averting a more terrible and abiding scourge," as he would go on to argue in *Sir Thomas More* (1:53). In this manner, Southey portrays illness and wellness as interchangeable in the larger providential plan. Hence his attraction to "vaccination." In Southey's understanding of vaccination, not only does disease *provide* the "cure unto diseases." Literally and figuratively, disease is *synonymous* with cure. The discovery of the vaccine for the pox by way of the pox seemed to confirm that this belief system had empirical validity.[24]

No wonder, then, the poet's curious treatment of smallpox in *A Tale of Paraguay*. In the scheme of things, smallpox plays a rather small role in *A Tale of Paraguay*, merely kick-starting the events to come by creating the conditions that isolate the Guaraní family from human society (it is not even the disease that kills the family at the end). Nevertheless, the *Tale* opens with an

---

23. Fulford and Lee demonstrate that vaccination also regularly appears in Southey's prose as a "reassuring political metaphor"; Britain would never experience a revolution at home, Southey argued, because the example of the French Revolution had "successfully inoculated her from the "disease" (Fulford and Lee 159; Southey qtd. in Fulford and Lee 159).

24. My reading of Southey's views on vaccination are in part derived from a letter he composed to his daughter, Bertha, in 1820: "<Catharine> Senhouse has got the small pox, & of a very bad sort, but it is supposed that like all the cases which have occurred after vaccination, it will stop at a certain stage of the disease" (May 1, 1820). That Southey expresses little concern for Senhouse despite what he admits is her "bad" case of smallpox is telling. It stands as testament to the fact that he saw the illness that accompanied vaccination as preventing a worse form of illness.

encomium to Jenner and a meditation about the *meaning* of smallpox itself: "Africa sent forth [the disease] to scourge the West, / As if in vengeance for her sable brood / So many an age remorselessly opprest" (*Paraguay* 24, 23). Here, Southey makes three arguments about the disease: (1) Smallpox is not European in its origin; (2) its appearance is a form of divine punishment for societal sins (in Europe's case, for the slave trade); and (3) it provides figures such as Jenner the opportunity to make discoveries like the process of vaccination, a discovery Southey calls the "triumph of an age," which presages mankind's "glorious destiny" when its "only war" will be "against the miseries that afflict mankind" (24). These arguments minimize European culpability for colonization's worst effects. Not only is Europe *not* responsible for smallpox's devastating appearance (Africa is), but the disease also ultimately contributes to the universal good. After all, it is a mechanism of divine justice *and* a driving force behind the eventual "blest consummation" of mankind's "glorious destiny" (24). Thus Southey assures his reader that the "spotted plague" responsible for the near-extinction of a "feeble nation of Guarani race"—"how brought among them none could tell, or whence"—"work[ed] the Lord's mysterious will" (25). Jenner's vaccination, then, not only eases Southey's "colonial guilt." Metaphorically understood as a process by which disease "grows cure unto disease," vaccination appears to legitimate a providential understanding of colonial disease in which the very appearance of the disease (and, most troublingly, the resulting deaths) finally is reason for celebration, not mourning.

This prepares us for the conclusion to the poem, in which the members of the family perish in quick succession: First Monnema, the mother, expires, followed by her daughter, Mooma. Against all odds, Yeruti, the son, makes a full recovery from the illness that takes his mother and sister; however, he ultimately *chooses* to die after he secures his baptism from Dobrizhoffer. That the Reductions have such a deadly effect initially undermines the earlier implicit argument of the poem, that native "submission" to Christian rule is "easy," natural, and even emancipatory. So tragic are the deaths that even Southey's heroic missionary expresses some doubt that he has done right by the family: "Was it then for thus that he had brought / That harmless household from their native shade? / Death had already been the mother's lot; / And this fair Mooma, was she form'd to fade / So soon,—so soon must be in earth's cold lap be laid?" (*Paraguay* 131).

But Southey dismisses these doubts. In the next stanza, Dobrizhoffer decides that there is nothing to regret. Indeed, the poem intimates, to regret would be tantamount to questioning the wisdom of God. "Yet [Dobrizhoffer] had no misgiving at the sight; / And wherefore should he? he had acted well, /

and Deeming of the ways of God aright, / Knew that to such as these, whate'er befell / Must needs for them be best" (*Paraguay* 132). Providential order, the poem insists, ensures that the family's death is for the "best," an assertion Southey makes not once, but twice (133, 136). The climax of the poem in this manner echoes the themes presented in the opening: Colonial disease and native deaths ultimately work for the greater good.

But the deaths are not just for the "best" because they fulfill some grand providential order. The poem further suggests that for the family itself, death is actually a cure for an even worse malady. The Guaranís must die in order to be made *more* free, *more* Christian, *more* well. Looking for a reason for the family's quick demise, Southey attributes their "malady" to an inability to adapt to their new life: "Those old habits suddenly uproot / Conform'd to which the vital powers pursued / Their functions, such mutation is too rude / For man's fine frame unshaken to sustain" (*Paraguay* 123). According to the stanza, some natives simply will never adapt to Christian practice and belief—it is "a mutation too rude" for their sensitive constitutions. At least, this is the case *in life*. Death, however, gives natives the opportunity to be the perfect Christians they cannot hope to become while they live. If Monnema and Mooma cannot adapt mentally or physically to their Christian lives in the Reductions, once they die they are admitted into the "pale of Christ without delay" and "call'd away to bliss" (140, 134). Native deaths therefore are not occasions for pity or regret ("Mourn not for her!" Southey thunders at the reader when Mooma finally perishes [133]. "Who would keep her soul from being free! / Maiden beloved of Heaven, to die is best for thee!" [133]). Instead, in Southey's hands, native death is transmuted from missionary failure into the direct fulfillment of two missionary objectives. It is a means not only to freedom but also by which unsuccessful converts can be made *wholly* Christian as they are ushered into "the pale of Christ without delay."

Southey extends this language to justify the death of the son, Yeruti. On recovering from the malady that killed his mother and sister, Yeruti realizes that infirmity, not death, is the great evil to be avoided: "He understood / Something of death from creatures he had slain / But here the ills which follow in the train / Of age, had first to him been manifest,— / The shrunken form, the limbs that move with pain, / The failing sense, infirmity, unrest,— / That in his heart he said to die betimes was best" (*Paraguay* 136). He longs, then, to join his mother and sister, whom he sees in visions "as if they lived anew . . . feature, form and hue, / And looks and gestures . . . restored again" (137). Indeed, as Yeruti tells Dobrizhoffer, they are in death "as in life, the same, / Save only that in radiant robes arrayed" (141). In this manner, the poem makes the unlikely argument that dying is restorative, freeing, and the means of staving off the far more terrible illness of infirmity and old age. In other words, it acts like a vaccine. It protects the natives against the physical malady of old age and the spiritual malady of an imperfect Christianity. When Yeruti *chooses* to die at the end of the poem after being baptized, it's a decision rationally reached. The missionary notes no "mark of passion" or "derangement" when Yeruti discloses his wish to rejoin mother and sister (142). His pulse is "regular" and his mind "from all disorder free" (142).

The obvious parallel the poem draws between Jenner and Dobrizhoffer reinforces that the native deaths resulting from Christian colonization be considered not a moral wrong but a necessary part of introducing Christianity worldwide. Dobrizhoffer, notably, is described in terms that echo the opening encomium to Jenner. Each is described as having an "honour'd name" (*Paraguay* 23, 89). Each is deserving of "bles[sings]" or "homage" from "mankind" (23, 89). Indeed, the bizarre celebration of Jenner that opens the poem seems intended to prepare the reader for Dobrizhoffer's appearance; implicitly, we are invited to compare Jenner the medical doctor to Dobrizhoffer the spiritual doctor in the analogous service they perform to "mankind." But despite the intent of the poem to equate the missionary's scheme of Christian colonization to Jenner's vaccination, there is no avoiding the obvious: Where vaccination is meant to prevent death, the missionary ushers it in. In other words, the humanist principles that in no small part motivated Southey's original support of missionary work (to "free" oppressed and unhappy peoples) cannot be reconciled with what Southey intimates is colonization's expected, indeed welcome, outcome: namely, the mass death of native peoples.

While *Sir Thomas More* looks outwardly quite different from *A Tale of Paraguay*—the one a series of "colloquies" meditating on the social, political, and religious "progress" of the world, and the other a poem that dramatizes the death of a Guaraní family—I suggest that both works can be seen as participating in a common project. The providential logic by which native oppression and death are justified in *A Tale of Paraguay* finds its broader conceptual framing in *Sir Thomas More*. And, what's more, this conceptual framing finally is given a name: the "cosmo-political" idea, as advanced by Immanuel Kant.

Sir Thomas More

Thanks to Thomas Babington Macaulay's withering review of the work, *Sir Thomas More* is perhaps best remembered for its problematic claim that feudalism benefitted the working classes more than industrialism (see Bizup 84). When critics have revisited the text, it mostly has been to emblematize the political schism between Tory pessimism and Whig optimism regarding the growth of British industrialism and manufacturing.

Yet one can read *Sir Thomas More* as something more than a conservative screed against the modern economy. The text also, and more centrally, meditates on the function of religion in the current world. One of its primary concerns is what counts as rational Christian belief, that is, how religion accords with Enlightenment principles, as well as the ways that religious enthusiasm can be usefully "channeled" (in Southey's metaphor) to serve domestic and global stability. Identifying one of the central problems of modern society to be unbelief and viewing religion as the only means of "preserv[ing] our social system from putrescence and dissolution" (*STM* 2:89), *Sir Thomas More* looks to articulate a functional Christianity that threads the needle between religious "enthusiasm" and what it decries as the "triumph of liberal opinions" absent the moderating influence of religious education (1:83, 1:35; see 1:133 and 1:144).

Written in what Southey calls a "Boethian" form, *Sir Thomas More* is composed of a series of conversations between the character of Montesinos, a representative of Southey's contemporary moment, and (literally) the ghost of Sir Thomas More.[25] As the older and wiser of the two men, More is a tempering influence on Montesinos's religious optimism. Armed with centuries of knowledge and intimate with figures such as Martin Luther and Isaac Casaubon in the afterlife, the ghost of More guides Montesinos toward a religiosity more firmly based in skepticism and careful observation of global political, social, and cultural developments. In this spirit (no pun intended), Montesinos and More discuss a multitude of issues, ranging from the desirability of ladies' associations to the undesirability of Irish freedom, from the benefits of feudal society to the drawbacks of Spanish imperialism. Undergirding all these conversations are two questions introduced in the first colloquy: whether "the world will continue to improve, even as it has hitherto continually been improving," and if so, whether the "happy consummation" of this progress is the result of free will, or rather something "appointed, [which] must come to pass" (*STM* 1:27, 1:28).

Montesinos, the religious optimist, is convinced that the world is *always* improving (which he takes to be synonymous with becoming more Christian),

---

25. Some critics express doubt that there exists any real reason for this strange conceit, noting that the two characters are more alike than different in their thoughts, opinions, and modes of expressing themselves. Montesinos reads as "Southey in disguise," and More, David Craig notes, also "sound[s] suspiciously like Southey" (Storey 315; Craig 131). Wohlgemut's description most accurately captures the dynamic between the two men when she writes that generally "More agrees with Montesino [sic]," but through dialogue he "refine[s] and qualifie[s] Montesino's initial assertion" (145).

an opinion he derives almost solely from his faith in Providence. "The progress of knowledge and the diffusion of Christianity will bring about at last, when men become Christians in reality, as well as in name, something like that Utopian state of which philosophers have loved to dream," he remarks in the opening to the colloquies (*STM* 1:27). More, in turn, cautions Montesinos against an overreliance on faith, observing that such a disposition belongs more to "enthusiasts" and "madmen" than to civilized Christians. "Consider this," argues More, "that the speedy fulfilment of those promises has been the ruling fancy of the most dangerous of all madmen. . . . It becomes a Mahommedan rather than a Christian to rely upon Providence or Fate alone" (1:35, 1:56). *Real* knowledge of world history and recent events, More asserts, shows that the "notion of the improvement of the world [is] a mere speculation, altogether inapplicable in practice; and as dangerous to weak heads and heated imaginations as it is congenial to benevolent hearts" (1:37). His warning is taken to heart by Montesinos, who ultimately qualifies his belief in Providence to satisfy More. In doing so, Montesinos illustrates a key takeaway from this tedious "Boethian" debate: Belief and mere "speculation" will not do. They must be backed by material evidence and "rules" deduced from actual social and political developments over the course of human history.

The revised providentialism in *Sir Thomas More* thus borrows from strands of thought that appear in Southey's earlier writing. First, it displays that aversion to religious "enthusiasm" and its approval for merging religion with rationality and empiricism, which had appeared in Southey's journalism on missionary societies. Second, insofar as it represents a secularized conception of Providence, it resembles the natural, providential design described in *A Tale of Paraguay* (as I will discuss further below).

The unlikely name Montesinos gives to his revised providentialism is "cosmopolitanism," or, more precisely, "Kant's idea of a Universal History on a Cosmo-Political plan" (*STM* 2:409). In the conclusion to *Sir Thomas More*, Montesinos explicitly cites Kant's idea to answer the questions that opened the text. "Here Sir Thomas," he declares, "is the opinion I have attempted to maintain concerning the progress and tendency of society, placed in a proper position, and inexpugnably entrenched there according to the rules of art, by the ablest of all moral engineers" (2:407). Notably, Montesinos does not consider Kant's "cosmo-political plan" to be a radically new addition to his thinking. Rather, he is thrilled to discover the essay because, as he puts it, it seems to articulate the very "opinion" he has "attempted to maintain" all along. What excites Montesinos, in other words, is not the novelty of the "cosmo-political plan" but instead the way that it frames the ideas he already has.

His summary of Kant's essay emphasizes, then, the rationality of this "cosmo-political" providentialism:

> The sum of his [Kant's] argument is this: that as deaths, births, and marriages, and the oscillations of the weather, irregular as they seem to be in themselves, are, nevertheless reduceable [sic] upon the great scale to certain rules; so there may be discovered in the course of human history, a steady and continuous, though slow development of certain great dispositions in human nature: and that although men neither act under the law of instinct like brute animals, nor under the law of a preconcerted plan like rational cosmopolites, the great current of human actions flows in a regular stream of tendency toward this development: individuals and nations, while pursuing their own peculiar and often contradictory purposes, following the guidance of a great natural purpose, and thus promoting a process, which even if they perceived it, they would little regard. (*STM* 2:409)

The "discovery" of "certain rules" underlying irregular events, the "slow development of certain great dispositions in human nature," the existence of a guiding "natural purpose"—these terms, of course, evoke natural theology, which posited that divine order could be observed in the workings of the natural world. Yet, in delivering this speech, Montesinos does not at all position himself in relation to natural theology, despite its popularity in the 1820s thanks to figures such as William Paley and James Cowles Prichard. Instead, he frames his opinion by way of an Enlightenment *philosophe,* whose essay includes no direct reference to Christianity or God. As Roberts aptly reminds us, there is a considerable distance, then, between Southey's conservative defense of Anglicanism in *Sir Thomas More* and his enthusiastic support of Kant's "revolutionary and secularist vision" (46).

To account for the bizarre appearance of Kant's "cosmo-political" idea in the text, Roberts argues that *Sir Thomas More* represents an attempt by Southey to amalgamate his "earlier radicalism" with "the pessimism of experience" (47). No doubt this is part of the story. The other part of the story, however, almost certainly has to do with changing valences of "cosmopolitanism" in the early part of the nineteenth century. As Wohlgemut observes, by the 1820s "cosmopolitanism"—even Kant's controversial version of the ideal—did not connote "revolution" or "secularism" in the manner it had in the 1790s (146).[26] Indeed, the utter lack of *any* political or philosophical hedging in

---

26. For more on conservative screeds against cosmopolitanism, see chapter 1.

Southey's adoption of Kantian cosmopolitanism indicates that the erstwhile revolutionary ideal perhaps *already* had been domesticated to suit nationalist, conservative tastes.

Wohlgemut attributes this shift to the "general post-Napoleonic re-opening of British thought to Continental literature" (146), but another source for the domestication of "cosmopolitanism" must include the missionary texts, which so freely invoked cosmopolitan ideas and which so fully captured Southey's imagination. As shown in chapter 1, for years prior to the publication of Thomas De Quincey's translation of Kant's "Universal History" in 1824 (from which Southey drew), missionaries had been using "cosmopolitan" ideas and terms in reference not to revolution but missionary work. The Christian was a "citizen of the world" and the "only true cosmopolite" (Bogue, "Circular Letter" 3). Considering his voracious appetite for missionary writing, Southey was probably primed to see Kant's "cosmo-political idea" through a Christian lens by the time "Universal History" was published in England.

Still, considering how fervently Montesinos and More argue for the importance of Christian belief in all societies, it is striking that Southey endorses a text that omits explicit religious arguments (though, of course, these arguments are still instantly recognizable as religion barely sublimated into a more secularized framework, as made clear near the conclusion of the piece when Kant states that one of the benefits of a world history written in light of the "cosmo-political" idea would be its justification of "Nature, or rather of Providence" [qtd. in De Quincey 443; see also 444]). Indeed, one of Kant's foremost goals in writing "Universal History" and its follow-up, "Toward Perpetual Peace" (1795), was to argue for a teleological view of history without reference to God or a higher power. As Martha Nussbaum notes regarding "Perpetual Peace," when Kant brings up Providence, it is only to remind "his readers that we must not speak of providence with any confidence, since that would be to attempt to transcend the limits of human nature" ("Kant" 41). Given More's reprimand that Montesinos ought to avoid any appearance of religious "enthusiasm" and not "rely upon Providence or Fate alone," it therefore seems likely that Kant's essay attracts Montesinos precisely because it sublimates religion into a relatively nonreligious schema. God becomes a "great natural purpose," and Providence is a "process." Thus in Montesinos's adoption of Kantian cosmopolitanism—which, he says, puts his original "opinion" in its "proper position"—we see an attempt to create a scientistic account of Providence. More's demand that Montesinos ground his faith in natural processes and observable human history essentially forces Montesinos to "filter" his religious language (in Habermas's formulation); for the elder statesman More, only such "'translated' . . . contributions" count. Similar to the strategy adopted by missionary societies in their attempt to gain traction among the polite classes, Southey tempers religious concepts by way of Enlightenment ideas and rhetoric to give these concepts more political and scientific validity.

However, by the end of the "Conclusion," Southey leavens Kant's secularism with a measure of Christian religiosity. Here he revises Kant's "cosmo-political plan" so that it overtly includes God and, even more, the importance of Christian education. "I must diverge from him," says Montesinos of Kant, "and what in his language is called the hidden plan of Nature, in mine will be the revealed will of God" (*STM* 2:412–13). Deploring the ascendance of "Impiety" in the world (2:413), and no doubt uncomfortable with the complete absence of God in Kant's plan (as well as, one imagines, Kant's declaration that "religious liberty" eventually must be "established" if mankind eventually is to reach global "Illumination" [qtd. in De Quincey 440]), Montesinos finds a central place for God in Kant's universal history. *Sir Thomas More* thus concludes that while Kant was fundamentally correct in seeing "the history of the human race, as a whole" as ineluctably proceeding toward a "perfect state of civil constitution for society," he was incorrect to ignore the "revealed will of God" in this process, which demands that man act in accordance with Christian principles and institutions (*STM* 2:413).

Though Southey argues that the alteration is mostly rhetorical rather than substantive—as he puts it, he has simply substituted what Kant calls "the hidden plan of Nature" with his own term, "the revealed will of God"—there are, unsurprisingly, profound implications in claiming that the "hidden plan of Nature" includes a religious mandate, specifically a mandate for compulsory religious education. For one thing, his revised cosmopolitanism ends up riven by the same contradiction that undermined all his other arguments for Christian colonialism. Again, his idealized emancipatory Christian society is portrayed as achievable *only* by means of oppressive institutional power. Thus, on the one hand, he endorses Kant's scheme because it enshrines a commitment to individual freedoms in its providentialism. As Montesinos notes, Kant's "cosmo-political idea" predicates "the establishment of a universal civil society" exactly on individuals' diverging beliefs and action. After all, it is man's natural "antagonism" toward other individuals, rather than his agreement with them, that prompts the creation of "social arrangements founded in law" and drives mankind toward a more just, peaceful world (*STM* 2:410). But, on the other hand, *Sir Thomas More* also insists that a "system of Government, conducted in strict conformity to the precepts of the Gospel" is indispensable for carrying out "the system of Nature, in other words . . . the will of God" (2:412, 2:411). As More puts it, "The will is revealed; but the plan is hidden. Let man dutifully obey that will, and the perfection of society and of human nature will be the result of such obedience; but upon obedience they depend" (2:413). Never does he explicitly remark on the degree to which this endorsement of total "obedience" to theocratic power conflicts with Kant's belief in "individuals and nations . . . pursuing their own peculiar and often contradictory purposes" (2:409). While asserting his total agreement with Kant's "universal history," then, he simultaneously treats total "obedience" to a centralized (not to mention, earthly) authority as central to mankind's progress, seemingly unaware that such compulsion undermines the raison d'être of a "universal history" in the first place.

In an effort, perhaps, to resolve this contradiction, *Sir Thomas More* devotes significant energy to describing this scheme for mandatory yet also non-oppressive religious education. To do so, he relies on those "naturalizing metaphors," which had also appeared in their troubling extremes in *A Tale of Paraguay*. "Religion," declares Montesinos,

> ought to be so blended with the whole course of instruction, that its doctrines and precepts should indeed, "drop as the rain, and distil as the dew, as the small rain upon the tender herb, and as the showers upon the grass;" . . . the young plants would then imbibe it, and the heart and intellect assimilate it with their growth. We are, in a great degree, what our institutions make us. (*STM* 2:425)

In effect, *Sir Thomas More* envisions a plan of religious education in which people are *unconscious* of being religiously indoctrinated. Because Christianity is to be "blended with the whole course of instruction"—rendered inseparable from social institutions—mandatory and state-sponsored religious education is therefore organic and wholly noncoercive. Unsurprisingly, this plan resembles the course of Christian instruction established by the Jesuit missionaries in the Paraguayan reductions. In both cases, it is implied that mandatory religious instruction belongs to the "hidden plan of Nature" or (to use the phrase from *Paraguay*) "unerring Nature's order." And both schemes, in forcefully implementing what More calls elsewhere in the text "the rituals of social religion" (*STM* 2:179), supposedly give "Sufficient scope" to each individual, leaving "free the will" (to return to *Paraguay*).[27] Moreover, both works take the same view of the social ills that accompany European colonization. No longer are they reason for pessimism; instead, such iniquities are to

---

27. In this section, More argues that this "well-rooted principle of religion" acts "as a strong corrective" against the civilizational decline of colonists. When this "preservative fails," he continues, the colonists "fall into a state, which, if it be in some respects better than that of the wild-men whom they displace, is in other respects as certainly worse" (2:179).

be regarded as part of the broader "remedial process" (*STM* 2:244). Southey's "cosmo-political" scheme, in other words, ends up echoing his schemes for missionary-led Christian colonialism.[28]

In detailing Southey's explicit and implicit arguments for colonialism in his journalistic writings, *A Tale of Paraguay,* and *Sir Thomas More,* my purpose has not been simply to show how and why Southey came to be an unlikely supporter of the missionary movement. I have also traced how Southey appropriated missionaries' understanding of Enlightenment-influenced ideas and rhetoric for his nationalist and imperialist ambitions. Thus, while he openly applauded the manner in which the missionary societies came to focus on more pragmatic and rational concerns like social welfare, civil rights, and freedom from the despotic rule of priests and "heathen" customs—those "great and obvious temporal advantages of Christianity"—he nonetheless took issue with their hesitation to embrace colonization as a means of diffusing these "advantages." Relying on individual changes of heart and conversions of the native elite to "improve" society seemed impossibly idealistic; in his view, Western institutions alone had the power to compel individuals to reshape society. Hence the importance of colonialism, of instituting something like authoritarian rule in the missionary field. To justify this position, and thereby preemptively respond to missionary concerns regarding colonialism as a means of expanding Christianity, Southey advanced the secular providential-

---

28. This accords with the various schemes for colonial expansion and social stability described in *Sir Thomas More,* in which Southey argues that the stability of *any* society, whether in the center or periphery of empire, is based either on perpetual economic prosperity (impossible to guarantee) or, better, on the "willing obedience of a free people . . . by religion enjoined" (2:198). "In colonizing," More thus advises, "the vow should be remembered which David vowed unto the Almighty God of Jacob: 'I will not suffer mine eyes to sleep, nor mine eyelids to slumber, neither the temples of my head to take any rest, until I have found out a place for the temple of the Lord.' The chief reason why men in later times have been worsened by colonization . . . is, that they have not borne this in mind" (2:272). Thus the same fundamental vision of Christian colonization led and enforced by the British faithful—delineated originally in Southey's early-1800s journalism on missionary societies—finds expression years later in *Sir Thomas More.* These themes are also reiterated in his 1830 review of *Polynesian Research* for the *Quarterly Review*:

> Little expecting, at the commencement of their career, that they should ever be involved in such secular concerns, and little desirous that any such honours should be forced upon them, the course of things has led [missionaries] to become the legislators of these islands, and practically to acknowledge, what perhaps they would not be willing in theory to admit, the importance and necessity of a connection between the government and the religion of a country. ("Art. I" 40–41)

The review postdates *Sir Thomas More,* and to avoid redundancy, I have relegated it to this footnote. But it's worth noting that Southey returned again and again to the same arguments for Christian colonization in relation to missionary work.

ist metaphors of the "hidden plan of nature" and "vaccination" in *A Tale of Paraguay* and *Sir Thomas More*.

For Southey, these metaphors were put in their "proper position" in the concept of cosmopolitanism. In Kant's "Idea of a Universal History on a Cosmo-Political plan," he felt he had found something like the original soil for his ideas regarding Christian expansion. Yet in trying to graft his arguments for mandatory religious education and Christian colonialism onto the providential framework of Kant's "cosmo-political" idea, he fundamentally transformed this idea. Kant's emancipatory ideal, which held out individual "freedom" as the means and end of cosmopolitan society, in Southey's hands became justification for the most atrocious iniquities of British colonialism—that is, the subjugation and, if need be, the death of native people. In other words, Kant's Enlightenment-inflected providential scheme became a vehicle by which Southey could justify native oppression and death as part of "the hidden plan of Nature." It also helped him make the argument that native death, in fact, fulfilled the missionary goals of making natives into model Christians, "freeing" them from their subjugation to arbitrary customs and tyrannical rulers. And, as John Eimeo Ellis's account suggests, it was Southey's take on missionary work that became ascendant. Moving into the mid-century, missionaries began to see themselves not as agents of native emancipation, but "trustees" meant to oversee and help direct native societies. It is in tracing the legacy of missionary work alongside Southey's interest in missionaries that we start to see a shift in the connotations of cosmopolitanism—a move away from its secular and revolutionary associations, toward an agenda of Christian colonialism. And, as we will see in the next chapter, a similar transformation was occurring in missionary conceptions of "universal kinship," as missionaries' intermarriages began exposing, thus solidifying, the very real limits of the evangelical conception of the global human family.

CHAPTER 3
===

Universal Kinship and *Jane Eyre*

OVER SEVERAL MONTHS, the missionary St. John Rivers campaigns to mold Jane into his ideal wife. "I have made you my study for ten months," he declares when he proposes marriage. "In the tractability with which, at my wish, you forsook a study in which you were interested, and adopted another because it interested me [and] in the unflagging energy and unshaken temper with which you have met its difficulties—I acknowledge the complement of the qualities I seek" (*Jane Eyre* [1847] [*JE*] 449). Numerous critics have turned to missionary history to explain this moment of St. John's bizarre proposal.[1] Where much has been said on Jane's motivations for defying St. John's "despotic ambition" (Thomas 55), however, scant attention has been paid to the most pressing and perplexing issue of this episode: St. John *needs* a wife and, for motives that are not obviously clear, only Jane will do.

In fact, while St. John offers a litany of reasons Jane should become a missionary's wife for her sake, he says little as to why a wife is so indispensable to *his* work. True, he gives one reason for his wish to wed Jane—that "as a conductress of Indian schools, and a helper amongst Indian women, your assistance will be to me invaluable"—but Jane's helpfulness alone little justifies the vehemence with which St. John presses his case, especially considering that Jane, using words that St. John calls "violent, unfeminine, and untrue," proves

---

1. See, for instance, readings by Thomas; Gibson; and Cunningham.

not at all the "docile" creature St. John desires in a partner (*JE* 449, 459). Ultimately, he departs for India unmarried, reflecting that he "himself has hitherto sufficed to the toil" (502)—a concluding statement that indicates that if St. John cannot wed his cousin Jane, his next best option is to take no wife at all.

Why should marriage to Jane specifically represent such a burning issue for St. John? Several answers seem readily available: Jane's unique capacity for suffering and "labour" attracts and excites him (*JE* 448); he wants to mortify himself by turning from an ideal image (in Rosamond Oliver) to a "real" one (in Jane), just as Jane mortifies herself in drawing Blanche Ingram's picture and comparing it to her own mirror image; or he wishes for a "familiar marriage," to draw on Talia Schaffer's term, to guard against the temptation to pursue a sexual relationship with one of the "Indian women" he anticipates meeting in the mission field (1–2). Yet none of these explanations fully account for why any other Englishwoman—trained in missionary work, seized by evangelical fervor, and, of course, adequately plain and hardy—would not make a suitable, if not preferable, substitute to the unwilling and unruly Jane. After all, there were women who aspired to be matched with a missionary, as well as missionary societies and clergymen willing to facilitate these pairings.[2] Perhaps most importantly, these explanations do not entirely make clear why the novel takes such pains to juxtapose the near marriage between St. John and Jane with an emphasis on their being kin, relations so closely connected that they even share the same name ("You are not, perhaps, aware that I am your namesake?—that I was christened St John Eyre Rivers?" [*JE* 428]).

To comprehend St. John's fixation on marrying his "namesake," as well as the stress the novel places on the fact of their being blood relations,[3] we must

---

2. There are records of single women who offered their services in the CMS and LMS in the very first years of the societies' operations (Murray 6). Indeed, by the first decades of the nineteenth century, such women were known enough to be satirized in a short story titled "The Missionary Bride" (1838). Appearing in *Bentley's Miscellany*, "The Missionary Bride" opens with the narrator remarking, "There are not a few instances of young females of respectability and accomplishments educating themselves for the avowed purpose of becoming the wives of missionaries" (Hoffman 330).

3. In other works published around the same time as *Jane Eyre*, the marriage (or near marriage) of cousins might be complicated, but not on account of the characters' *cousinship*. Examples include the speaker and his cousin Amy in Lord Tennyson's "Locksley Hall" (1840); Caroline Helstone and Robert Moore in *Shirley* (1849); Richard and Ada in *Bleak House* (1852–53); Henry Esmond and Lady Castlewood in *The History of Henry Esmond* (1852); Aurora and Romney Leigh in *Aurora Leigh* (1857); and Rachel Verinder and Franklin Blake in *The Moonstone* (1868). Thus *Jane Eyre* is somewhat unique in representing St. John and Jane's cousinship as a significant and complicating factor in their contemplated union. Talia Schaffer points out that perhaps one of the only other novels to foreground and work through the ambivalent ramifications of cousin-marriage to a similar degree is that other famous Brontë novel, *Wuthering Heights* (148–55).

focus our attention on St. John's vocation as a *missionary*—a vocation that the novel marks as being in tension with Jane's and St. John's ideas of kinship. Of course, it is critical commonplace that family and marriage are vexed issues in Brontë's novel. As Mary Jean Corbett notes, the novel prompts interest in these issues because it seems so intent to foreground how "kinship, far from being given or fixed, is historically created and culturally contested" (ix). Yet little critical attention has been paid to what *Jane Eyre* insists is a major complicating factor in Victorian ideas of kinship: the extent to which kinship was mediated by missionaries' influential understandings of cosmopolitanism, as materialized in their efforts to unite "the whole human race in one harmonious and affectionate brotherhood" (*Report of the Directors* [1821] 1). According to early nineteenth-century missionary supporters, scripture demonstrated that the varying skin colors and cultural differences across the world constituted nothing more than an "accidental, epiphenomenal mask concealing the unitary Adamic origins of a single, extended human family" (Kidd 26). Influenced by this exegetical tradition, missionary societies theologically and rhetorically grounded their projects in concepts of kinship that resonated with the moral cosmopolitanism promulgated by figures such as the Pietist-influenced Christoph Martin Wieland, who declared in his "Das Geheimniβ des Kosmopoliten-Ordens" (1788), "The cosmopolitans . . . regard *all peoples* of the earth as just so many *branches* of a *single family*" (qtd. in Kleingeld 508).[4]

This definition of cosmopolitan feeling, which modeled British Christian responsibility to the globe on established Christian understandings of familial love and responsibility, not only helped British Christian readers feel kinship with otherwise unfathomably foreign people in the South Seas, India, or elsewhere. It also constituted an instantiation of the broader missionary project to domesticate Enlightenment cosmopolitan ideas, dissociating them from Continental revolutionary fervor and aligning them instead with Christian sentiment and British nationalism, as I've previously discussed. Where late eighteenth-century figures such as Edmund Burke had insisted that the "new philosophy" of cosmopolitanism stood to destroy the "natural" ties of family ("A Letter" 35), early nineteenth-century missionaries cultivated among their readers and supporters a cosmopolitan sentiment that saw the entire world as their "natural" family writ large. Grounding the ethical treatment of oth-

---

4. For the ways that notions of kinship worked to organize and legitimate missionary projects abroad, see Cleall 29. For more on Enlightenment *philosophe* efforts to unify the "brotherhood of mankind" without recourse to religious authority, see Schlereth 90–91. I should also mention that where Kleingeld finds the roots of Wieland's moral cosmopolitanism in the precedent of the Cynics and the Stoics, I see Wieland as also indebted to his spiritual mentor, the apostolic Johann Adam Steinmetz (1689–1762), whom W. R. Ward identifies as a central figure in the "enthusiastic character [of the] new piety" in Central Europe (77).

ers in relations of kinship, this instantiation of missionary cosmopolitanism exalted the idea of the Christian family, reinforcing the notion that "kinship" constituted the ideal bond of sympathy, openness, and fellow-feeling between people.

This moral emphasis on universal kinship manifested itself in a particularly startling way with respect to missionary marriages, though rarely has its full significance been appreciated. Before the 1820s and the writing of *Jane Eyre*, some missionary society directors not only permitted but encouraged missionaries to interracial marriage. Seeing unions with converted native women to be fiscally desirable, politically strategic, and morally praiseworthy, they urged their missionaries to enter into marriages with converts. Assuming that influence flowed from husband to wife (in keeping with Victorian notions of the patriarchal nature of marriage), some missionaries acted on the recommendation of their societies.

By the second decade of the nineteenth century, however, these marriages had produced unanticipated repercussions for missionary work. Although they literalized the metaphor of universal kinship (as indigenous women became part of white missionaries' families), they also proved more reciprocal in terms of influence than missionaries had originally anticipated. As such, intermarriage began to undermine assumptions of British Christians' innate superiority over "natives," assumptions that underwrote missionary work in the first place. This situation produced something of a dilemma for missionary societies. While their continued support for universal kinship in principle meant that intermarriage could never be explicitly prohibited, the destabilization caused by interracial unions was alarming enough to provoke a profound shift in missionary practice. By the 1820s, then, intermarriage was actively discouraged. Seeking to uncouple universal kinship from their former acclaim for intermarriage, missionary societies increasingly portrayed interracial unions as dangerous, seductive moral pitfalls.

This fraught phase of the missionary movement informs the thematics of kinship developed throughout *Jane Eyre*, and, further, unifies the novel's anxious focus on family formation and interracial marriage—most obviously in Rochester's marriage to the racially ambiguous Bertha Mason—with its sustained interest in missionary work. Thus where many prominent readings of the novel's treatment of race in the colonial context tend to concentrate on Bertha,[5] I suggest that there exists a crucial link between the Bertha-Roches-

---

5. See, for instance, readings by Berman; Plasa; Azim; and Meyer. Feminist readings of *Jane Eyre* do tend to mention St. John as well as Bertha (J. Sharpe 54), but mostly insofar as the missionary represents an obstacle to (and thus an opportunity to define) Jane's feminist agency and "ascendency into power" (Kaplan 186; Perera 85–89; J. Sharpe 54).

ter interracial marriage plot and the later St. John missionary plotline.[6] *Jane Eyre*, I propose, makes clear that St. John's proposed endogamous union to his kinswoman represents the conceptual alternative to Rochester and Bertha's "incongruous" intermarriage (*JE* 350). If the novel disparages Rochester's marriage to someone (at least coded) as racially other, it criticizes just as vehemently St. John's singular determination to wed Jane, a woman who literally shares his blood and name.

In its juxtaposition of St. John's resolve to wed someone who, in the narrowest possible sense of the term, is of his own "race" with his lofty evangelical dedication to the universal human "race" (*JE* 23; "The Missionary" 292),[7] the novel not only displays its attunement to missionaries' sentiments concerning universal kinship. It also underscores how missionaries, in their attempt to realize those sentiments in practice, were forced to reject their societies' initial support for interracial marriage in favor of less "corrupting" unions with more appropriate "kin." The novel, then, ultimately exposes the ways that the history of missionary marriages legitimated *and* problematized evangelical understandings of universal kinship.

To develop these arguments, the remainder of this chapter unfolds in four sections. The first recounts the relationship between the concept of kinship and the concept of marriage as set forth in *Jane Eyre*, demonstrating that the novel figures the marriage bond as exemplifying feelings of kinship, while also expressing anxiety that this bond exceeds and surpasses ties of mere kinship to sometimes troubling effect. The next two sections delve into the larger missionary context of these anxieties, detailing, first, the ways in which universal kinship became a central precept of missionary cosmopolitanism, and second, how missionaries sought to actualize—and then moved away from—these imagined ties by way of intermarriage. In the final section, I return to St. John's desire for his kinswoman in order to argue that this context is integral to understand fully the argument of Brontë's novel. One purpose of *Jane*

---

6. Spivak's influential "Three Women's Texts" represents the most prominent and sustained attempt to link what she terms the distinct narrative registers of "childbearing" (in the novel's marriage plots) and "soul making" (in the novel's attention to the work of "civilizing" colonial others). Yet even Spivak admits the irreconcilability of "childbearing" and "soul making" within the narrative logic of the novel, calling the latter "a sort of tangent in *Jane Eyre*, a tangent that escapes the closed circle of the *narrative* conclusion" (248). A focus on the ideological structures motivating missionary work, I suggest, closes this distance and makes evident the connection between the novel's foci on familial relations and missionary culture.

7. Brontë played with the various meanings of the word "race," using the term to refer to the larger "race" of mankind (as in "The Missionary," where she writes, "pagan-priests . . . Crush our lost race" [292]) and at other times using it to demarcate a small group bound by family and blood (in *Jane Eyre*, for instance, Jane asks, "How could [Mrs. Reed] really like an interloper not of her race?" [23]).

Eyre, I contend, is to explore the contradictions inherent in British Christian cosmopolitan notions of kinship and marriage, contradictions that the novel suggests are most evident in the ways that missionaries' efforts to obstruct any interracial mixing belied their outward devotion to the idea of "universal kinship." In making its missionary St. John one of the primary foci in its exposition on these issues, Brontë's novel explores the distance that had opened by the 1820s between the inclusive beliefs initially touted by missionary supporters and their increasingly prejudiced practices.

"Close Union! Intimate Attachment!": Kinship and Marriage in *Jane Eyre*

Jane Eyre has as a central theme the analysis of certain essential contradictions in a constellation of ideas concerning nineteenth-century kinship and race. The first and perhaps most striking of these contradictions is the discrepancy that exists between Jane's idealized expectation of kinship as automatically conferring intimacy and "full fellow-feeling" and the tenuousness of the family bond in practice (*JE* 432). One even could say that Jane's longing to find family repeatedly is offset by the novel's insistence that the family ties are conditional, fragile, and little worth having. Take, for instance, Helen, who tells Jane before she dies, "I leave no one to regret me much: I have only a father; and he is lately married, and will not miss me" (94). Or Rochester, who suffers "family troubles" and has "broke[n] with his family" (145). There is also the Rivers siblings' father, who quarreled and "never reconciled" with his brother (400). Adèle is "forsaken by her mother," and Mrs. Fairfax says of her distant relation to Mr. Rochester, "It is nothing to me" (165, 115). Moreover, Eliza Reed—further driving home the realization that blood is no guarantor of family—renounces her relationship to her sister Georgiana, declaring, "I wash my hands of you: . . . you and I will be as separate as if we had never known each other" (265). In the world of the novel, Jane's strained familial relation with the Reeds is not exceptional but well within the norm.

The distance between Jane's idealized notion of kinship and the feebleness of kinship in practice is most distinct in the St. John Rivers plotline. When Jane discovers that Diana, Mary, and St. John are her "kindred," she exclaims, "I want my kindred: those with whom I have full fellow-feeling" and asks St. John to "say . . . you will be my brother" (*JE* 432–33). Jane's notion of kinship—influenced by the supposition that to be kin is to be intimate equals—is most prominently on display in her insistence that St. John, Diana, Mary, and she herself are all entitled to equal portions of the inheritance bequeathed to Jane after her uncle's death. Remonstrating against St. John's objections, Jane argues, "I, wealthy—gorged with gold I never earned and do not merit! You, pennyless! Famous equality and fraternization! Close union! Intimate attachment!" (432). Her association of "fraternization" with "equality" (as well as with "close union" and "intimate attachment") is significant: Kinship, Jane believes, ought to confer parity, closeness, and union.

Yet St. John refuses to return Jane's enthusiasm. Instead, he gives a measured and relatively cold response: "I think I can [be your brother]. I know I have always loved my own sisters; and I know on what my affection for them is grounded—respect for their worth, and admiration of their talents. You too have principle and mind . . . your presence is always agreeable to me; in your conversation I have already for some time found a salutary solace" (*JE* 433). He finally decides, "I feel I can easily and naturally make room in my heart for you, as my third and younger sister" (433). The deliberateness of St. John's response belies his professed "ease" and "naturalness" in feeling kinship with Jane. Where in Jane's imagination "kindred" necessarily signifies "full fellow-feeling," St. John makes clear that kinship, for him, promises no such sympathy. Rather, he ties his affection—not to mention his acceptance of being related to Jane—to certain conditions: "respect for [her] worth," "admiration of [her] talents," and the agreeability of her company.

St. John again underscores the tenuousness of family ties when he asks Jane to go with him to India as a missionary wife. Arguing that she must accompany him as his spouse and not as his sibling, he asserts that the bond between brother and sister is a "loose tie" (*JE* 452). "I . . . do not want a sister," he adds; "a sister might any day be taken from me" (452).[8] St. John's choice of phrasing is especially piquant in light of his earlier calculated acceptance of Jane as his "sister." In a moment when Jane asserts her sisterly relation to St. John, he denies wanting the familial tie and adds that the bond between brother and sister is one easily dissolved. Though Jane delights in her newly discovered relationship to Diana, Mary, and St. John, and though the reader is to understand this as the fulfillment of what Jane calls her lifelong "craving" for family (432), Brontë still depicts these familial ties as conditional, uncertain, and, at times, barely binding. Thus the novel foregrounds the vast distance between the ideal of kinship and how family is actually practiced

---

8. On the one hand, St. John obviously refers to the Christian edict that no other family relation takes precedence over that of the marriage tie. If Jane were to marry in India, she would certainly be "taken" from St. John. On the other hand, St. John never makes this concern explicit. Tellingly, Jane's insistence that she shall never marry has little impact on St. John's determination that kinship ties are "loose."

and experienced, even—or perhaps especially—by its missionary and most staunchly Christian character, St. John.

In contrast to its depiction of the "loose" ties among kin and family, *Jane Eyre* treats marriage as a remarkably binding and potent relationship (not least because of the impossibility of divorce, as illustrated in Rochester's indissoluble union to Bertha and in the novel's allusions to biblical prescriptions against divorce). The premise that marriage for better or worse establishes radical oneness between husband and wife is central to the narrative of *Jane Eyre* and, in fact, generates much of its plot. In the larger context of the nineteenth-century marriage plot, the peculiarity of this narrative design becomes exceptionally pronounced. Where most marriage plots feature some "meaningless and blissful" union (to use George Steiner's wry characterization of Celia and Sir James's coupling in *Middlemarch* [265]) to serve as the foil to the ideal marriage to be achieved by the end of the novel, *Jane Eyre* is intent on denying that any such "meaningless" marriage could exist. In the world created by Brontë, marriage necessarily means becoming "one person . . . not sentimentally or poetically, but with the profoundest sense of reality and seriousness," in Margaret Oliphant's apt phrasing (581). In other words, the virtues *and* problems arising from marriage in *Jane Eyre* are always tied to permeability and becoming "one" with another—not only in the eyes of society but also mentally, culturally, and spiritually.

The "oneness" of marriage in the novel, moreover, is regularly figured in terms of kinship and blood, a formulation that evokes the British Christian understanding of marriage as the realization of ideal kinship. Jane, for instance, draws upon the language of kinship to express her romantic feelings for Rochester: To Jane, her bond with Rochester is as corporeal as it is spiritual. Thus when he says to her that they "must become one flesh without any delay," or when she describes herself as "akin" to him and "absolutely bone of his bone, and flesh of his flesh" once they marry (495, 199, 500), their language not only brings to mind the original union between Adam and Eve. Significantly, it also draws on a particularly embodied notion of universal kinship as used by missionary societies and alluded to by St. John to prompt Christian sympathy for the unified "race" of mankind (501).

Jane and St. John's hypothetical marriage is imagined in similar terms of "influence," identification, and kinship but to disastrous ends. Despite having no amorous feelings for Jane, St. John nevertheless describes marriage as a "physical and mental union," indeed as the "only union [with] a character of permanent conformity" (*JE* 453). Such sentiments give new significance to an earlier statement made by the missionary when he reveals to Jane their relationship as cousins. "But, Jane," he tells her, "your aspirations after family ties and domestic happiness may be realized otherwise than by the means you contemplate: you may marry" (432). Though Jane rejects his suggestion out of hand—"Nonsense . . . I don't want to marry, and never shall marry!"—St. John never fully dismisses the subject (432). As he reveals with his proposal to Jane, marriage constitutes not just *a* means of establishing "family ties"; it is, rather, the very basis of any "permanent" familial union. He wishes to "influence" her, as he puts it, and insists to Jane that in marriage, "a part of me you must become" (452, 453).[9]

The union of Rochester and Bertha earlier in the novel makes most clear what is at stake in St. John's choice of spouse. That Rochester and Bertha's marriage is one of corruption and contamination is no original insight; critics have often observed their relationship is described as one of "infection" and "penetration" (Thomas 41; McKee 70–71; Buzard 449). "Rochester," contends Sue Thomas, "represents his contact with Bertha's depravity as a contamination of his being . . . and carries her contagion inside him as a corporeal memory and as a monitory presence" (40). In becoming "a part of" Rochester after they wed, the racially ambiguous Creole Bertha undoubtedly influences her husband's character. Generally overlooked, however, is how this language of "penetration" and "contamination" corresponds with descriptions of the novel's *other* marriages, in particular Rochester and Jane's successful partnering.

To convey the horror of his marriage to Bertha, Rochester describes their "daily" intimacy in terms of "mixing air." "I saw her and heard her daily," Rochester admits to Jane. "Something of her breath (faugh!) mixed with the air I breathed" (*JE* 346). In her reading of the passage, Patricia McKee notes that "air" and "spirit" are closely associated throughout *Jane Eyre* (71). As Brontë was aware, the word "spirit" derives from the Latin *spirare*, "to breathe."[10] Seeming to draw on Robert Burton's famous pronouncement in *Anatomy of Melancholy* (1621), "Such as is the air, such be our spirits" (237), Brontë capitalizes on the linguistic relationship between "spirit" and "air" to convey Roches-

---

9. Brontë hints that this "influence" may not be one-way. Despite St. John's certainty of his mastery over Jane and Jane's professed sense of inferiority to St. John, the novel leaves open the possibility that if the cousins were to marry, they would be more "equal" than either foresees. When she contemplates marriage to her cousin, Jane suddenly apprehends that "revelations were being made" (*JE* 452). A "veil," she recounts, falls from St. John's outward "hardness and despotism," and having "felt [St. John's] imperfections" for the first time, Jane realizes she is "with an equal" (452). The removal of a "veil"—reminiscent of the wedding veil—reveals to Jane that there could be parity between St. John and herself. One wonders if St. John fully appreciates that by marrying Jane, he risks becoming as much "part of" her as she would of him.

10. Incidentally, Gaskell mentioned Brontë's particular virtuosity in playing with words in different registers, valences, and languages. Charlotte, she wrote, "would wait patiently, searching for the right term, until it presented itself to her. It might be provincial, it might be derived from the Latin" (323).

ter and Bertha's corporeal and spiritual closeness as married couple. The trope later recurs when Rochester describes his psychic reunion with Jane: Feeling a "gale" upon his brow, he could have sworn, "in some wild, lone scene, I and Jane were meeting. In spirit, I believe, we must have met" (*JE* 496). Though Rochester's spiritual "mixing" with Bertha is "gross" and "impure," in contrast to his airy "meeting" with Jane (346), the metaphor of mixing airs suggests a vital similarity shared by these outwardly unlike relationships. In both unions, partners become like one spirit (a phrase, we'll soon see, that was used by the *Evangelical Magazine* to describe marriage).

In addition to their spiritual intermingling, Bertha and Rochester also share the same "flesh," albeit in a peculiar sense. Bertha, the novel stresses, physically mirrors Rochester. In "stature [she] almost equal[s] her husband" and is as "athletic as he" (*JE* 328). With their "dark" countenances and similar black "manes" of hair (476, 328, 486), we find in Bertha someone who not only acts as "Rochester's double," as Thomas observes (49), but who also resembles him. When she transforms into something like a "Vampyre" after wedding Rochester, even attempting to "la[y] her teeth" into him, she similarly literalizes the act of securing a "good race" or bloodline by way of marriage (*JE* 317, 328, 343).[11] In Bertha, then, we see how the qualities that make for an ideal marriage tip into the stuff of nightmares: "Union" becomes "corruption," "influence" becomes "contagion," and oneness with another means a catastrophic loss of identity and self.

Bertha and Rochester's doomed union thus is a sort of perverse realization of Jane and Rochester's marriage. Not only is Bertha united in "flesh" and "assimilat[ed]" by "blood and nerves" to Rochester (as Jane describes her own marriage at the novel's end). In their mingling of air and spirit, Bertha and Rochester's marriage also prefigures Jane's spiritual, airy (re)union with her future spouse—a commonality suggesting that different as these marriages appear, the institution of marriage invariably possesses certain attributes. "As far as my experiences of matrimony goes," Brontë wrote in an 1854 letter to her friend Ellen Nussey, "I think it tends to draw you out of, and away from yourself" (qtd. in Glen 92n). As though in anticipation of this thoroughly ambivalent sentiment, the marriages and near-marriages of *Jane Eyre* appear

---

11. The scholarship on *Dracula* anticipates my argument. The vampire, taking "the body and blood of the innocent and transmut[ing] them into [her] own identit[y]," enacts the metaphors associated with matrimony (Malchow 124). Associated with sexual pleasure, securing her bond to another by "body and blood," and demanding the obliteration of her victim's previous identity and connections in the making of the new bond, the vampire embodies and exaggerates the qualities normally celebrated in marriage.

premised on one central idea: Marriage, for better or worse, necessarily means profound "physical and mental union."

Thus a dizzying array of contradictions appears in the novel's treatment of kinship and marriage. Contrary to Jane's belief that family means "full fellow-feeling," the novel portrays such familial ties as "loose" and impermanent. Marriage, on the other hand, is the "only" relation that realizes the otherwise empty promises of kinship. Bringing these issues into sharpest focus in St. John's behavior toward Jane, the novel gestures toward the history of kinship and marriage as enacted in missionary writing. We must put ourselves in possession of the background information that Brontë no doubt had in mind to understand the forces at work here.

Universal Kinship and Missionary Work

Dependent on the voluntary contributions of their supporters, missionary societies preoccupied themselves with a central problem: How could feelings of sympathy be engendered in the British Christian heart for faraway peoples? What "definite idea" (to use the phrase from an 1832 issue of the *Scottish Missionary Register*) could enlarge "compassion for the heathen" and make tangible the Englishman's moral responsibility to the multitude of lost souls around the globe ("Introduction" iii)? In much missionary writing, universal kinship emerged as this "definite idea." "Suggesting to those at 'home' that they had familial connections with unknown 'heathen' kin overseas," the language of kinship with what missionaries called the "universal human family" constituted a primary "means of identifying with those who otherwise seemed remote" (Cleall 29; "The Peace" 393; Cleall 29).

Judging from its ubiquity, the language of universal kinship must have garnered missionary societies considerable support. Repeatedly, societies construed British Christian responsibility to others in terms of kinship and what they felt to be the natural corollary of kinship, sympathy. "Sympathy," announced the *Baptist Magazine* (a periodical affiliated with the BMS), "is one of the most amiable feelings which glows in the bosom of man.... Shall we not feel, deeply feel for those who are 'bone of our bone, and flesh of our flesh'[?] ... Shall we not extend our view to the whole world?" ("Jesus Wept" [1826] 504, 506). In its annual report for 1827, the LMS similarly declared, "It was the design of the Creator, that a feeling of universal brotherhood should bind together the whole human family" ("Thirty-Third General Meeting" 266). Finding perhaps its best expression in the abolition motto "Am I Not a Man and a Brother" (which enjoyed particular popularity in the years during which many of the events of *Jane Eyre* take place),[12] Christian universal kinship disseminated the notion that common "man"-hood indicated common "brother"-hood and, moreover, that this revelation of common kinship would stimulate pity, compassion, and sympathy for the distant "heathen."

The donation lists included at the end of each issue of the *Evangelical Magazine and Missionary Chronicle* offer a striking example of how far missionary societies went in cultivating feelings of kinship between British Christians and foreign "heathens." In exchange for donations, the LMS allowed its subscribers to give Christian names to newly converted children.[13] Regularly (and more than a little surprisingly), donors bestowed their family surnames onto these children. A brief glance over a single issue of the *Evangelical Magazine* reveals that the practice, while not frequent, was fairly common. For just over £3, for instance, a "Mrs. Jacomb" from Cheltenham could give the name Nathaniel Pierce Jacomb to a "Boy in Calcutta" ("Missionary Contributions ... December 1842"). A month earlier, records indicate, a Mrs. Schroder donated £5 to the LMS to have a "Nat. Girl" renamed Sarah Schroder ("Missionary Contributions ... November 1842").

The colonial preoccupation with renaming, of course, participated in the broader imperial effort to overwrite indigenous cultural systems and consolidate imperial control. Undoubtedly, some missionaries' insistence that native converts change their original names served a similar function. Heike Liebau, for instance, observes that by taking a Christian name, the convert symbolically assured missionaries (as well as their British readership) that he had truly "chang[ed] religious identity. . . . Since the original name of a local person represented that person's former faith, it could not be used when that person became a Christian" (81). Yet, that missionary supporters were willing, even

---

12. Sue Thomas demonstrates that Jane meets St. John in 1833, the year that saw the death of William Wilberforce and the passage of the Slavery Abolition Act (11). Thomas continues, "According to this dating, Bertha Mason and Rochester married in 1819; Bertha was born in 1792, Rochester in 1797, and Jane in 1814" (11). Thus Brontë sets significant moments in the novel at a time when, arguably, the missionary rhetoric of universal kinship had reached fever pitch due to evangelical campaigning for abolition.

13. The CMS also renamed African children after their supporters, a practice that the missionary historian Charles Hole dates to 1812:

> On December 11, 1812, the Committee had intelligence of the Rev. William Marsh having collected 95*l*. 9*s*. 9*d*. at Reading; and as Mr. Marsh expressed the wish of himself and his friends, that an African boy should be redeemed from slavery and named Launcelot, in compliment to Mr. Launcelot Austwich, the Mayor of Reading, for his kindness in promoting the collection, the missionaries were to be instructed accordingly. This was the first instance of the African children of the Society being named in compliment to English friends of the Mission. In the present instance it was a Christian name that was transferred; later it was surnames as well. (237)

eager, to give foreign children their *own* family names suggests the sincerity with which these supporters aspired to those feelings of universal kinship espoused by missionary societies.

The popularity of universal kinship almost certainly is due to its success in masking an ideological contradiction inherent in the missionary project. On the one hand, missionary work drew much of its popular appeal from the Christian "ideal of equality," the notion that all men, being made by God, possessed souls that were equal in His eyes and as such deserved the same fundamental rights and freedoms on earth (Agathocleous, *Urban Realism* 41). The power of this idea should not be underestimated. Missionaries and their supporters derived much of their moral high ground from positioning themselves against the worst excesses of authoritarianism and bigotry. On the other hand, universal kinship also facilitated the "ideology of colonial paternalism" (42), allowing "'free-born' Britons" to govern their heathen "kindred" without feeling themselves to be despotic or bellicose (Thorne 37–38). It comes as no surprise that when missionaries invoked the family of mankind, they tended to portray indigenous people as "their younger brothers and sisters (occasionally as their children), not as equals" (Cleall 30).

Demonstrating, to borrow a phrase of Madhavi Kale's, "the prolific instability of empire as a discursive resource" (5), the language of universal kinship masked a rent between the equality it exalted on a moral plane and the hierarchization it facilitated de facto. So long as "equality" remained an abstract ideal rather than concrete practice, British Christians easily believed themselves both equal with *and* superior to all other people around the globe. In regarding his fellow man to be his own kin—as like himself, as knowable and sympathetic—the British missionary supporter could bask in the "majesty of the ideal of global kinship" without having to face realities of cultural, national, racial, and moral difference (Agathocleous, *Urban Realism* 107). Predictably, any course of action derived from the idea of universal kinship was "destined never to fulfill its normalizing mission because the premise of power was preserving the alienness of the ruling group" (Chatterjee 10). Perhaps this dynamic is nowhere better illustrated than in the troubled history of missionaries' interracial marriages, a history of which *Jane Eyre* is cognizant.

Intermarriage in the Mission Field

Moments before proposing to Jane, Rochester asks, "Are you anything akin to me, do you think, Jane?" (*JE* 283). His question, together with Jane's reciprocal insistence that Rochester is "akin" to her, draw on a discursive tradition in

British Christianity that linked romantic love to feelings of kinship. Marriage, needless to say, played an important role in British Christian society not least because it was what "created kinship" in the first place (Marcus 197). Yet marriage occupied an even more curious role within the evangelical scheme of kinship than has been fully appreciated. Not only was the institution regarded as the foundation of family (an 1841 missionary report, for instance, defined the institution as "the basis of family ties" [Timpson xlviii]); it was also considered the bond that *epitomized* feelings of kinship, as Rochester's question to Jane indicates. If kinship meant feeling for another as though they were (to use the words of the *Baptist Magazine* mentioned earlier) "bone of our bone, and flesh of our flesh,'" marriage was the preeminent expression of this feeling.

The bond of marriage, moreover, was not only kinship par excellence; it was also the relation that in being the "basis of family ties," clarified and superseded in importance all other family relations. "Under the shelter of this domestic economy," argued Jerome Alley in *Vindiciae Christianae* (1826), "new or better relationships spring up. The duties due to father and mother, or by them, are more clearly ascertained" (qtd. in "Art. I" 9). Drawing from Matthew 19:5, Alley asserted, "No other relationship of life is to be suffered to interfere between [the married couple]. They are to leave father, and mother, and sister, and brother, rather than suffer the sacredness of their common engagement to be impaired. They are to become one; to be united in the sameness of interest and of heart" (8). The passage, then, makes two crucial arguments regarding marriage. It suggests that conjugal relations in some sense not only extend but supplant older family ties in the creation of new ones. Simultaneously, it also stresses that marriage is, at its heart, a relationship of "sameness" as well as one of "mutuality" and "equal and impartial duty" (in Alley's words) (8, 9).

As Ruth Perry demonstrates, the late eighteenth and early nineteenth centuries saw a shift from a kinship system based mostly on consanguineal relations to one that privileged conjugal ties. The new stress on the "second family" over the family of origin certainly helps account for the rise of a rhetoric that emphasized the importance (and, crucially, the inescapability) of complete identification between spouses. If Victorians tended to conceive of marriage according to "the Christian notion of husband and wife constituting 'one flesh'" and "the Platonic notion of soul-mates as two halves of a single being" (Ablow 10), evangelical writers in particular advanced these ideas with unparalleled descriptive force. *The Evangelical Magazine and Missionary Chronicle*, for instance, asserted that marriage meant the joining of "kindred souls in body and spirit [who], uniting before the throne of grace . . . seem like one spirit," in a formulation reminiscent of the "mixing airs" metaphor employed in *Jane Eyre* ("On Marriage" [1816] 48). And, in *Theology; Explained and Defended* (1818), Rev. Timothy Dwight praised marriage as "*the most intimate union which exists in the present world*" (74).[14] According to such formulations, once man and woman had become husband and wife, they were to aid and empathize with each other, becoming totally permeable to the influence of their partner in the process. When the evangelical Sarah Lewis argued in her popular treatise *Woman's Mission* (1836) that female "influences" in motherhood and matrimony "act by a sort of moral contagion, and are imbibed by the receiver as they flow from their source, without consciousness on either side," she reinforced the already prevalent notion that openness and unconscious reciprocity of influence characterized the best Christian marriages (94).[15]

The British Protestant imagination thus attributed three remarkable qualities to marriage. First, it held up marriage to be the foundation and exemplification of feelings of kinship. Second, it suggested that new family ties created by marriage superseded older ties in significance and importance. And finally, it maintained that marriage established a "sameness" or reciprocity between husband and wife that was a natural result of each being open to the other's feelings and sentiments.

I specify these attributes because they underpinned debates surrounding missionary intermarriage and universal kinship that took place in the early nineteenth century. In fact, it was because these marriages appeared to confer relations of mutuality and openness between racially different spouses that they so deeply unsettled missionary societies. In her study on missionary intermarriages in southern Africa, Julia Wells notes, "Within such relationships, all suggestions of inherent European superiority melted away, as African women became not only intimate partners, normally accorded equal status of their husbands, but also the mothers of bicultural children" (2). The phenomenon she identifies is generalizable: As travelogues and missionary reports made public stories of South Sea and African missionaries who had "married non-Christian women and defected from the mission, in effect going native," missionary societies expressed ever shriller alarm that their missionaries identified too much with their native wives (Cox, *British* 107–8). Taking

---

14. Dwight's sermon was reprinted in the appendix of Rev. John Morison's *Counsels to a Newly-Wedded Pair* (1830). Morison served as the editor of the *Evangelical Magazine* and throughout his life was an enthusiastic supporter of the LMS.

15. Brontë read a review of Lewis's tract in an 1850 issue of the *Westminster Review*. In a letter to Gaskell, she remarked, "I got hold of a number—for last January—I think—in which there was an article entitled 'Woman's Mission' (the phrase is hackneyed) containing a great deal that seemed to me just and sensible" (*Selected Letters* 173).

to heart the evangelical exhortation to view racial others as cousins and kin, missionaries treated (or appeared to treat) native wives as partners and peers. In doing so, their marriages threatened to destabilize the hierarchy between "Christian" and "heathen," "primitive" and "civilized," and "Us" and "Other" upon which missionary work was predicated.

In light of their collusion in the imperial project of mapping difference along racial and civilizational lines, it's perhaps surprising that at the turn of the century, missionary societies not only tolerated but encouraged interracial unions. In a 1796 speech, for instance, the LMS director Rev. Haweis suggested that missionaries in the Polynesian islands would "do well [to build] matrimonial connexions" with their early converts (qtd. in Cleall 68). As Wells notes in regard to the African missions, "It is clear that the LMS in its early years did little or nothing to dissuade its missionaries from marrying African women. . . . In those days, missionaries wrote home about the exemplary achievements of colleagues who had African wives, often giving credit to the women for their role in smoothing over cultural difference" (19).

At least three considerations motivated the early tolerance of missionary societies for intermarriage. First, from an economic standpoint, unmarried missionaries and missionaries with native wives were cheap to provide for, certainly cheaper than a British missionary family. Second, missionary alliances with the families of native leaders made political sense: To paraphrase a recommendation issued by LMS director Joseph Hardcastle, by taking "indigenous women, ideally from within the ruling aristocracy" as their wives, single missionaries would "cement relationships between mission society and local powers" (qtd. in Cleall 68).[16] The third consideration, however, was religious. Simply put, missionary societies in their early years felt bound to recognize and even embrace intermarriage. As James Cowles Prichard's *Researches into the Physical History of Man* (1813) strongly suggests, the very veracity of biblical history was evinced precisely in the propagation and viability of "mixed breeds in the human kind" (150).

In his history on the subject, Damon Salesa makes clear the religious stakes of intermarriage and "mixed breeds." In the 1770s, writers such as Henry Home, Lord Kames, and the planter Edward Long brought the monog-

---

16. The same considerations led trading companies to tolerate intermarriages. Thus while "the Hudson's Bay Company frowned on intermarriage between Europeans and the Indian peoples with whom they traded . . . the North West Company (formed in Montreal around 1779 to challenge the Hudson's Bay Company), and the American Fur Company (1808) had a more tolerant view. Theirs was also a pragmatic policy because intermarriage of voyageurs and traders with Native American women forged family ties that often reinforced trading networks" (Olmanson 7).

enist account of human origin into dispute, a development that focused particular attention on racial crossings and made the issue "a proving ground for debates about humans, species, races and the natural and divine" (3–4). Faced with such religiously skeptical polygenists, who distanced themselves from the biblical account of mankind's origin and labeled miscegenation as degrading and unsustainable, groups such as the LMS found themselves backed into supporting racial crossings in the process of defending biblical authority. In this way, "Christian universalism and Christian teaching on the sanctity of marriage converged to uphold the legality if not the wisdom of interracial marriage" (Cox, *British* 107), making intermarriage, as the LMS missionary Thomas Lewis argued in defense of his own marriage to a Polynesian woman in 1798, appear "essential to faith and practice" in the early years of missionary work ("Otaheitean Journals" 65).

In seeming to achieve a degree of intercultural sympathy and openness, however, these unions exacerbated concern that the missionary—and, by extension, British morality itself—did not improve but degenerated upon contact with foreign women. "The 'foreign field,'" observes Cleall, "was feared to harbor forces of corruption and contamination which, through the family, could corrode the very identities of the missionaries" (27). When in 1817 the *Evangelical Magazine* called on British Christians to "*pray for the Missionaries who are employed in pagan countries . . . that their purity may be preserved immaculate amidst the peculiar temptations to which they are exposed*" ("A Call" 7), it implicitly expressed this growing unease. To the extent that intermarriage actually attained and realized the unification of "kindred souls in body and spirit" between spouses, it was seen as an exceptional threat to missionary purity.

The case of missionary Thomas Lewis exemplifies this dilemma. Although LMS directors had urged their South Seas missionaries to form unions with native women, the missionaries, upon reaching the islands, instead decreed all Polynesian women to be "harlots" ("Otaheitean Journals" 16). "From the manner in which the children of the natives are brought up," they declared, "it is probable that there is not a female on the island, above the age of twelve years, that is not debased" (58). According to this convoluted logic, all Polynesian women being thus "debased" were also necessarily "heathens," and thus, "to marry an heathen woman was directly contrary to the word of God" (16). When Lewis took a Polynesian woman as his wife in 1798, his fellow missionaries, predictably, refused to acknowledge or perform the rites for his marriage. Insisting that his union was unsanctioned, the missionaries excommunicated Lewis from their community.

Lewis in turn rebutted these charges, asserting that the sanctity of his marriage was determined not by the missionary community but by God and the common "consent" of the nuptial parties:

> I am informed . . . that marriage is a civil ordinance of the God of nature: and the following description is very similar to that which Mr. Eyre was pleased to give once—"Marriage is the conjunction of man and woman, importing an inseparable custom of life. That conjunction is rather of the minds than of bodies, for the consent makes the marriage." ("Otaheitean Journals" 132)

Quoting the preeminent evangelical and LMS director John Eyre, Lewis drew upon the missionary ideal of marriage as "an inseparable custom of life" born of mutual agreement to argue for the legitimacy of his marriage. In doing so, however, Lewis inadvertently exacerbated his fellow missionaries' dread of corruption.

Believing their authority to derive from the moral and cultural distance between themselves and the natives they sought to convert, the Tahitian missionaries resented what they saw as Lewis's transgression. Where Lewis should "have shone in a conspicuous manner among these dark heathen," they complained, he instead "endeavour[ed] to make friends with the world" and "sunk into the arms of a poor idolatress" ("Otaheitean Journals" 81, 110). The language chosen by the missionaries is revealing. Rather than make himself "conspicuously" distinct from the "dark heathen," Lewis, so the missionaries alleged, had yielded to the sexual temptations of a "harlot" and assimilated himself into the heathen "world." Small wonder that Lewis's assurance of having "an inseparable custom of life" with his wife failed to win over the Tahitian missionaries. Such "inseparability," far from being a missionary aim, was what missionaries feared. Rather than accept the marriage, the missionaries "summarily tabooed" Lewis "lest [his] contamination infect anyone else" (Herbert, *Culture and Anomie* 179).

The missionary George Vason, who married a Polynesian woman, took to wearing the native dress, and joined in native "amusements" (Vason 110), further exacerbated British anxiety that intermarriage threatened to breach the cultural and moral barriers separating white missionaries from the "uncivilized" islanders. In a repentant autobiography published in 1810, Vason admitted, "My marriage, which for a time rendered me very happy, threw down every barrier of restraint, which hitherto conscience had opposed to my inclinations. . . . I lament to say, that I now entered, with the utmost eagerness, into every pleasure and entertainment of the natives" (112). Yet, he asserted, there was a lesson to be learned: "My case may . . . show the expediency of sending married men chiefly as Missionaries, or else of not sending them to such tremendously alluring scenes" (113–14). Missionaries, Vason's narrative implies, become whom they marry: If a missionary marries a British wife, he shall remain properly British abroad.[17] A union with an "alluring" native wife, however, portends mental and cultural fusion with her people. The curious cases of Vason and Lewis—the former narrated by a repentant returnee to England, the latter recounted by hostile missionaries after his death—thus appear to impart the same message. Because intermarriage makes a wife "a part of" her husband ("associat[ing]," to use Rochester's description of his marriage to Bertha, a "nature most gross, impure, depraved . . . with" that of her spouse [*JE* 345]), such a union precipitates the intellectual and moral "contamination" of the white missionary.

Similar cases arose in South Africa, as the once celebrated marriages of missionaries to African women became a source of vexation for the LMS. The abandonment of British cultural forms in favor of those practiced by his wife, for instance, made the missionary James Read an object of ridicule, as accounts of him living barefoot in a clay hut with a Khoekhoe wife trickled back to London (Elbourne 214; Lichtenstein 238).[18] Perhaps most shocking to British audiences was the apparent "backsliding" of the missionary Johannes van der Kemp. There was a certain irony to this scandal, as just a few years earlier the LMS had looked to Van der Kemp to improve its prospects after the public relations disaster of its first mission to the South Seas (caused partly by Lewis).[19] Yet in 1806, just a few years before his death, an elderly

---

17. Interestingly, the CMS never openly embraced a policy of intermarriage in its mission to New Zealand, probably in order to "avoid any repeat of George Vason" (Wanhalla, *Matters* 35). However, the society did see its share of problematic unions. For instance, Thomas Kendall, a missionary to New Zealand, was dismissed from service for his 1822 affair with the daughter of a high-ranking Maori chief as well as for his role in sanctioning an intermarriage between Maria Ringa and the Norwegian Peter Tapsell in 1823 (Wanhalla, "The Natives" 31). Such behavior among Church missionaries attracted the attention of the House of Lords in 1838, which formed a committee on New Zealand partly to investigate claims that the "Conduct of One or Two" missionaries "has been such as to undo much they could have done themselves, and to have thrown Dishonour upon their Names" (Polack qtd. in Wanhalla, *Matters* 24).

18. The German physician and explorer Henry Lichtenstein characterized Read as "extremely ignorant" and claimed that "nobody could be made to believe that he married [his wife] from inclination" (238). Lichtenstein's account provoked a fierce response among missionary supporters. A letter to the editor of *The New Monthly Magazine* argued, for instance, "that other African missionaries have married native women and live happily with them; and I certainly think it tends to promote the cause of Christianity, when men, who devote their whole lives to its propagation among Heathen nations, can do it from principle; for there are no *casts* in the religion of Christ" ("Professor Lichtenstein Corrected" 519).

19. The first issue of *Transactions*, which contained an account of the alleged fiasco of Lewis's marriage, opened with the assurance that though the South Sea missionaries have been

Van der Kemp wed a thirteen-year-old Malagasi girl (Elbourne 217). Reports of the union scandalized the LMS back in England and decimated Van der Kemp's reputation in the British press. Van der Kemp, sneered the conservative-leaning *New Monthly Magazine and Universal Register,* "took unto himself a Hottentot Venus of thirteen, and, like the Santon Barissa, sacrificed a long life of piety and benevolence to a few days of spiritualized concupiscence which he was unable to gratify, and fell a hasty victim to the impotent attempt" (J. R. 32).

However, what finally provoked the LMS to curb the practice of interracial marriage in South Africa was not (just) the union of Van der Kemp and the thirteen-year-old Sara. Of much more concern to the society was the strained relationship between the LMS and the Cape Town settlers caused by these missionary intermarriages, which, in the eyes of the slaveholding white settlers, undermined the "master-servant" hierarchy they had established over the broad Khoisan population (Wells 2). Indeed, evidence suggests that what bothered the white settlers in particular was less these unions in and of themselves, than the genuine mutuality, even affection, to which the missionaries aspired in their interracial unions (Elbourne 221; Wells 2–11).[20]

The LMS missionary Michael Wimmer provides one of the most compelling examples of the tension between the (relative) equality that missionary societies called for in marriage and their growing collusion with the racial hierarchies of white settlements, which ran counter to those calls. In an 1815 letter to his LMS superior Johannes Seidenfadden (a missionary who had married into and settled among the Cape Town colonists), Wimmer defends his decision to marry a "native" woman despite the objections from both local government officials and those missionaries who had allied themselves with the colonists, such as Seidenfadden. In affecting terms, Wimmer describes his wife Susannah's despair at being told of the "unlawfulness" of their union and his efforts to console her. Notably, he recounts reassuring Susannah that since their problems were "only because you are a Hottentot woman and no other reason is in the way, will you do as I; here is my hand, I take you this evening to my wife, and so she did the same" (qtd. in Wells 8). The letter thus not only appeals to Seidenfadden's sympathy (in its portrayal of a loving and heartbroken wife) but also implicitly criticizes Seidenfadden and his colleagues for prohibiting the marriage on the grounds of racial difference

---

"attended with the infirmities incident to our fallen nature," "the illustrious Vanderkemp [is] about to establish a Hottentot Village . . . for the purpose of civilizing and collecting such of the natives as are willing to hear the Gospel of the Kingdom" ("Otaheitean Journals" xvii, xviii).

20. The evidence that still exists of these unions suggests that missionaries such as Van der Kemp and Read *did* in fact have fairly harmonious marriages (Elbourne 219).

alone ("only because you are a Hottentot woman and no other reason is in the way"). Wimmer's arguments for his marriage thus resonate with the justifications earlier made by Lewis for his own intermarriage. Both missionaries invoke the British evangelical ideal of marriage while also implicitly reminding the LMS that racial difference should not matter in establishing new conjugal and familial ties.

In practice, however, race *did* matter, as the issue threatened to split concord between those missionaries who sought to live with and among indigenous converts and those who saw Christian conversions more efficaciously attained by cooperation with white colonists and imperial authorities. In 1817, Seidenfadden and the LMS missionary George Thom convened an informal missionary synod to curtail what they termed "the evils which have resulted from marriages beyond the colony" (qtd. in Wells 11). In what constituted a rather remarkable rhetorical feat, the 1817 synod effectively called for an end to missionary intermarriages while managing to sidestep all explicit mention of race in its recorded proceedings. The omission, Wells notes, "openly suggests [that synod participants] were aware that their views were not necessarily shared by the LMS Directors in London or by other local missionaries" (11).[21] Hence the synod culminated in the carefully coded recommendations that the LMS cease sending unmarried missionaries to South Africa and, furthermore, that "no Missionary should be allowed to marry beyond the limits, but to marry in the Colony according to the law to prevent evil" (qtd. in Wells 11). The LMS largely adopted the synod's recommendations despite knowing of the synod conveners' sympathies with the slaveholding colonists.[22] Without

---

21. A host of other "evils" were cited as reasons for the society to forbid "marry[ing] beyond the limits." "Settler opinion" emerged as the "chief problem," along with legal "irregularity in the ways the marriages were contracted." In South Africa, as well as in the South Seas, much of this "irregularity" stemmed from prejudiced missionaries' refusals to perform necessary marriage rites (Wells 19). The refusal of colonist-sympathizing missionaries to recognize missionary intermarriages allowed them to condemn indigenous wives as "concubines" and such marriages as unlawful and adulterous. Take, for instance, a series of letters authored by these missionaries to the LMS directors in London to take action against those such as Wimmer and Read. "Deplorable is the state of affairs," writes Thom. "Four Missionaries stand charged of adultery and damnation not by the *Boors*, not by *Lichtenstein* but by Missionaries themselves. James Read's conduct is the worst of all. . . . [R]eports fly about that he was always an adulterer and yet this man can write *a long letter* and speak against these Sins in Caffraria while he hugged his Concubine in his bosom." Another letter alleges Wimmer "has been guilty of living with a Hottentot without being married for a considerable time" (Ullbrecht, Messer, Brownlee, Evans, and Hooper).

22. Neither Seidenfadden nor the white colonists of South Africa had particularly good reputations in LMS circles in London. The LMS, for instance, dismissed Seidenfadden from his missionary post when it was revealed he had been systematically oppressing the indigenous people for years. An internal investigation found he "had been running the Caledon missionary

expressly forbidding the practice, the LMS ceased encouraging missionaries to marry indigenous converts and, in an even more striking about-face from earlier practice, mostly stopped sending single missionaries abroad.

Thus by the 1820s, mixed marriages were shunned. "Native" wives, far from making exemplary partners for the missionary, instead were regarded as both evidence of *and* the catalyst for the missionary's moral and social degeneracy. "A connexion so unequal," proclaimed an 1823 missionary history extrapolating from Van der Kemp's case, "not only sinks a man in the eyes of the world, but tends insensibly to debase the tone of his own mind and manners" (Brown 414). To account for this "debasement"—which was so contrary to missionary societies' original expectations of these intermarriages—indigenous women were increasingly represented in missionary literature as irresistible, inherently corrupting objects of sexual desire. White missionaries could not but be tempted by such "tremendously alluring" women in such "tremendously alluring" scenes.

One imagines that a neater solution to the difficulties presented by interracial marriage would have been for missionary societies simply to forbid the practice of these unions. Yet, as Jeffrey Cox observes, the ethical standard explicitly adopted by missionary societies to shore up their moral authority made banning intermarriage outright a difficult endeavor. "Unable or unwilling to rule out racial intermarriage in principle," missionary societies instead quietly worked to "stigmatiz[e] interracial marriage without outlawing it" (Cox, *British* 110). Thus alongside their strategy to portray intermarriage as fundamentally degrading, missionary societies also began to exalt the importance of taking a wife before leaving England and maintaining a proper British Christian family while abroad. In his "Introductory Essay" for the American edition of *Memoir of Mrs. Mary Mercy Ellis, Wife of Rev. William Ellis* (1836), for instance, the influential missiologist Rufus Anderson argued that the missionary in possession of a British or American wife would "bear up better against adverse circumstances than one who is unmarried, will be more of a man, a better christian [sic]" (x). Moreover, he insinuated, such a wife would

---

institution for his own financial gain, forcing the Khoi residents to build irrigation canals on land from which he then evicted them and farmed for his personal use." He also was "found guilty of selling Khoi children to collect on trivial debts" (Wells 17). That Seidenfadden was held in esteem by the Cape Town colonists was hardly a mark in his favor, as many LMS directors found the Boers distasteful. After completing a tour of the South African missions, the LMS director John Campbell reported, "I had been accustomed from my youth to hear, even from the pulpit, the expression, 'As savage as a Hottentot.' Hottentots are not so savage or dull as our peasantry, or as in the Dutch boors. The wife of a boor may be seen in the morning, singing her hymn, with her psalm-book in one hand, and the *sambuk* in the other, lashing her slaves" (qtd. in Philip 420).

protect the missionary from "temptations" that "violate[d] the laws of purity" (R. Anderson x, xi). One suspects Anderson had in mind missionaries such as Vason, whose marriage by his own account "threw down every barrier of restraint."

If we view this history of controversy in a different light, it becomes clear that what alarmed missionary societies—and what also prevented them from banning intermarriage explicitly—was the fact that these interracial marriages did not fail. On the contrary, they lived up to the expectations placed on them. In producing bicultural, biracial children, these marriages concretized the racial intermingling implicit in the ideal of "universal kinship." Moreover, the conversion of wives to Christianity (in many cases) and the transformation of husbands' "minds and manners" to accommodate the cultures of their wives demonstrated the sympathy and openness that characterized ideal Christian marriages. A spouse was indeed "a sort of moral contagion," and marriage, creating actual rather than metaphorical bonds of kinship, was undeniably the union of "kindred souls in body and spirit." No matter the author's stance on the morality or advisability of intermarriage, nearly all accounts of missionaries' marriages reinforced this remarkable message. The language of kinship and mutuality used to defend interracial unions in missionary and evangelical publications dovetailed with the rhetoric deployed to denounce them.

Intermarriage and the "Incorruptible" St. John Rivers

As she makes evident in her poem "The Missionary" (1846) as well as in *Jane Eyre*, Brontë was fascinated by missionary work in general and the conjugal challenges faced by missionaries in particular.[23] In stark contrast to the relatively asexual missionary figure imagined, for example, in R. M. Ballantyne's novels, Brontë's missionaries teem with barely contained sexual longing. The titular figure from "The Missionary" represses what he calls his "carnal will" to carry out his duty, "dissever[ing] English ties" (most notably his "tie" to his love interest Helen, of whom he says, "I could not—dared not stay for thee") in favor of what he characterizes to be the "hot action" of India ("The Missionary" 32, 51–52, 5). Similarly, below his icy demeanor, St. John Rivers "almost rave[s] in [his] restlessness," vowing to "overcome" his "last conflict with human weakness" (as he unflatteringly refers to his feelings for Rosamond) (*JE* 398, 405). Brontë, in other words, perceived that foreign missionary work

---

23. In his edition of her poems, Victor A. Neufeldt suggests that Brontë heavily revised the "The Missionary" in 1845, roughly contemporaneous with her composition of *Jane Eyre* (xli).

strained national, familial, and romantic "ties," and she was aware that even the most respected single missionaries struggled to check amorous feelings.

This struggle would have been no secret to those acquainted with missionary narratives and periodicals written in the early nineteenth century, as the Brontës were. Both Patrick Brontë and Aunt Branwell shared an admiration of missionary societies and society founders of various denominations (Thormählen 16; Cunningham 96; Carens 171n12). Moreover, Charlotte herself was as much "brought up in Church-Methodism as a kind of surrogate Dissenter" as she was in the Church of England (Cunningham 96).[24] She gravitated especially toward the story of Henry Martyn, the renowned missionary affiliated with the CMS who worked in India in the first decades of the nineteenth century and who helped sponsor her father Patrick Brontë's education at (the significantly named) St. John's College, Cambridge (Gibson 433; Cunningham 96; Peterson 93). As Stanley and others have demonstrated, the "forbiddingly pious figure of St John Rivers" is "certainly modelled on Martyn" ("Ardour" 109).[25]

Martyn's memoir would almost certainly have led Brontë to the stories of Van der Kemp and Read in South Africa.[26] More importantly, however, it also would have alerted her to the ways that missionaries struggled to reconcile the demands of their "calling" with their romantic feelings and familial aspirations. Indeed, one of the most fascinating aspects of Martyn's narrative was the numerous difficulties he faced in his decision to pursue a life of celibacy as a missionary. At a meeting of the Eclectic Society in 1805, for instance, Richard Cecil, the renowned Evangelical associated with the Clapham Sect, warned Martyn that he "should be acting like a madman, if he went out unmarried," and Martyn himself admitted that having no female company "in a scene and climate of such temptation" as India was a formidable prospect (qtd. in Stanley, "Ardour" 12). His misgivings proved justified, as after spending just a year

---

24. Patrick Brontë particularly admired Henry Venn, one of the original founders of the CMS, who exhibited the more ecumenical leanings that tended to distinguish missionary movement supporters from the stricter denominationalism exhibited by other eighteenth-century Dissenters (Thormählen 16, 21).

25. In fact, her depiction of St. John so closely resembled the real-life missionary that "when her father read *Jane Eyre* he believed he was being presented with old family stories and that Charlotte had had Henry Martyn in mind when she conceived of St John" (Cunningham 96–97).

26. Charlotte likely read John Sargent's memoir of Martyn (Cunningham 96), in which Martyn repeatedly mentions his admiration of Van der Kemp and his elation at finally conversing with him and Read in Cape Town in January 1806 (Martyn 133). Omitted from the memoir is any mention of these missionaries' marriages, although the marriages were hardly secret. If Brontë was familiar with Martyn's biography (see Gibson), she probably would have been aware of these two missionaries who both eventually became controversial within the LMS.

in India, he called for his English love interest Lydia Grenfell to come join him as a missionary's wife. Lydia, it is worth mentioning, never came.[27]

It is unsurprising, then, that both "The Missionary" and *Jane Eyre* display awareness that the institution of marriage represented a particularly contested site in missionary work. Regarding intermarriage to be a looming threat to the "cultural boundary" between "'civilised' and 'uncivilised'"—a boundary from which missionaries drew what they considered to be their moral, intellectual, and spiritual authority (Cleall 49)—missionary societies began to guard against the allure of intimate unions with racial others. Consequently, standard practice increasingly called for missionaries to marry before heading to the mission field, in order to maintain British "family and household structures" while overseas (27). To return to Rufus Anderson's 1836 words, the married missionary was now considered less likely to be "led into such temptations" as exist among heathen peoples (xi). A wife, moreover, in "secur[ing] [for the missionary] regularity and comfort in his establishment, and such food, clothing, and retirement as habit has made necessary," would support the missionary in being "a better christian [sic]" (ix, x). Not only did the adoption of this policy help mission societies head off charges that their missionaries, in taking "native wives," had themselves "gone native." It also conveniently obviated the necessity of banning intermarriages because of explicit racial prejudice. Thus where the "native" woman was portrayed as inherently sensual and corrupting—seducing the missionary away from the practice and "purity" of his faith and culture—the English missionary wife was increasingly figured as *de*-sexed, uncorrupt, and *in*corruptible. Culturally, racially, and religiously alike to the missionary and maintaining the "regularity and comfort in his establishment," she was "expected to contain the potentially disruptive male sexuality of her husband, while not, apparently, being a desiring [or desirable] subject herself" (Woodward 92).[28]

---

27. In the late 1810s, missionaries were still documenting their struggles to resist the "temptations" of indigenous women. In 1818, the LMS missionary to South Africa, Robert Moffat (father-in-law to David Livingstone), petitioned his fiancée to join him in the mission field to prevent him from "taking a native [wife]." "I could not easily brook the idea," Moffat added, "but rather than fall into sin, feeling that I am mutable I shall say little and I have seen Missionaries more set against marriing [sic] a native than myself and have married" (qtd. in Woodward 91). There is a certain richness in Moffat's admission, as a year earlier he had declared his intention to resign his missionary post if those who had taken native wives, "Andrew Verhoogd, Michael Wimmer, John Barlett and James Read, remain as Missionaries" ("A Copy").

28. Hence why St. John "lacks" romantic desire for Jane (Peterson 103). As his barely contained desire for Rosamond is intended to demonstrate, St. John's problem is not that he cannot discern "real" from "counterfeit" sentiment (Peterson 103). Rather, attention to missionary writing reveals that he probably chooses Jane *precisely* because he's not attracted to her—an example, I think, of the viability and desirability of "familiar marriage" identified by Schaffer.

It is therefore no wonder St. John insists upon a wife prior to leaving for India. Undoubtedly, he would have faced some pressure from his missionary society to procure a suitable partner before leaving England. More threateningly for the austere St. John, however, he would also have been cognizant of the well-documented "temptations" represented by the "native" women awaiting him in the mission field. The novel itself alludes to the existence of such temptations in its conflation of Rochester's sultry "West India" (*JE* 346) with the "hot action" of India in St. John's missionary work. Not only do the British holdings share similar names and climates in the novel, but Rochester also describes the voluptuous black-haired Bertha as his "Indian Messalina" (350). Given Rochester's sensuous "Indian" wife haunting the narrative, St. John's request—that is, for Jane to "help" him with the "Indian women" by becoming his wife—has added significance. Although he labors for the human "race" (396, 417, 501), a term that aligns St. John with the monogenism of the missionary movement, the novel intimates that St. John hopes to guard against the temptation of taking a racially other wife by marrying Jane as a prophylactic measure.

As a missionary who necessarily sought to *extend* universal kinship, then, St. John markedly *restricts* his choice of wife to one who is already understood to be, in the strictest sense, his kindred. In so doing, he in effect practices the most extreme form of what Ann Laura Stoler terms "white endogamy." For not only is Jane a close blood relative of St. John (being of "his race," in the sense that Mrs. Reed might use the term [*JE* 24]). She also, as mentioned above, already shares the same name as her cousin. Brontë thus suggests that St. John's lofty goal of realizing the universal human family is belied by how strictly he feels he must constrain his own marriage to one who is *already* his kin, who already holds his name, and who is, as he believes, already prepared to "think like [him]" and to "trust like [him]" (448). This disjunction—between St. John's laboring for the united human "race" (in the most expansive understanding of the term) and his singular determination not to mix or corrupt his "race" (in its most narrow, biological, familial sense) in marriage—is connected to the challenges facing early nineteenth-century missionary work. Drawing inspiration for St. John Rivers from prominent missionary figures such as Martyn, Van der Kemp, and Read, Brontë evokes a moment when the "universal kinship" exalted by missionary societies was being undermined by their simultaneous efforts to circumscribe missionaries' marriage partners according to ever stricter racial lines.

Here we begin to see why the question of whether Brontë endorses or critiques the missionary project has proven so difficult to decide. Written in the 1840s but looking back on the years when the practice of intermarriage was straining the missionary commitment to universal kinship, *Jane Eyre* threads a middle path between early nineteenth-century missionary enthusiasm for intermarriage and the excessive backlash against "connexion[s] so unequal" that subsequently took place in the 1820s and 1830s. Thus, on the one hand, the Rochester-Bertha plotline condemns "the risks, the horrors, the loathings of incongruous unions," thereby lending support to the 1820s missionary determination that interracial partnerings sink "a man in the eyes of the world [and] debase the tone of his own mind and manners" (*JE* 350; Brown 414). On the other hand, however, the Jane-St. John plot vehemently denounces the opposite extreme of the missionary's obsessive determination to marry a woman, who is, as he believes, *absolutely* like him—indeed, *so* much like him that she poses no risk of sparking inconvenient feelings of romantic desire. In Jane's final choice of marriage partner, then, the novel ultimately stresses the importance (to draw on Corbett's apt phrasing) of "marrying the [person] who is *like* a relation, rather than the [person] who actually *is* one" (110). Jane's union with Rochester can thus be seen as occupying an intermediate space between the interracial, "incongruous union" of Rochester and Bertha and that of complete and utter racial sameness represented in St. John's proposal.

Rejecting the idea that strong (and quite literal) kinship ties make for strong connubial ties, the novel thus positions itself as a key work in the conceptual transformation of Christian "universal kinship." Where it had been inseparable from interracial mixing in the early nineteenth century, by the late 1800s universal kinship had become a peculiarly "sterile" idea (Viswanathan 195). Indeed, as Viswanathan demonstrates, the metaphorical global family invoked by British religionists in the late Victorian period effectively "displace[d]"—rather than irrepressibly brought to mind—the "threatening aspects of interbreeding" (187, 190).

Jane Eyre, I submit, occupies and looks to represent a transitory moment between an early nineteenth-century "universal kinship" that necessarily involved sexual intermingling (in the novel's rather frank acknowledgment that St. John would indeed like to "mate" and would "scrupulously observe" his conjugal duties) and the "sterile" universal kinship of the late Victorian period identified by Viswanathan (*JE* 452, 451). For as antiseptic as St. John's proposal to his kinswoman is, the novel also makes clear that the marriage would hardly be sex*less*. In fact, part of what repulses Jane in contemplating a union with her cousin is the "monstrous" knowledge that once married to him, she would have to "endure all forms of love (which . . . he would scrupulously observe)" (*JE* 451). What makes Jane recoil, in other words, is exactly what St. John wants in proposing to someone he considers exactly "like him": a cousin-marriage with someone "of his race," sexual relations sans romantic desire, a coupling from which his "spirit [could be] quite absent" from the contaminating influences of matrimony (451). Using curiously clinical language that subordinates marriage to missionary vocation and makes sexual intercourse a matter of Christian responsibility rather than (potentially threatening) desire, St. John repeatedly insists in his proposal to Jane that it is not "the mere man, with the man's selfish senses . . . I wish to mate: it is the missionary" (452). If there is such a thing as "sterile" sexual intercourse, sex without the specter of commingling and corruption, certainly this proposed endogamous union is it.

Jane, of course, rejects St. John's proposal. And it is *here*, in the aftermath of this decision, that *Jane Eyre* suggests the full ramifications of the sterility of missionaries' universal kinship post-1820. At the end of the novel, ten years after Jane leaves Moor House to reunite with Rochester, we are informed that in contrast to Jane and his sisters, "St John is unmarried" (502). The sentence (as declarative and succinct as Jane's own famous pronouncement, "Reader, I married him") draws attention to the fact that even as the missionary "labours for his race," St. John's *own* "race," the Rivers family line, is doomed to extinction by his decision to remain an "uncontaminated" missionary in foregoing marriage entirely (498, 501)[29]—a fate St. John unknowingly presages when he declares to Jane that his vocation "is dearer than the blood in my veins" (418). That Brontë's missionary decides *never* to marry, since he cannot marry someone who in his view is essentially himself or at least of his own "race," indicates that Brontë perceived how missionaries' "incorrupt[ibility]" after the 1820s had become intimately connected to—and, even more, potentially threatened by—their choice of spouse (502). It also suggests the extent to which she saw the growing dissonance between the evangelical espousal of humanity's fundamental kinship and its increasing conservatism and "management" of evangelical conjugality and reproduction.

By establishing St. John's supposed purity in opposition to Rochester and Bertha's "impure" intermarriage, Brontë's novel interrogates missionary anxieties surrounding kinship and matrimony. Although during the early decades of the nineteenth century, missionary societies evoked the ideal of kinship in order to imaginatively extend British Christian responsibility and sympathies to the heathen abroad, *Jane Eyre* suggests that such evocations were ultimately cheap—mostly rhetorical rather than genuinely felt. Only the interracial marriages sanctioned during the first years of the century gave full evidence of

---

29. St. John relates to Jane earlier in the novel, "Rivers is an old name; but of the three descendants of the race, two earn the dependent's crust among strangers, and the third considers himself an alien from his native country" (*JE* 395). With Diana and Mary married at the end of the novel, only St. John remains of the Rivers line.

missionaries' belief in the creed of the fundamental oneness of mankind. However, as these marriages seemed to approach the complete identification and reciprocity between races exalted by the discourse of universal kinship, missionary societies and missionaries grew increasingly unnerved by what they saw to be the practical erosion of missionary authority, an authority predicated precisely on the distance separating the "civilized" Christian Englishman from the "uncivilized" native. Although these intermarriages instantiated the principles that helped legitimate the missionary movement—the equality of all believers in the eyes of God, the necessity of cultivating sympathetic bonds transcending race and nation, and the desirability of instantiating actual relations of universal kinship—their very success ultimately forced missionaries to abandon such unions in practice.

Thus, even as *Jane Eyre* stresses the traditional Christian notion that marriage constitutes the most complete expression of kinship, it also highlights the troubled experiences of missionaries—experiences in which the establishment of openness and union between spouses seemed dangerously close to "contamination," to loss of identity and the attenuation of older forms of cultural, national, even spiritual affiliation. In attending to evangelical universal kinship, then, the novel examines not only the communion promised by this ideal but also the threatening corollaries of achieving such openness. Foregrounding the vast distance between the embodied practice and abstract idealism of universal kinship that had opened by the 1830s, it also exposes the very real limits of the cosmopolitan "human family" missionaries supposedly wished to achieve.

CHAPTER 4

The Missionary, Luxima, and the Forging of a Post-"Mutiny" Cosmopolitanism

THOUGH SHE is best known for her Irish national novel, *The Wild Irish Girl* (1806), Sydney Owenson's imaginative foray into India with *The Missionary: An Indian Tale* (1811) was a sensation in its time. The Irish statesman Lord Castlereagh was an admirer of the work (qtd. in Dixon 2:48), and Charles Kirkpatrick Sharpe, a writer for the *Quarterly Review,* rhapsodized in a letter to his friend Sir Thomas Stapleton, "I have read Miss Owenson's things, till I dream of the moon beaming through a gauze curtain upon the immaculacy of a Circassion's back" (471–72). Most famously, Percy Bysshe Shelley declared himself a devotee of *The Missionary*: "It really is a divine thing. . . . Since I have read this book, I have read no other" (qtd. in Hogg 397). Over the next twenty years, the novel went through seven editions and earned its author over four hundred pounds—"no mean sum in early nineteenth-century publishing," as Julia Wright observes ("Introduction" 41). Despite receiving criticism for its "numerous conceits" and "frequently affected phraseology" ("Art. XII" 195), the novel helped cement Owenson's reputation in early nineteenth-century literary circles.[1] In 1859, Owenson, a now-married Lady Morgan, revised and reissued *The Missionary* under the

---

1. Critics of the day regularly referred to the "Owensonian school" as shorthand not only for Owenson's works but also the body of sentimental novels inspired by her style (see Lennon 142).

new title *Luxima, the Prophetess: A Tale of India*. Motivated by the charged political climate of mid-century (and perhaps a degree of opportunism),[2] Lady Morgan, so the preface to the new edition declared, "greatly altered, and re-modelled" her influential 1811 novel. It continued, "The story of 'Luxima,' will, it is presumed, prefer no ordinary claims to public attention, and the more particularly on account of the recent melancholy occurrences which have distracted a country with which we have so long had such extensive commercial relations" (*Luxima* iii, iv).[3]

At first glance, the preface seems to overstate the extent and profundity of Owenson's revisions. After all, the general plot of the novel remains the same, as do its footnotes (save for minor corrections in spelling), and many of its key passages. Rather than "greatly altering" her 1811 story, the bulk of Owenson's efforts seem expended on cutting sections of ornate and sentimental prose, sections that do little to establish the characters or advance the plot. No wonder, then, that on the rare occasion when the two versions of the novel are considered together (as a majority of scholarship focuses on *The Missionary* alone), the revisions tend to be dismissed as mostly stylistic and thus largely superficial: The original three-volume "novel of sensibility" merely is trimmed to a single-volume format intended to appeal to a "Victorian audience trained in [the conventions] of the realist novel" (Chakravarty 88; Wright, "Introduction" 55).

Nevertheless, there are reasons to heed Owenson's 1859 preface. A more sustained examination of the two novels makes clear that changing literary tastes are not the sole motivating force behind Owenson's revisions. Instead, her 1859 *Luxima* seems informed by a larger transformation in missionary sensibilities toward India and the knowability of the Indian people following the so-called Indian "Mutiny" of 1857 (see Herbert, *War* 7). From the 1790s to the early 1850s, missionary societies and evangelicals had championed a version of cosmopolitanism predicated on the Enlightenment faith in the fundamental similitude of all humankind. With the events of the "traumatic" Indian Mutiny, however, missionary societies experienced a profound crisis in this faith. Owenson's revisions, subtle as they are, nevertheless capture this epistemic shift in missionaries' "cosmopolitan" assumptions, as the evangelical

---

2. In its review of the reissue, for instance, the *Calcutta Review* noted *Luxima* "[is] published at this time in the hope that the new interest felt in India will ensure its sale" ("Luxima, the Prophetess" ii).

3. *Luxima* had "an almost ten-percent reduction in length" while "approximately one page of text was added." Moreover, "there are other minor changes besides corrections that are not easily quantifiable, but that appear at regular intervals in the novel" (Parsons 375).

belief in a universal human nature gave way to a nascent recognition of the irreducibility of cultural plurality—in essence, a *new* cosmopolitanism.[4]

That there *was* a shift in missionary thinking around the late 1850s into the early 1860s has been well documented. Adrian Wisnicki notes that David Livingstone, for instance, occupies a "transitional" space between the philosophies of conversionism and trusteeism. "Whereas older missionaries to Africa and elsewhere had championed the 'oneness of humanity' [and] espoused 'conversionism,' an '"incorporative" ideology' that represented the 'other' as open to conversion," Wisnicki writes, a new set aligned themselves instead with "trusteeism," the paternalistic view that considered the "superior races" to be responsible for overseeing and guiding *essentially* different and *fundamentally* unincorporable "inferior races" (261; Ross qtd. in Wisnicki 261). Moreover, Stanley argues that this development coincided with and was fed by a theological shift (*Bible* 74–77). The lack of progress in converting the "heathen" to Christianity, coupled with the upheavals in India, undermined missionaries' postmillennialist optimism that "evangelicalism was destined to succeed on an unprecedented scale, and as it did so the world would become a better place" (74). Considering the gulf between the different races—even between individual *people*—to be nearly insurmountable, an increasingly influential evangelical faction argued that global salvation would be accomplished not through missionary efforts to promote individual conversion but instead by divine fiat. Eventually their pessimism would coalesce around the ascendance of premillennial eschatology in missionary work, a view articulated by Graham Wilmot Brooke of the CMS in 1886: "I see no hope given in the Bible that wickedness in this world will be subdued by civilization or preaching of the gospel—until the Messiah the Prince come" (qtd. in Stanley, *Bible* 77). Partly underlying these shifts was the dawning of what I term a new "post-Mutiny" cosmopolitan outlook among missionary societies. This outlook departed from Enlightenment cosmopolitan assumptions of mankind's fundamental likeness and the existence of a common kinship hidden underneath superficial outward differences—assumptions that had guided earlier decades of missionary work, as my earlier chapters recount.

Of course, this post-Mutiny cosmopolitanism would come nowhere near approaching the progressive ethical concerns of the "new cosmopolitanisms"

---

4. Stocking's concept of "culture" in the late Victorian period offers a useful formulation for the phenomenon I identify in post-Mutiny missionary texts. Writing about Franz Boas, he argues that the anthropologist helped show "that the behavior of all men, regardless of race or cultural stage, was determined by a traditional body of habitual behavior patterns passed on through what we would now call the enculturative process" ("Franz Boas" 877; see also Lecourt, *Cultivating*). Permeating post-Mutiny missionary writing, I suggest, is precisely this anthropological idea, albeit in inchoate form.

conceptualized by critics such as Appiah and Robbins, as well as Vertovec and Cohen. Nevertheless, there is an aptness in calling this shift in missionary thinking a sort of incipient "new" cosmopolitanism in its own right. The "new cosmopolitanisms" that have proliferated since the 1990s tend to find common ground in their efforts to recuperate cosmopolitanism from its associations with the Eurocentric normativity of the Enlightenment. In a similar manner, the post-Mutiny line of missionary thinking evinced an "awareness of the inadequacy of the totalizing even while that ideal is being asserted" (Agathocleous, *Urban Realism* 120). And, also resonant with the new cosmopolitanisms of today, the beating heart of this new missionary cosmopolitanism was a reevaluation of cultural alterity. Rather than regarding it as a veneer obscuring humanity's fundamental similitude, missionary thinking in the post-Mutiny period newly privileged culture as constitutive of, and thus inextricable from, individual identity.

But to see this historical shift in Owenson's work, we cannot examine only one novel or the other in isolation. Instead, we need to cast our view to the dynamism of the "re-modelling" process itself, to the interplay between the different versions of novels. To contextualize and trace the discursive changes between *The Missionary* and *Luxima,* I divide the remainder of this chapter into four sections. In the first, I establish how the novels position themselves vis-à-vis the politicization of religion in the early nineteenth century, paying particular attention to the social ramifications of missionary work in the context of imperialism. Next, I challenge the idea that Owenson's revisions can be understood merely according to the extent to which they make the novel more or less sympathetic to British imperialism—the question in much criticism that seems the sole litmus test as to the value of examining Owenson's revisions at all, and a question that, I believe, ultimately proves unsatisfying in apprehending the underlying pattern of thought that informs the reconstituted *Luxima.* Instead, we should look to those discourses of "universal humanity" and cultural alterity that were shifting in missionary writing—discourses that buttress yet never cleanly graft onto anti-imperialist *or* imperialist sympathies. The sections that follow thus examine the archive of missionary writing from this period to trace the ways missionary societies grappled with these issues of cosmopolitanism and culture, providing one of the likely contexts for Owenson's own discussion. I conclude by examining Owenson's revisions. Tracking how she transformed her novel of sensibility to one more aligned with the conventions of realism, I argue that *The Missionary* and *Luxima*—the former rooted in Enlightenment conceptions of humanity's fundamental similitude, the latter grappling with the possibility that people of other cultures and races were radically "Other" and unknowable—together constitute a valuable artifact of changing cosmopolitan views following the 1857 Mutiny. In doing so, they provide one potential taproot of the sensibilities underwriting the "new cosmopolitanisms" of today.

Owenson and the Politics of Religion

Set in India in the seventeenth century, *The Missionary* and *Luxima* tell the story of the Franciscan missionary Hilarion, who leaves Spanish-controlled Portugal to proselytize in Goa. Upon reaching India, he focuses his efforts on converting the widowed Brahmin prophetess Luxima to Christianity in the belief that her conversion, "if once effected, might prove the redemption of her whole nation" (*Missionary* 96). In the process, however, he falls in love with her. Luxima reciprocates his love, and for Hilarion's sake she becomes Christian in name though not in spirit. The events leading to Luxima's demise are set into motion when officers of the Spanish Inquisition find the lovers sharing an incriminating embrace. The Spanish-Jesuitical officers, already suspicious of Hilarion's Portuguese-Franciscan loyalties, quickly convict the missionary of heresy and sentence him to be burned at the stake in Goa. On the day of his execution, Luxima—who has been separated from the missionary since his arrest—chances on the conflagration and in her distraught state confuses the auto-da-fé with the funeral pyre of her ex-husband. At the climax of the novel, she attempts to commit suttee but is saved by Hilarion. Meanwhile, the Hindu onlookers witness their priestess's heroic self-sacrifice and are roused to revolt against their European occupiers. During the fracas, Hilarion and Luxima attempt to escape. But as they flee the city, a Spanish soldier fatally stabs Luxima, and she eventually dies in Hilarion's arms. The story concludes with Hilarion's retirement to a remote region of India, where he lives his remaining days practicing what appears to be a sort of syncretic religion.

In composing a novel centered on missionary work in India, Owenson likely drew inspiration from her childhood encounters with the British missionary endeavor. Her father was the Irish Catholic actor Robert Owenson. Her mother, though, was a devoted follower of the prominent Methodist leader Selina Hastings, the Countess of Huntingdon (who patronized the unfortunate Rev. Thomas Lewis prior to his becoming a missionary in the South Sea Islands, as detailed in chapter 3). Owenson relates in her memoirs that her mother's cousin, the missionary Mr. Langley, attended her christening and "often dined at our hospitable table" (*Lady Morgan's Memoirs* 1:65).[5] As the sacrilegious plot of *The Missionary* makes evident, however, the pious sentiments of missionary societies had little to do with Owenson's reasons for composing the novel.

An Irish national and nationalist, Owenson witnessed the political and social repression Irish Catholics suffered at the hands of the English. The British imposition of the established church over Ireland (not to mention her own religiously eclectic upbringing) sparked her sympathy for religious toleration and her enmity toward colonial domination—themes she often revisited in her novels and journalism (see Wright, "Introduction" 9–19; Judson 202–3; Donovan). Here, surprisingly, we see where she might have made common cause with the missionary movement. In his account of the rapid politicization of the evangelical movement from 1811 to 1813, Rutz notes the overlap between Catholics and evangelical Dissenters in their protection and promotion of "religious liberty." Throughout the first decade of the nineteenth century, Lord Sidmouth, who served as prime minister from 1801 to 1804, bemoaned what he saw as magisterial laxness in granting licenses to Dissenting preachers. In 1811 he finally introduced a bill designed to address these so-called abuses of the Toleration Acts of 1689 and 1779 ("Politicizing" 191–92). However, what Sidmouth regarded a modest effort to clarify and control the religious "privileges" extended to Dissenters signified something quite different to evangelical Nonconformists. To them, Sidmouth's bill was nothing less than an attempt to rescind the principle of toleration itself (192, 198). As the bill became symbolic of a broad government attempt to curtail their freedom of conscience, evangelicals' determination to combat Sidmouth snowballed into a larger political movement.

Witnessing the powerful evangelical response, proponents of Catholic relief saw an opportunity to advance their own agenda (Rutz, "Politicizing" 200, 201). Their efforts to join forces with evangelicals were not unfruitful; in fact, they found some prominent voices, including the LMS director Rev. Rowland Hill, fully willing to "declare for the Catholicks" under the banner of religious freedom (Holland qtd. in "Politicizing" 201).[6] Looking back at these

---

5. Owenson also recounts why Mr. Langley's visits ended: "One day . . . to my father's infinite disgust, the reverend gourmand drew from his pocket a bottle of some very fine sauce which after pouring a little over his turbot, he re-corked and consigned again to his side-pocket. My father took no notice at the time, but when he was gone he said to my mother . . . 'Jenny, my dear, I'll be—if that canting cousin of yours ever puts his feet under my mahogany again!'" (1:65–66).

6. Evangelicals were not united in their support of Catholic emancipation. Among CMS-affiliated evangelicals, divisions ran deep. Stock's *History of the Church Missionary Society* notes that while prominent figures in the evangelical and modern missionary movement,

decades in an 1881 issue of the *Evangelical Magazine and Missionary Chronicle*, Rev. J. P. Gledstone, a London director of the LMS and prominent social purity reformer, would credit the work of Dissenters in helping to pass the Roman Catholic Relief Act of 1829. It was "a measure . . . required by simple justice, carried by a union of Nonconformists and Catholics," Gledstone writes, and he recounts with pride that the Irish populist Daniel O'Connell rendered the following thanks to Dissenting evangelicals for supporting Catholic emancipation: "I stand here, in the name of my country, to express our gratitude, in feeble, but sincere language, for the exertions made in our behalf by our Protestant Dissenting brethren" (735; qtd. in Gledstone 735).[7]

Owenson cared little about bringing the good word to lost "heathens," but the earthly political ramifications of the evangelical movement sparked her interest. Evangelicalism, she apprehended, had not just spiritual but social consequences. In her final novel, *The O'Briens and the O'Flahertys* (1827), she plainly articulated these interests:

> I anticipate . . . that I shall be accused of unfeminine presumption in "meddling with politics;" but while so many of my countrywomen "meddle" with subjects of much higher importance;—while missionary misses and proselyting peeresses affect to "stand instead of God, amongst the children of men," may not I be permitted, under the influence of merely human sympathies, to interest myself for human wrongs? (41)

---

such as "Wilberforce, Buxton, the Grants, young Lord Ashley, Dealtry, [and] Daniel Wilson, favoured the recognition of Roman Catholic claims," Rev. Josiah Pratt and Rev. Edward Bickersteth (who both served as CMS secretary at different times) "actively opposed the bill" (281). Michael Ledger-Lomas ably summarizes the reasons why Nonconformists also were of two minds on the issue: "Even if Dissenters were never the mainstay of 'constitutional-national anti-Catholicism' in the United Kingdom, because they disliked its conflation of Protestantism and establishment, they were disturbed at the ease with which 'Popery was putting its hand into the colonial treasury, for its support in Australia, Canada and other sections of the British Empire'" (5).

7. In the same essay, Gledstone soothes potential fears regarding a resurgence of Catholicism in England: "The principles of Nonconforming Christians compel them to grant a free and untroubled home to their Catholic fellow-countrymen," he argues, "but they are equally urgent in demanding that we make the dominance of Catholicism impossible" (736). Thus the essay evinces lasting Protestant suspicions of Catholicism, underscoring the unease that characterized the Dissenting-Catholic alliance more broadly. Owenson herself disapproved of O'Connell's populism, though, as Donovan notes, she "tempered the venom against [him] with lofty words of praise in the 1846 preface to *The Wild Irish Girl*. Here she lauds the Catholic Association, founded by O'Connell in 1823, as 'the greatest league of genius, patriotism, and courage, that Ireland ever had associated in her cause'" (193). Here, again, we see Owenson's penchant for making common political cause with movements with which she otherwise disagreed.

There's no mistaking Owenson's scorn for "missionary misses and proselyting peeresses." But even as she asserts her difference from these proto-Mrs. Jellybys, she also draws attention to them for a reason. Attuned as she was to issues concerning Irish politics and religious freedom, Owenson no doubt perceived the politicization of evangelicalism (i.e., the fervor of "missionary misses") presented an opportunity to boost the Irish cause, as well as address other "human wrongs."[8]

However, Owenson was also quick to perceive that evangelical fervor was Janus-faced; the emancipatory potential of the movement was balanced on a knife's edge against its equal potential to augment repressive colonial power.[9] As debates thundered around issues of "religious freedom" and governmental oppression, India became the focal point for assessing the social and political impact of the missionary presence in particular.[10] For Owenson, this made India the natural stand-in for exploring in what capacity Dissenting missionaries might (or might not) stand on the "right" side of history in advocating for the liberty—including the religious liberty—of colonized people.

Despite being set in an exoticized and clearly fictive seventeenth-century Spanish-controlled India, then, *The Missionary* attempts to intervene in pressing contemporary debates. The stance it takes is explosive: The uprisings of colonial India, it suggests, might spring less from the "religious bigotry of the natives" than from the "tyranny" of Christian colonization. Footnoting a passage in which the "coercive tyranny of the Spanish Government" is faulted for "excit[ing] in the breasts of the mild, patient, and long-enduring Hindus, a principle of resistance" (*Missionary* 241), Owenson explicitly equates contemporary Britain with Inquisitorial Spain:

> An insurrection of a fatal consequence took place in *Vellore* so late as 1806, and a mutiny at Nundydrag and Benglore, occurred about the same period:

---

8. Invariably, Owenson "horrified conservatives," as she "advocate[d] liberal opinions ... in the cause of civil and religious liberty" (Wright "Introduction" 13; *Lady Morgan's Memoirs* 1:x).

9. I partly depart from Franklin's certainty that Owenson was "firmly in line with the (substantially) Whig opposition to missionary activity in India" (197). Taking into account Owenson's political savvy and her sympathetic portrayal of Hilarion—a "dissenting" missionary in his own right—it seems likely that Owenson held a more nuanced view of missionary activity in India. To the extent that missionaries could aid in advancing an agenda centered on freedom of conscience and national liberation, she appears to have been allied with evangelicals who supported missionary work in India under the banner of religious freedom. But she seems leery of the ways that missionary work, when aligned with imperial power, could repress this freedom.

10. For one view of how this played out, see Ahmed. For another perspective, see Carson, *East India Company*.

both were supposed to have originated in the religious bigotry of the natives, suddenly kindled by the supposed threatened violation of their faith from the Christian settlers. (241n)

The footnote shifts this sentimental work of historical fiction into "commentary on political rebellion" (Parsons 376). Religious bigotry, Owenson suggests, is the product of religious persecution (the latter "kindles" the former), and furthermore, this lesson from the past must be applied to the present moment. Of interest to me is the particular blame she puts on "Christian settlers"—a phrase that evokes, though to confusing ends, the fierce debates raging between the East India Company and missionary societies in the late eighteenth and early nineteenth centuries.[11] Certainly Owenson appears to echo the sentiments of the antimissionary faction of the East India Company, which attributed the Vellore Massacre to missionary interference in native faiths (Franklin 184).[12] Yet the repetition of the word "supposed" signals a degree of skepticism of the East India Company's narrative—skepticism likely born of some antipathy to the company's consolidation of imperial power, some sympathy with evangelicals' emancipatory rhetoric, and some cognizance of missionary claims that the company's "religious neutrality" privileged the rights of Hindus and Muslims at the expense of native Christians."[13] In other words, Owenson's footnote opens its political leanings up to interpretation: To what extent are missionaries implicated in the forms of governmental "tyranny" that lead to insurrection?

Judging from her portrayal of the missionary Hilarion, her answer appears to be: It depends. Capturing the potential of the evangelical missionary movement to seesaw between emancipation and repression, Owenson fashions her missionary as an ambivalent character; in his "devotional zeal and fervid enthusiasm," he vacillates between "oppressor and oppressed" (*Missionary* 74; Rangarajan 92).[14] Undeniably, he is an agent of Spain, prominent enough to

---

11. See chapters 2 and 3 in Carson, *East India Company*.
12. This opinion was famously captured in Sydney Smith's diatribe against the Baptist missionaries, in which he called them "little detachments of maniacs" who were "quite insane and ungovernable" (61, 58). The missionaries, he continued, "would deliberately, piously, and conscientiously expose our whole Eastern empire to destruction for the sake of converting half a dozen Brahmans" (58).
13. Converts "lost everything on conversion: home, livelihood, and essential services," and Baptist missionaries found "their catechists suffered even greater hardships" (Carson, *East India Company* 61–62).
14. Rangarajan, however, argues that Hilarion's ambivalence "parallels the involvement of dispossessed British soldiers in the conquest of India[,] . . . the active role Irish troops played in the Vellore Massacre" rather than seeing evangelicalism's mixed mandates as the source of the missionary's "dual identity" (92).

"receive an audience from the Bishop and Grand Inquisitor of Goa" upon his arrival in India (82). But he is also at odds with the colonial structure that enables and supports his mission: He is Portuguese rather than Spanish, Franciscan rather than Jesuit.[15] His national loyalties and religion thus make him a "dissenter" in his own right, uniquely primed to sympathize with the Indians repressed by Spanish theocratic forces despite being explicitly employed to advance those forces. His capacity for understanding the Brahmin prophetess Luxima in their shared religious "enthusiasm" (and mutual physical attraction, of course) leads him to fall in love and identify with her, but his "enthusiastic" determination to Christianize her also sets in motion the events leading to her tragic demise and the resulting rebellion of the "Hindoos."

But the point here isn't that Hilarion definitely colludes with colonial power. Instead, it is to note that Hilarion is unmistakably a *missionary*—not only "an amalgam of the Romantic poet, imperialist, and Orientalist" (Freeman 21) but also a representation of *actual* Dissenting missionaries in terms of their marginalized political positions at home, their ambivalent positions in the realm of colonial politics, and (let's not forget) their troubled history of interracial unions.

Though Owenson never admitted to creating *Luxima* because of the 1857 Mutiny, the original novel's reference to the 1806 Vellore Massacre makes credible her editor's assertion that the revised novel is linked to "recent melancholy occurrences" in India. By self-consciously joining that "great volume of writing about the Indian war that thronged the Victorian literary marketplace from the start" (Herbert, *War* 206), the new novel, like the original novel, comments on the present by re-presenting the past. As Gautam Chakravarty observes, "In *Luxima* Goa and Vellore together prefigure the rebellion of 1857–9.... [They] construct a paradigm of cultural encounter [extending] from the seventeenth to the mid-nineteenth-century" (88). The release of *Luxima* in 1859 suggests that Owenson saw her novel as challenging the supposed "suddenness" of the events of 1857. Instead she felt the "Mutiny" somehow had links to those of the seventeenth and early nineteenth centuries. But what were those links? And how does *Luxima* represent them?

---

15. Owenson opens her novel by underscoring Portugal's degradation under Spanish domination, and she nationalizes the Catholic sects by aligning the Franciscans with Portugal, the Jesuits with Spain. "Under the goading oppression of Philip the Second, and of his two immediate successors, the national independence of a brave people faded gradually away, and Portugal, wholly losing its rank in the scale of nations, sunk into a Spanish province," she says. "The Jesuits governed with the Spaniards; the Franciscans resisted with the Portuguese" (71). Thus Hilarion is introduced by an account of politicized religion, embroiled in colonial unrest.

"Identical in All but the Title"?

Though today the 1806 and 1857 uprisings are ascribed similar causes (Parsons 376), the 1857 Mutiny provoked a level of shock, horror, and soul-searching among the British public that outstripped anything experienced after the Vellore Mutiny. One imagines that Owenson was cognizant not only of the similarities between the rebellions but also their stark differences. But the nature of those differences, as perceived by Owenson, has been a subject of recurring debate.[16]

One body of scholarship dismisses the editorial changes as cosmetic, even immaterial. Concluding that the 1859 novel is "little different" from *The Missionary* (Wright, "Introduction" 53), critics in this camp argue that *Luxima* transposes the anti-imperialist sensibility of the 1811 novel onto the 1857 Indian Mutiny. Chakravarty, for instance, claims that *Luxima* is "identical in all but the title" to *The Missionary* and argues from this somewhat misleading premise that the 1859 reissue of *Luxima* "extends the original series" of colonial rebellions to encompass the seventeenth to mid-nineteenth centuries "without modifying the basic explanatory model" (88). As such, *Luxima* offers a "counterpoint to the proactive martial heroism" of the post-Mutiny period (91). Wright's analysis of the 1859 revisions, delimited to Owenson's excisions of bloated prose and alterations made to the first three chapters, argues *Luxima* only "further authorizes" the conclusions reached by *The Missionary* regarding the "futility and immorality of proselytization" in colonial holdings ("Introduction" 56; see also 53–57).[17] *Luxima*, then, is little more than a mid-century reprint of *The Missionary*, which essentially and only recapitulates the message of the 1811 novel: Imperial domination and overzealous evangelism provoke violence.

Another body of scholarship assigns more significance to Owenson's revisions. Parsons and Viswanathan, for instance, argue that the 1859 *Luxima* amends the original novel better to capture the changed sensibilities of the mid-century moment. Focusing on the new title of *Luxima, the Prophetess*, Viswanathan concludes, "Luxima's displacement of the missionary as the plot's

---

16. Most critical readings of *The Missionary* actually neglect *Luxima* (see, for instance, Judson; Freeman; Ahmed; Reynolds; Franklin; and Burgess). Rajan mentions the existence of *Luxima* in passing, but only to drive home the popularity of the original novel (123). I am indebted to this scholarship for offering insight into the early nineteenth-century imperial context that informs the novel. Yet that so much critical attention has been paid to *The Missionary* without consideration of Owenson's serious attempt to revise the novel with *Luxima* perhaps says something about boundaries subtly encouraged by periodization.

17. She further speculates that revisions to *Luxima* were to address "critics who argued that her early work was marred by overwrought language" (55).

main figure is Owenson's concession to the progressive irrelevance of missionaries immediately preceding and following the 1857 rebellion" (27). Parsons offers the most careful analysis of Owenson's revisions. Observing that even the briefest textual comparison immediately makes clear that "*Luxima* and *The Missionary* cannot simply be read as identical novels," he goes on to contend that the changes "taken together . . . indicate a major attempt to revise every part of the novel" (374, 375). Ultimately, he pegs the significance of the newly released *Luxima* to the distance it establishes between itself and "the vague cosmopolitanism of romantic orientalism," which also works to distance it from "the violent, triumphalist imperialism of the period after the 1857–58 rebellion" (373–74).

But several problems attend both critical camps. For one thing, if Luxima "displaces" the missionary in the 1859 title of the novel, she doesn't displace him in the plot; in fact, Hilarion arguably is made an even more central character, as Owenson excised many key scenes featuring Luxima (the significance of which I discuss below). Moreover, any claim that *Luxima* is more "distanced" from imperial sentiments compared to its predecessor is similarly problematized by two befuddling revisions of the novel's climax. In 1811, the natives are described as rebelling against their European occupiers to "avenge the long slighted cause of their religion, and their freedom" and, just a few sentences later, for "religion and their liberty" (250). *Luxima*, on the other hand, removes any mention of "freedom"; "religion and vengeance" rather than "liberty" spark revolt (*Luxima* 309). What has happened to "liberty"? If Owenson was revising her novel to denounce British imperialism in the post-Mutiny period, why is India's claim to "liberty" as a cause for revolution jettisoned in the 1859 text?

In light of these and other dissimilarities between the two novels, a different perspective might prove helpful. The revisions cannot be attributed entirely to renewed fervency against imperial excesses during the Mutiny, nor are they steered by Owenson's sense of missionaries' diminishing significance in the British Empire (indeed, with the celebrity of David Livingstone and the success of *Missionary Travels and Researches in South Africa*, missionaries arguably had never been more visible). I propose the revisions instead are guided by shifting understandings of cultural alterity—changes that were particularly prominent in missionary discourse. Taken together, *Luxima* and *The Missionary* register the passing of a missionary cosmopolitanism more inflected by Enlightenment commitments and the emergence in its place of a post-Mutiny cosmopolitanism more sensitive to the inescapability of *situatedness*.

This first sense of cosmopolitanism, what I term "Enlightenment cosmopolitanism," refers to the early nineteenth-century missionary conviction that all people, in sharing a common origin, also necessarily shared the same desires, needs, and wants, as well as the same stages of "civilizational" development. This conviction was evinced in the missionaries' reliance upon the supposed universality of reason and common sense, in the monogenist theories to which they adhered, and also in their belief that all people, no matter their race, nation, or culture, would welcome the introduction of Western commerce.[18] *The Missionary* builds on and propagates these ideas. In one key scene, for instance, Hilarion adopts a perspective that in no small part resembles the Enlightenment conception of cosmopolitanism as that "luxuriously free-floating view from above" (Robbins, "Introduction" 1). In language reminiscent of Rev. Bogue's 1804 recommendation that each Christian "extends his views . . . towards the community, of which you form a part, and also towards all the nations of the earth," Owenson's missionary stretches his "imagination . . . beyond the limits of human vision" as well as "over those various and wondrous tracts, so diversified by clime and soil, by government and by religion, and which present to the contemplation of philosophy a boundless variety in form and spirit" (*Missionary* 80). His imagined apprehension of such diverse "forms and spirits" unites his own "spirit" with nothing less than the universe itself: "His spirit, awakening to a new impulse," we learn, "partook for a moment the sublimity of the objects he contemplated, the force of the characters he reflected on, and, expanding with its elevation, mingled with the universe" (81). "Expanding" his view upward and outward in this manner, Hilarion becomes the ideal cosmopolite, the man who transcends "chauvinistic national loyalties or parochial prejudices" (at least in his own mind) (Schlereth xi). The corollary of the privileged cosmopolitan perspective bestowed on Hilarion is the cosmopolitan ethos that permeates the rest of the novel. As Wright notes, *The Missionary* participates in the project of cultivating a distinctly "Enlightenment sensibility." It endeavors to "imagine a fundamental similitude between human beings . . . grounded in sympathy and affect rather than a shared culture" (*Ireland* 2–3)—a sentimentality dependent on and resonant with the conviction of the "Enlightenment cosmopolite" that "human nature is essentially the same at all times and among all nations" (Schlereth 71).

---

18. As Lecourt observes, missionaries saw the apparent "universality of religion" regardless of geographic locale or culture as evidence of "humankind's origins and of each individual's ability to be educated into a thinking and reflective subject" (*Cultivating* 34). Even rival religions, then, were reasons for missionary optimism regarding universal human nature and the prospects of Christianity's eventual triumph.

But if *The Missionary* evinces an early nineteenth-century "Enlightenment sensibility," the post-Mutiny *Luxima* seems to reflect "a historic shift in [this] sensibility" (to use Herbert's words) (*War* 58). One of the most prominent sites of this shift can be found in missionary and evangelical culture, as the "incomprehensible" horror of 1857–58 compelled missionary societies not only to question their faith in Enlightenment cosmopolitanism and the existence of a universal human nature but also to confront the possibility that cultural differences were irreducible, embedded, perhaps even legitimate. In other words, they found themselves contending with the reality of "the ethnos as well as of the species" (Hollinger 230). When one recalls Owenson's familiarity with missionary enterprises as well as her interest in the politics of religion, it seems likely that her 1859 revisions took place in this broader context—for her optimistic vision of an imminently realizable human unity is moderated, scaled back, in *Luxima*. To comprehend the contours and implications of this shift more fully, we might do well to attend to evangelical and missionary writing.

"Vague Cosmopolitanism": Assumptions of Human Unity in Missionary Thought

As Wright compellingly demonstrates, *The Missionary* is shot through with the concept of a "universal humanity . . . that mitigated, or at least potentially countered, rising imperialist pressures to essentialize difference" ("Introduction" 27). Arguably, there was no larger, unified public movement that more vocally championed the idea of a "universal humanity" than the modern missionary movement.[19] Seeking "to fulfill what they saw as a divine injunction concerning doctrines about common humanity," the missionary movement of the early nineteenth century was "convinced that ideals about intrinsic equality were to be more than mere metaphysical abstraction" (Frykenberg 13; see Stocking, *Victorian Anthropology* 44 and Lecourt, *Cultivating* 34).

Thus, as detailed in chapter 1, Protestant missionaries emerged as some of the key promoters of cosmopolitan thought insofar as the idea expressed the

---

19. Strikingly, the novel was published the very year that some missionary societies were hailing the cessation of the Inquisition in Goa. An 1811 issue of the *Evangelical Magazine*, for instance, proclaimed, "The Inquisition at Goa is to be abolished. . . . If this be correct, every Protestant, and every other lover of religious liberty, will rejoice" ("Inquisition in Goa" 351). That Hilarion considers himself to be a purveyor of religious liberty, in contrast to the "tyrannical" Inquisition, aligns him with the ethos of the Protestant missionary movement.

universalist assumptions of Enlightenment humanism.[20] As the LMS director Rev. Samuel Greatheed put the matter, missionary societies predicated their evangelizing on the belief that the foreign "heathen"—far from being essentially different from the Englishman—instead "hold[s] out a faithful mirror of our own natural face" (104). Such attitudes remained popular with evangelicals through the 1850s. The Scottish evangelical William Gillespie, for instance, denounced polygenist theories of human development in his pointedly titled *An Exposure of the Unchristian Principles Set Forth in Mr George Combe's Work* (1836), disparaging Combe's contention that "certain savage tribes are incapable of so slight a thing as civilization" (115). Richard Watson, a Church clergyman writing in the 1840s, claimed theories positing "essential distinctions of inferiority and superiority" went contrary to religious feeling (63), and in a prefatory letter for David Livingstone's Cambridge lectures, Rev. Adam Sedgwick put the point more strongly: "The poor African is our untaught brother created by the God who made us; and knit together, soul as well as body, out of elements undistinguishable from our own" (68). Indeed, the commitment of missionary societies to a "notion of a universal humanity of mankind" meant that evangelicals held the conviction that "culture rather than race . . . explained racial differences" (Price, *Making Empire* 23, 30)—a view that not only illuminated *why* differences existed but also implied that culture was not intrinsic to identity. The belief in the fundamental similitude of humanity—and, relatedly, in the missionary's unique position to apprehend this larger picture—coalesced in the proclamation that opens this book: The missionary, being "at home in the islands of the Southern Seas, in the wilds of Caffraria, in the heart of India," is the world's "only true cosmopolite."

These Enlightenment humanist assumptions underwrote missionaries' interest in the traditions and cultural practices of the peoples to whom they proselytized. In fact, the success of Orientalists in translating Hindu texts into English and Indian vernacular languages,[21] rather than being viewed as an inherent threat to missionary authority, at times fortified evangelical convictions that intimate knowledge of Indian culture would reveal essential

---

20. To borrow Agathocleous's formulation of the differences between Enlightenment cosmopolitanism and the "new cosmopolitanisms" of today, missionary cosmopolitanism in the early nineteenth century never implied an "ethos attentive to difference" ("Cosmopolitanism" 454).

21. Leask observes, "British 'orientalists' . . . sought to interpret—or construct—Indian society according to their ideal of an indigenous classical past" and "rationalized British intervention in India as a project aimed at restoring Hindu culture to its 'original purity'" (9, 100).

commonalities between Britons and Indians. Though at odds with Orientalists who aligned themselves with the East India Company's policies to restrict the missionary presence in India, evangelicals nevertheless and perhaps surprisingly hailed the "progress which has lately been made in Hindoo Literature" as "being likely to lead to the happiest consequences" ("Home Proceedings" 14). "Much of what is really inculcated in the Hindu sacred books bears a strong, though disfigured resemblance to the leading doctrines of the Gospel," declared the archdeacon Thomas Fanshaw Middleton in an 1814 speech for SPCK. He continued,

> It may reasonably be hoped that as the genuine doctrines and traditions of Hinduism shall be more fully ascertained, they will furnish positive and direct arguments, by which the Hindus may be brought to know the only true God, and Jesus, whom He hath sent. ("Home Proceedings" 15)

A fuller knowledge of Hinduism, in other words, promised to reveal its prevailing tenets to be in accordance with British Christianity. Hinduism and the "natives" were regarded as *knowable,* and close attention to indigenous thought and practice was thought to uncover a "common humanity" underlying the trappings of race and culture—a humanity, of course, that would eventually and inevitably accept the undeniable "truth" of Protestant Christianity. Thus missionary societies reinforced a message that already had traction among evangelicals: Culture was a "form of variation shallow enough not to challenge a vision of human commonality" (Lecourt, *Cultivating* 49).

Keeping with this philosophy, Middleton urged SPCK missionaries "to converse with [the natives] familiarly on every subject, which may present itself; to enter into their sentiments, feelings, associations, and prejudices; and to be altogether such as they are, except only in their ignorance, their superstitions, and their vices" ("Home Proceedings" 16). Fifteen years later, William Ellis described the ideal missionary in similar terms. "The business of [his] life is with the people among whom he is stationed," wrote Ellis in *Polynesian Researches* (1829). Thus "every thing related to their history is, at least, interesting; and the origin of the islanders has often engaged our attention, and formed the subject of our enquiries" (2:37). Again and again, missionary sermons and narratives dwelled on this central message. By thoroughly "enter[ing] into" the history, feelings, and society of the people to whom he evangelized, the missionary would better perceive the fundamental inward commonalities shared between himself and the "heathen" (commonalities that would become evident once the "heathen" had converted to Christianity).

This faith in an Enlightenment-informed conception of universal human nature also found expression in an 1854 essay published by *The Eclectic Review*, a periodical founded by British Dissenters and whose profits benefited the British and Foreign Bible Society. The central question of the missionary enterprise, asserted *The Eclectic Review*, was

> whether charity in its best sense cannot be exercised as to make Christians more and truly Christian, and to conciliate the most prejudiced of other faiths, whether we Christians cannot ourselves follow out genuine Christian principles, and, at the same time, profit by all that is good in men of other creeds; whether, in that case, the Moslem and Hindoo, the Chinese and Pagan, will not view the general superiority of our social system with favour and adopt it with zeal; finally, whether a cosmopolitan spirit will not spring up vigorously wherever once spread, so as to foster all reforms and promote ever welcome change? ("Christianity and Mohammedanism" 644).

In the scenario sketched by this series of questions, the missionary need only embody "genuine Christian principles" to make converts of the "Moslem and Hindoo, the Chinese and Pagan." No force or any strenuous effort is required of the missionary. Rather, the author presumes, a "cosmopolitan spirit"—in this context, used as a synonym for liberal missionary Christianity—will naturally "spring up" in any country that encounters British Christianity. Integral to this vision is the presumption that common human nature, rather than racial and cultural affiliations, dictates the needs, desires, and values of all people. No wonder, then, that little distinction is made between "Moslem" and "Hindoo," "Chinese" and "Pagan." In the formulation presented by *The Eclectic Review*, cultural differences are slight and, in the larger scheme of history and human progress, temporary.

The evangelical belief in a universal humanity helps account for what Jeffrey Cox calls the "contradictory nature of the missionary relationship to imperialism" (*Imperial Fault Lines* 14). On the one hand, this belief distanced the missionary movement from the worst excesses of imperialism. As discussed in chapter 3, missionaries and their supporters condemned polygenists such as Edward Long and Georges Cuvier, whose theories were often used to justify the consolidation of European authority, the practice of slavery, and the extermination of other racial groups. On the other hand, "the flip and darker side of this civilizational and universalist discourse was . . . its intrinsic resistance to ideas of cultural plurality" (Stanley, "From 'the Poor Heathen'" 4). As Colin Kidd observes, "So much discussion of race was framed by the question of monogenesis that it distorted western ethnology in an anti-pluralist direction . . . inhibit[ing] a full acceptance of racial diversity" (25). The cultural tolerance championed by *The Eclectic Review* and the SPCK, in other words, both emanated from and reinforced the pervasive Enlightenment view that culture ultimately did not matter. Instead, what was perceived as critical was the "civilizing mission" by which mankind's fundamental oneness finally would be revealed.

Adhering to the conviction that local culture shrouded a "genuine" humanity shared by all, missionaries unsurprisingly viewed "the sentiments, feelings, associations, and prejudices" of those to whom they proselytized as alterable and finally dispensable. Indigenous "culture"—though undeniably a subject of great interest—seemed to attract the attention of the missionary movement to the extent that it was regarded as transient and destined to pass (a passing, of course, also urged on by a number of missionaries who had the express goal of abolishing indigenous culture as rapidly as possible).[22] Nowhere were these seemingly contrary sentiments better captured than in the flurry of correspondence surrounding the importation of "Hindoo" idols and objects to evangelical museums in England, as detailed by Daniel White ("A Little God" 105).[23] "I [intend] to send a box by the ships of next season," wrote the missionary John Fountain in a 1798 letter to BMS committee member John Webster Morris, "containing some of the implements, utensils, and idols, of the Hindoos; which may serve as useful illustrations *when the present customs, manners, and superstitions of these tribes shall be known only in history*" (qtd. in White, "A Little God" 105; emphasis mine). As Fountain's letter makes evident, the missionary effort to study and preserve cultural relics and traditions presupposed the passing of the culture whence they came.

Thus, the "vague cosmopolitanism" championed by missionary societies simultaneously challenged *and* fortified the public support of British imperialism. As Wright maintains, in one sense the evangelical conviction that "moral sentiments are universal and unite humanity despite apparent difference" helped garner public sympathy for the plight of disenfranchised and oppressed peoples overseas (*Ireland* 22). However, such cosmopolitan feeling also grounded itself in a Eurocentric objectivity of values and an assumption that cultural plurality was an irrelevant, not to mention undesirable, goal. To borrow Thomas Schlereth's observation of the Enlightenment cosmopolitan project, the "penchant for uniformity and universality" also meant the dissolution of "idiosyncratic . . . or particularistic traditions, practices, or beliefs"—a

---

22. See Herbert, *Culture* 150–203.

23. For more on the circulation of Indian religious objects in evangelical museums, see White, *From Little London* 73–82.

dynamic that too easily "became perverted into [the] militant national chauvinism" that would feed British imperialism in India and beyond (126, 133).

"Mutual Comprehension . . . Is Simply Impossible": Post-Mutiny Cosmopolitanism

The events of 1857–58 in India, along with the failure of Livingstone's attempts to settle and commercialize territories around the Zambezi River in Africa in the 1860s, brought the long-held missionary faith in an imminently realizable "universal humanity" into crisis.[24] Years spent accumulating knowledge of local culture, language, and customs and fostering relationships with "natives" had done nothing, it appeared, to make foreign countries more amenable or legible to British missionaries. Missionary societies and their supporters were forced to recognize the limits of universalizing theories and the possibility that local institutions—no matter how strange, distasteful, or incomprehensible—would perhaps have to be confronted *as they were,* on their own terms.

The Mutiny in particular compelled missionaries to reassess their belief in an essential human nature, as well as their own capacity to be fully "at home" in a foreign culture. By almost all British accounts, the uprising—which first erupted in the Meerut Cantonment on May 10, 1857, before quickly spreading across northern and central India—was experienced as abrupt and unforeseen. The public imagination seized on these "shocking" bloody events; "for months the London papers, when not filled with accounts of English gallantry, . . . inked their pages with descriptions of native atrocity" (Baucom 75).[25] Vivid descriptions of the sepoys' "betrayal" and the gruesome revenge

---

24. The Scottish missionary James Stewart contributed to Livingstone's downfall in public influence. Traveling through the Zambezi River region in 1861, he found Livingstone's glowing accounts of the area's fecundity and native hospitality entirely mistaken. Famously, he cast Livingstone's *Missionary Travels* into the Zambezi while proclaiming, "So perish all that is false in myself and others" before departing back to Britain (Jeal 388). Stewart's expedition marked a turning point in official British government attitudes: "Livingstone had based his opinion on a belief in the essential identity of character in all races. He was convinced that Africans and Asian could easily be made Christians, customers and valuable produces [sic] of raw materials. . . . But from the early 1860s the official view was changing fast. The 1857 Rising and the Taiping Rebellion provided evidence from India and from China that the reaction to European expansion might be more complex than had been originally imagined" (McCracken 54, 55). Despite his denunciation of Livingstone, Stewart later came back around to Livingstone's views.

25. Chakravarty notes that the British could not stop writing about the Mutiny: By the end of the century, "the literary yield of the rebellion surpass[ed] in volume the literary representation of [all] the other conflicts during the long nineteenth century of expansion" (3).

exacted by British troops astonished British Christians. If the Mutiny proved "a moment when educated Britons suddenly were afforded a deeply disillusioning view into the national soul and found that they could never return afterward to their prelapsarian state of unawareness" (Herbert, *War* 15–16), for British evangelicals this disillusionment comprised the realization that efforts to "enter into" indigenous culture had not revealed a knowable, predictable human nature.

Instead, the events of the 1857 uprising seemed to show that years spent accumulating a supposedly thorough knowledge of Indian culture only indexed the utter inscrutability of the "native mind." "How suddenly calamities supervene!" lamented *The Church Missionary Gleaner* in an essay characteristic of post-Mutiny missionary writing. "Who could have imagined in May last . . . that our country men in India were on the point of being plunged into scenes of horror from which death has proved to many a welcome refuge?" ("Delhi" 99–100). Placing emphasis on the "suddenness" and "unimaginability" of the Mutiny, such essays drove home that no amount of familiarity with the "sentiments, feelings, associations, and prejudices" of the "natives" could have prepared British Christians for their "treachery" (100).

As a result, evangelicals in India and England increasingly questioned whether "good fellowship" and "mutual comprehension" could ever be achieved between Indians and Englishmen. One missionary featured in an 1863 LMS report on India bemoaned the difficulty of establishing relationships of affinity and trust with the "native heathens": They "seldom . . . really speak out their mind [and] a foreigner can hardly know when they do so," he ranted (Mullens 185). The Rev. James Kennedy, a missionary in Benares (Varanasi), similarly affirmed the difficulty of establishing "real attachment and good understanding" (8). Recounting the difficulties faced by English officers overseeing sepoy regiments, he wrote, "[The officer] wishes to be kind to the men, he learns their language, talks with them, and in every possible way aims at conciliating their good-will. In such cases a kind of attachment springs up, and yet a barrier exists which cannot be surmounted" (8). Back in England, the renowned theologian and, at the time, chaplain of Lincoln's Inn Frederick Denison Maurice devoted a series of five sermons to the crisis of faith provoked by the Mutiny. "A general maxim or theory of the universe does not meet individual cases," he reflected in the opening sermon. "It breaks down, the moment the particular instance occurs to which we need that it should be applied" (5).

Unsurprisingly, the "naivety" of pre-Mutiny universalists emerged as a popular target of post-Mutiny ire. The 1857 uprising, asserted a strident group of critics, made plain that attempts to find common ground between Hindu and Christian values were not only fruitless but dangerous. Such efforts, they warned, obscured the underlying and profound "enmity of the human heart in the Hindoo [against] the pure doctrines of Christianity" ("India" 686). Thus an anonymously authored pamphlet entitled *Lay Thoughts on the Indian Mutiny*, released by the influential London publisher James Nisbet, attacked "the peace-prophets and philanthropists (the blindest of all the mole-eyed race)" for "'much bemus[ing]' themselves with anticipations of perpetual international reciprocations of good fellowship"—an indignation especially aimed at the optimistic fervor that peaked "somewhere about the year 1848," but which no doubt also applied to the earlier predictions of the inevitability of a global "cosmopolitan spirit" made by periodicals such as *The Eclectic Review* (A Barrister 3). Building on this body of criticism, the Bombay-based missionary John Murray Mitchell censured the Romantic taste for translating and publishing "classical" Hindu texts. In *Indian Missions; Viewed in Connexion with the Mutiny and Other Recent Events* (1859), he inveighed against what he called the "tendency to speak in terms of very mitigated condemnation, not to say approbation of heathen religions." He ranted,

We have heard much of

> "The intelligible forms of ancient poets,
> The fair humanities of old religion.
> The power, the beauty, and the majesty,"—

as Coleridge, translating Wallenstein, expresses it.... This grievous folly is now checked, if not extinguished.... On a wide and gloomy stage the heathen religions have been suffered to enact a most gloomy tragedy, to reveal their genuine character in the sight of the nations. Humanity turns shuddering from what looks like the saturnalia of fiends, rather than the doings of men. (Mitchell 6–7)

The "genuine character" of Hinduism in Mitchell's account contrasts starkly with the "genuine doctrines and traditions of Hinduism" that were so approvingly described and endorsed by Thomas Middleston in 1814. Where the latter saw resonance between Christian doctrine and a newly unearthed, "genuine" Hinduism, the former censures the Romantic effort to make Hinduism "intelligible" as nothing more than a futile attempt to "mitigate" the condemnation Hinduism deserves.

In a startling turnaround from missionaries' pre-Mutiny faith in universal kinship and a shared human nature, post-1857 missionary discourse went so far as to question (and in some instances even deny) the humanity of Indian "heathens." Mitchell, for one, proclaimed that because unconverted Indians were closer to "fiends" than to "men," "sympathy between India and Britain—mutual comprehension—attachment, is simply impossible, until a total revolution takes place in the mind and training of India" (11). The Benares-based Kennedy reached much the same conclusion. "Their mental world is antipodal to ours," he argued. "While their habits remain what they are, they can neither understand us, nor be attached to us" (36). Pervading some significant strands of missionary discourse, then, was the contention that true Christian faith, instead of being the natural conclusion of preexisting sympathies and ties between Indian and Briton, was the necessary precondition of any sympathy at all. The work of evangelizing would have to be built on an assumption of cultural difference instead of an assumption of shared human nature.

Realizing that they had underestimated the difficulty of understanding and modifying local perspectives and practices, a significant number of missionaries and missionary societies began endorsing a proselytizing practice that reflected their new reality. New guidelines emerged for missionary work, which recommended that "any association of Western culture with Christianity should be minimized" and that "missionaries should assimilate themselves as far as possible to the native ways of living" (Porter, "Overview" 54). The 1857 missionary conference in Benares offers a striking example of missionary efforts to address the emergent problem of the seemingly impenetrable partitions of culture. Taking place just months after the outbreak of the Mutiny, the conference saw missionary societies resolving to rely less on British-born missionaries and reaffirming the need for native lay preachers who were thoroughly fluent in the native "vernacular."[26] Native preachers, missionary societies reasoned, were "familiar with . . . native modes of thought, native illustrations, native objections, and with that native literature, the doctrines of which they will have continually to refute and explode" ("Missionary Conference at Benares" 264).[27] Following the precedent set by the conference in Benares, the BMS further outlined its plan to stress "indigenous initiative" over the use of missionaries at the 1860 Liverpool missionary conference. The missionary's "position, habits of thought, education, his belonging, in many

---

26. To be clear, "native preachers" were always imagined as playing a key role in the triumph of global Christianity. Yet the post-Mutiny period saw a reemphasis on their centrality to the missionary project.

27. Consider how starkly this recommendation contrasts not only with Macaulay's "Minute on Indian Education" (1835) but also with the opinion of the evangelical MP, Clapham Sect member, and East India Company chairman Charles Grant: "The first communication, and the instrument of introducing the rest, must be the English language; this is a key which will open to [the Hindoos] a world of new ideas" (qtd. in Wright, *Ireland* 287).

parts of the world, to the dominant race," declared the BMS, "place him too far apart from the mass of the people," while native pastors, on the other hand, could "harmonise with the customs, habits of thought and expression . . . prevailing in their own country" (Tretrail 282, 283).

The BMS went so far as to discourage the amalgamation of Hindu and "English notions," as they termed it. "As far as possible, [native pastors] should be kept from the English tongue," recommended the BMS home secretary Frederick Tretrail.

> English literature, especially biblical . . . is filled with strange idioms and illustrations—and its whole structure and style, are very different from the languages of the East, especially—[thus] it is not to be denied that the main body of native preachers are not prepared either to appreciate or use it. (283)

In emphasizing the preferability of "native pastors" over British missionaries, the BMS reinforced an idea that had gained currency in the wake of the Mutiny. English thought and culture were simply beyond the "appreciation" and grasp of native preachers, and conversely, British missionaries, steeped as they were in their own particular "English notions," could never relate to "the mass of the people" in India. If Christianity were to make inroads in India, missionary societies would need to recognize (however rudimentarily) and accommodate (however grudgingly) the sheer impregnability of cultural difference.

Together, these conferences highlight the extent that missionary societies came to regard "local knowledge" as elusive, innate, and largely opaque to missionaries born outside that culture. In other words, proselytization in the latter half of the nineteenth century was underwritten less by a belief in a "shared brotherhood of humanity" that simply needed to be brought to light and more by the conviction that cultural differences were, to a degree, irreducible—a shift in missionary attitudes that subtly, but significantly, departed from the universalist emphasis of earlier missionary discourse. The heathen, then, was not a "faithful mirror" of the unsaved Englishman. Rather, the foreigner, not to mention the Englishman, was an inevitably encultured subject whose "modes of thought," "illustrations," "objections," and "literature" could only be fully understood by those born into the same culture as himself.

Of course, there was an enormous ideological contradiction at the heart of this proselytizing strategy. In order to "refute and explode" native beliefs and practices, missionary societies increasingly relied on native pastors who knew and could speak to the "customs, habits of thought and expression" of their people. In this sense, the campaign to dismantle indigenous culture and customs also relied on the preservation of these cultures and customs—a preservation that induced some missionaries to interrogate their own "European preconceptions," as they came to recognize that what had seemed universal truths were but culturally specific values (Herbert, *Culture and Anomie* 175).[28]

Thus the insufficiency of the idea of a universal human nature compelled missionary societies to accept what we might identify as an embryonic "new cosmopolitanism"—that is, an understanding that "any cosmopolitanism's normative or idealizing power must acknowledge the actual historical and geographic contexts from which it emerges" (Nussbaum qtd. in Robbins, "Introduction" 2; Robbins 2). For while these societies obviously refused to embrace cultural plurality in the manner endorsed by Robbins, the newly formulated missionary cosmopolitanism of the post-Mutiny period nonetheless possessed a trait evinced by the new cosmopolitanisms of today. Rejecting Enlightenment assumptions regarding the fundamental commonality of mankind but refusing to give up the normativizing potential of cosmopolitanism entirely, the post-Mutiny cosmopolitanism of some missionary thought sought to account more effectively for the constitutive and inescapable role of culture in the development of identity. Thus becomes clear, to use Geoffrey A. Odie's understated phrase, "a difference between the religious situation before and after 1857" (181).

Owenson's Revisions

Somewhat ironically, this sense of the fundamental impregnability of culture became most entrenched at a moment when Britain arguably had never felt herself to be more knowledgeable about India. This was certainly true on the missionary front. Porter observes that even as the 1850s witnessed missionary societies establishing "the first systematic statistical charting of missionary progress," the "upheavals of 1857 brought home the limits of evangelical endeavours" ("Overview" 54). The technological triumph represented in the quantification of missionary success was undercut by the realization that

---

28. Herbert observes that the missionary Thomas Williams's *Fiji and the Fijians* (1858) captures something like the dynamic I'm describing here. He argues, "Williams's determination to achieve an impartial and unprejudiced view of these people stained with crimes leads him to postulate something approximating what anthropologists call 'culture': a set of irresistible collective forces by which an individual is unconsciously molded" (176). But where Williams's relativism ultimately resolves in a reassertion of the ephemerality of culture—discovering, after all, that the Fijians are but "a mirror of ourselves"—I suggest a slightly different view was emerging in India regarding the individual's ability to shake those "irresistible collective forces" of culture (177).

this abundance of knowledge had somehow proven an insufficient measure of missionary understanding. Similarly, decades of Orientalist scholarship—produced by missionaries and secular scholars alike—had not anticipated the scale and suddenness of the Mutiny. The vast British apparatus for knowing India had failed to apprehend the true state of Indian hearts.

Owenson's reissued *Luxima* seems intent on reflecting this state of affairs, on the one hand conveying a more extensive intermingling between the novel's imperial nations (Spain and to a lesser degree Portugal) and the colonized one (India), and on the other, portraying its missionary as far less capable of making any meaning of this increased knowledge. In 1811, for instance, Hilarion has no acquaintance with Indian customs, language, or religion prior to his arrival in India, giving the impression that his journey is to a degree unprecedented. In 1859, however, Owenson adds a new character, "an old brother of the order of St. Francis" who is also "a converted Hindoo, a Brahmin by descent, and long a professor of Indian learners" (*Luxima* 4). Thanks to him, Hilarion acquires fluency in the "Hindoo language and Sanscrit" before leaving for India (11). The addition of this "old" character suggests Owenson's interest in depicting Portugal and India as already having a lengthy shared history predating the events of the novel. Moreover, the appearance of this Brahmin in a Portuguese monastery implies that the relationship between the countries is one of cooperation and mutual influence. In breaching India's borders, Europe has also opened its own to the people, culture, and language of India. No wonder, then, that where it is Hilarion's "*Imagination*" that stretches over the "various and wondrous tracts" of India in 1811 (80), these same "shores and mighty regions of the East" present themselves to Hilarion's "*memory*" in the 1859 *Luxima* (15). In the former, we are presented with a world to be discovered; in the latter, a country and culture already known, charted, and explored.

But if the "world" of *Luxima* is more interconnected, it is also more resistant to universalizing suppositions and theories. Within the first chapters of *Luxima*, we see Hilarion more than once defeated by the project of "conjecture," the term used only in the 1859 version to designate the missionary's attempts to perceive the principles that invisibly unite the world and all its people. In *The Missionary*, Hilarion is always "connecting, or endeavouring to connect, his incongruous ideas, by abstract principles" (a project that, the 1811 novel implies, he pursues ardently despite his ultimate failure to reach any concrete conclusions) (76). In *Luxima*, by contrast, Hilarion is described as "weary of conjecture" even before attempting to connect his "incongruous ideas." Twice in the same chapter, in fact, Owenson adds to the 1859 version the peculiar phrase, "weary of conjecture" (9, 18). The ultimate effect of this repetition is to impress on the reader that Hilarion, prior to even trying, has perhaps concluded that the project of finding universal connections is in vain. Thus even as *Luxima* implies a long history of interaction between Europe and India, it also suggests the futility of finding any "abstract principles" that would unite all that is "incongruous."

In another instance, Owenson substitutes the word "spirit" for "soul" in a passage describing Hilarion's ambitions to "penetrate into those regions . . . which the hallowed footstep of Christianity had never yet consecrated" (*Luxima* 22). Instead of attacking the "vital *soul*" of Hinduism as he did in *The Missionary*, Hilarion instead attacks the "vital *spirit*" of the religion in *Luxima*. The substitution cannot be dismissed as cosmetic, not least because the word "spirit" is now inelegantly repeated twice in the sentence. A more likely explanation can be found in a minor but ongoing theological debate concerning the difference between the spirit and soul.

Though many evangelicals used "spirit" and "soul" interchangeably when addressing the broader public, an anonymous 1800 letter to the British *Evangelical Magazine* (later republished in an 1803 American "best of" collection entitled *The Beauties of the Evangelical Magazine*) demonstrates that some took issue with this slippage. The letter writer takes pains to distinguish "spirit" from "soul," identifying the former as "immortal" and therefore "*superior*" to the latter ("Critical Remarks" 128). Considered together with the 1859 addition of a passage that describes India as a place in which "every where, religion, under some material form, proclaimed her influence over the mind or ignorance of man," Owenson's replacement of "spirit" for "soul" suggests the permanence of Hindu religiosity in India. If "soul" can pass, "spirit" cannot, and Hinduism is given a "vital *spirit*" in 1859, is "every where" in the Indian landscape, suggesting that the presence of the religion in India is eternal, enduring, inextricable from the land itself.

Within the first three chapters alone, then, the 1859 novel emphasizes two crucial shifts in British attitudes toward India after 1857. First, it registers the greater degree of self-doubt in the post-Mutiny British psyche: If India is more known and knowable in terms of its languages, customs, and cultural practices, the Indian "mind," paradoxically, is all the more illegible to the European outsider. Second, *Luxima* surpasses *The Missionary* in advancing the notion that the "old habits and ideas" of Hinduism are difficult to "uproot" (in the words of an LMS missionary)—a textual shift that maps onto broader cultural shifts in missionary thought (Rice 267). For no longer did missionary societies believe that the "multitude of Heathen" in India was imminently "prepared to welcome . . . Divine Grace" ("Foreign Intelligence" 454). The events of the Mutiny finally convinced many of them instead that Hinduism was woven into the very fabric of Indian thought and tradition. "No one ever expected Brahminism to descend from the position which it has held for ages without a struggle," pronounced the *Missionary Magazine* in its November 1857 issue (Rice 267). Seeing the "natives" as unbreachably different from rather than fundamentally like themselves, the missionary movement entertained new doubts regarding whether India would ever embrace Christianity—doubts that led to growing support for trusteeism over conversionism.

The character of Luxima brings into view the new unease regarding the legibility of "heathens." The Brahmin priestess is more inscrutable in the 1859 *Luxima* and seemingly more wedded to her native religion. As already mentioned, Viswanathan suggests that the new title of *Luxima* registers the "new centrality of the female protagonist, Luxima" (27). However, if the new title seems to shine a spotlight on Luxima, the novel's new content shrouds her, making her character and states of mind more difficult to decipher. Excisions of what initially appears mere florid prose in fact relate to Luxima's emotional state. A comparison of the two novels reveals at least twenty-six instances in which the text abbreviates, omits, or makes more obscure the state of Luxima's feelings.[29]

To give an example of this pattern, in the 1811 novel the narrator relates: "Some moments of unbroken silence passed away . . . [and] the tender Indian was now soothed, under her affliction, by the consideration of him for whose sake she had incurred it: for to suffer or to die for him she loved was more precious to her feelings than even to have enjoyed security and life, independent of his idea, his influence, or his presence" (*Missionary* 189–90). While Owenson retains "some moments of unbroken silence" in 1859, she removes all description of Luxima's feelings in these moments (*Luxima* 205–6). To Hilarion as well as the reader, Luxima is all the more opaque, and her affections for the missionary, all the more ambiguous.

Midway through the novels, Hilarion inadvertently glimpses Luxima without her awareness of his presence. However, only in the 1811 version does Luxima "[draw] aside her veil," granting Hilarion a view of her face "animated by suspenseful love [and an] intelligence of beauty which rushes upon the countenance from the heart that is filled with a pure and ardent affection" (*Missionary* 162). In 1859, by contrast, Hilarion never sees Luxima's unveiled face and thus never receives this assurance of her affection. Adding to the mystery of the priestess's emotional state, the revised novel omits an impassioned speech Luxima delivers immediately following the missionary's moment of voyeurism. Meeting him, she declares her soul "one" with Hilarion's.

---

29. My thanks to my research assistant, Carly Lewis, for bringing this to my attention.

> "Oh no!" returned Luxima, endeavouring to conceal her tenderness and her tears: "Oh no! Part we cannot. Go where thou mayst, my life must still stand upon thine! My thoughts will pursue thee. Indissolubly united, there is not but one soul between us." (*Missionary* 178)

Keeping with early nineteenth-century optimism that mutuality and sympathy could be achieved between British missionaries and converts, *The Missionary* envisages an "indissoluble union" and a "single soul" shared by Hilarion and his only proselyte. But with the excision of this passage, the 1859 novel provides a very different Luxima. Rather than an "affectionate" priestess who perceives herself "one" with the European missionary (not to mention, who "endeavours" rather than succeeds in "concealing" her feelings), the post-Mutiny Luxima is veiled, inscrutable, and emotionally subdued.

No wonder, then, that where Luxima exclaims, "My beloved, I come!—Brahma receive and eternally unite our spirits!" in the climactic auto-da-fé of the 1811 novel, she instead cries in 1859, "Brahma receive and eternally unite our spirits" (*Missionary* 249; *Luxima* 307). In the former instance, Luxima's act of self-sacrifice is undoubtedly for Hilarion, as the description of the auto-da-fé proves an ironic fulfillment of Luxima's prophetic avowal of love made earlier in the novel (proving her a prophetess, indeed). Her wish to "unite" with Hilarion by way of mutual immolation recalls her earlier pronouncement, "My life must still stand upon thine. . . . Indissolubly united, there is not but one soul between us."

By removing this critical speech and "My beloved," *Luxima* obfuscates why and for whom Luxima determines to sacrifice herself. No longer can we be certain that she hopes to die for Hilarion's sake. Rather, as Parsons observes, it's implied that Luxima's martyrdom may be spurred by her allegiance to Brahma, not her love for the missionary. Thus in what constitutes her "most assertive moment in the novel" (378), the post-Mutiny Luxima potentially denies any "oneness" between herself and her European lover. Far from having embraced Hilarion's Christianity or Hilarion's love, Luxima's attempted suicide suggests that her "eternal" loyalty has always been to her own religion.

Further reinforcing the impossibility of achieving "mutual comprehension" between the lovers, Owenson revises her description of Luxima's death in the dénouement of her novel. Where Luxima is described as "smil[ing] *languidly* on [Hilarion]" in the 1811 conclusion (252), *Luxima* describes the Brahmin priestess as "smil[ing] *wildly* on him" (314). That Luxima would be "languid" in the moment of her impending death in some sense is expected; no one would be shocked to discover that listlessness results from mortal wounding. Luxima's "wild" smile, however, is more enigmatic. Though she "smiles" upon Hilarion, the "wildness" of her smile suggests an intrinsically rebellious, savage nature, one maintained until the moment of her death. This alteration in the 1859 text, then, belongs to a larger pattern guiding Owenson's revisions, a pattern in which Luxima is rendered less comprehensible and, consistent with post-Mutiny missionary discourse, perhaps all the more "wild," untamable, and indecipherable.

Corresponding with Luxima's increased inscrutability, *Luxima* suggests Hilarion as similarly immured in his culture, religion, and nationality. Shaped by his own inevitable enculturation, the missionary is rendered incapable of attaining anything close to a genuinely universal perspective. In *The Missionary*, for instance, Hilarion is described as "eloquent in the cause of religion" without the narrative specifying *which* religion (74). The 1811 wording thus opens the possibility that Hilarion could be, one day, as capable an advocate for Hinduism as he is for Christianity—a possibility foreclosed entirely in 1859 by Owenson's specification that Hilarion is only "eloquent in the cause of his church" (*Luxima* 7).

Taken together, revisions such as these suggest lost faith in the idea of a "universal humanity," particularly as a means of negotiating understanding across difference in the context of imperialism. Casting religious divergences as more firmly entrenched in and culture more formative of one's genuine nature, her revisions dissociate the original novel from the Enlightenment faith in mankind's fundamental similitude—the very faith that had marked *The Missionary* as a novel of sensibility (Wright, "Introduction" 95–98). Instead the new *Luxima*, while never being realist, begins to approach a mentality more characteristic of late Victorian realism, as it hesitatingly explores the ineffability of individual character and the near impossibility of achieving mutual comprehension despite the presence of genuine affection.[30]

But the fact that the revisions never fundamentally alter the plot perhaps speaks to Owenson's ultimate refusal to abandon the totalizing vision of *The Missionary*; Luxima and Hilarion still fall in love, and Hilarion still leaves his previous religious dogmatism in search of (what we imagine must be) a more fulfilling syncretism. Hence we are still presented with the promises of cosmo-

---

30. Rachel Hollander's reading of *Daniel Deronda* captures this dynamic in late Victorian realism in terms especially illuminating when considered alongside the universalist sympathy Wright describes as constitutive of Enlightenment sensibility. If Enlightenment sensibility tried to imagine the "fundamental similitude between human beings" despite differences of race, religion, and culture, the sympathy practiced by Eliot's characters instead "respect[s] . . . the extent to which the other cannot be assimilated or even understood" (Wright, "Introduction" 2–3; Hollander 63). *The Missionary* and *Luxima* together perhaps chart precisely this change in characterological conventions. But Owenson's novels maybe do more than this, in linking growing skepticism of Enlightenment ideas of human nature to this generic shift.

politanism—only now we find them tempered with a nebulous recognition of the irreducibility of cultural difference.

In this sense, the revisions in the cosmopolitan visions presented in Owenson's novels are analogous to those presented in missionary discourses of the time. Keeping this comparison in mind, we come to recognize that in Owenson's novel, as in missionary thinking, the new cosmopolitan view did not necessarily correspond with anti-imperialist sentiments. For as evangelicals lost faith in the notion that all humanity, being fundamentally the same, necessarily pursued, and indeed, were entitled to, the same objects—that is, liberty, representative government, and "civilization" in general—the impetus to realize those objects on behalf of indigenous people diminished. This meant, as Stanley notes, that missionary societies and evangelicals increasingly abandoned the project of battling more insidious and immoral forms of imperial control in the name of so-called universal rights. Rather, they came to focus their attentions on introducing the gospel by any means possible, with less immediate regard for individual freedom and political representation (Stanley, *Bible* 75–77). Hence the desire for "liberty"—that great ideal of Enlightenment humanism—as a catalyst for Indian revolt drops out of the 1859 text where it was once so prominently featured. The substitution of "vengeance" in its place not only suggests Owenson's sensitivity to the massive British outrage at the Indian "mutineers" (keeping "liberty" in the novel, no doubt, would have been seen by British readers as an effort to excuse and justify the killing of British soldiers, women, and children). It also newly implies that the "long-enduring Hindus" are *so* fundamentally different from Europeans that they lack the capacity to desire "liberty"—indeed, might not even know what "liberty" is.

In the preceding chapters, I have discussed several of missionaries' cosmopolitan experiments. Derived from Enlightenment assumptions of mankind's fundamental similitude and bolstered by the evangelical commitment to monogenism, these cosmopolitan experiments—whether promoting mankind's faculty for "reason" and "reasonableness," endorsing (however briefly) interracial marriages, or asserting the ephemerality of cultural difference—were predicated on missionaries' unshakeable conviction in a "universal humanity." I finish here, at the historical moment in which we see this conviction begin to waver. By reading Owenson's novels together, against the backdrop of changing missionary attitudes toward culture's relationship with Christianity, we can perceive the 1859 revisions as crystallizing how missionary cosmopolitanism had, indeed, "greatly altered." The twentieth- and twenty-first-century afterlives of this alteration are the subject of my coda.

CODA

The Afterlives of Missionary Cosmopolitanism

IN THE latter half of the nineteenth century, Brian Stanley observes, "the marriage of the Evangelical Revival and the Enlightenment was falling apart" (*Bible* 77). But even as missionary societies distanced themselves from their original Enlightenment optimism regarding mankind's fundamental unity, they never abandoned cosmopolitanism as a structuring ideal of their movement.

The noisiest claims to cosmopolitanism manifested themselves in the writings leading up to and surrounding the World Missionary Conference of 1910. Held in Edinburgh, the conference repeatedly was described (and described itself) as "cosmopolitan" in both its organization and ambitions. The London-based periodical *The Mercury*, for instance, marveled at the "cosmopolitan character of the World's Missionary Conference" and its "Many Strange Tongues and Dresses" ("Missionary Conference in Edinburgh" 5). In a similar vein, contemporary missionary periodicals hailed "the vast cosmopolitan throng of people" attending the event, describing scenes of "Europeans, Americans, Asiatics, and Africans rubb[ing] elbows," the sights of "various and often picturesque garbs," and the sounds of "more languages [being] spoken than at the Pentecost" (Patton 351). Such coverage, one imagines, must have been immensely gratifying to the chairman of the 1910 conference, John R. Mott, who prophesied, "The Edinburgh Conference will be cosmopolitan, and representative of the aggressive forces of Christianity to a degree which has not characterized any other Christian assembly" (927).

But this cosmopolitanism seemed superficial at best, deeply disingenuous at worst. In terms of attendees, the World Missionary Conference proved considerably more geographically and culturally homogenous than *The Mercury* implied. Stanley notes, "Of the 1,215 official delegates, 509 were British, 491 were North American, 169 originated from continental Europe, 27 came from the white colonies of South Africa and Australasia, and only 19 were from the non-western or 'majority' world (18 of them from Asia)" (*World* 12). Moreover, conference documents were littered with familiar nineteenth-century paeans to the greatness of Western religion and civilization, as well as well-trod expressions of condescension and regret that the foreign heathen was so irretrievably "primitive [and] childlike" (Stanley, *World* 13). The eight preparatory "Commissions" (convened in advance of the conference to examine and produce single-volume reports on issues deemed of critical importance to twentieth-century missionary work[1]) appeared only to bolster prevailing stereotypes of the natural "vigorous[ness]" of "'progressive' European races" contra the "inert and idle" "oriental" ones (Stanley, *World* 162). Tellingly, the one black African Christian to attend (Mark C. Hayford of Ghana) never even had his name listed among the official delegates. In the context of the World Missionary Conference, it seemed fairly easy, then, to see why "cosmopolitanism" was being deployed by missionary societies and their sympathizers: The term lent an air of enlightened universalism to an event in fact grounded in a conviction of Western exceptionalism.

But then I read the report of Commission 4, "The Missionary Message in Relation to Non-Christian Religions," as well as the original testimonies from which the report was compiled. True, the report's conclusion championed a troubling and militaristic vision of Christianity, cheering for "the spectacle of the advance of the Christian Church along many lines of action to the conquest of the five great religions of the modern world" (*Report of Commission IV* 274).[2] However, a deeper dive into the report, especially into the testimonies of a certain set of missionaries from India, revealed an undercurrent of

---

1. For instance, "Carrying the Gospel to All the Non-Christian World" (Commission 1); "The Church in the Mission Field" (Commission 2); and "The Preparation of Missionaries" (Commission 5).

2. To be clear, such language was not unique to the World Missionary Conference. Rather, it represented a continuation of the muscular Christianity movement, which popularized a masculinist and militaristic rhetoric that also found expression in (and was further popularized by) William Booth's Salvation Army and the YMCA (Van der Veer 89). In fact, several attendees of the World Missionary Conference belonged to the YMCA.

missionary thought seemingly at odds with the self-satisfied triumphalism of this conclusion, not to mention the conference as a whole.[3]

Specifically, these missionaries seemed to envision a new Christian universalism, one freed from the trappings of Western culture and capable of embracing new, non-Western forms, whatever those forms may be. "I think ... we have been inclined to identify too much Christ with the forms of Western Christianity, forgetting that our Christianity has its limitations," reflected Rev. James Mathers of the LMS mission to Bangalore, for instance. "We ought to start with the fact clear before us, that our Western Christianity is not the final form of our religion" (29, 31). Similarly, the renowned LMS missionary Thomas Ebenezer Slater contended, "We have made the fatal mistake of bringing to India a Christ from outside, a foreign and Western Christ, and one set in *our* theological systems; and not rather an Eastern Christ, as He really was—though He was, of course, the *universal* Christ, in Whom 'there is no East or West'" (Bangalore 17–18). And J. H. Messmore of the Methodist Episcopal Church cautioned that the missionary should "always remember that he himself has no monopoly on truth and that there is much valuable truth in all the great non-Christian religions" (3). On the one hand, this universalism appeared profoundly self-reflexive, as though the result of a profound missionary reckoning with a loss of faith in Enlightenment conceptions of a universal humanity aspiring to the same fundamental values, rights, and forms of governance. Yet this universalism was also undeniably forward-looking, optimistic, and, even more, prophetic of the final dissolution of Christendom with the rise of world Christianity.[4]

It is *this* emergent cosmopolitan Christianity that has proven the legacy of the 1910 conference. We do best to heed it, if we are to understand the enduringness of missionary work, as well as the resurgence of religious universalism in our current moment. Religious universalism, as expressed in contemporary Protestant missionary work, is not a rigidly dogmatic, conservative, and inward-looking reaction to a postmodern, pluralistic, and globalist society—at least, not in the manner we might initially imagine. Rather, in its rhetoric and tactics for bridging religious and cultural divides, this new religious universalism mirrors the "new cosmopolitanisms" of today.

---

3. I'm hardly the only person to feel this way about the Report of Commission 4. According to Kenneth R. Ross and David A. Kerr, "Commission Four provided what was perhaps the most strikingly original of all the Reports and the one which attracts the greatest interest today.... It is remarkable for the degree to which it scotches the idea that Western missionaries were iconoclasts bent on the eradication of existing religion in order to impose their own understanding of Christianity" (310).

4. For an account of the late nineteenth- and twentieth-century decline of Christendom, see Walls, *Cross-Cultural*, chapter 3.

The New Christian Universalism of the 1910 World Missionary Conference

It is no surprise that this new Christian universalism arose primarily among a subset of missionaries in India. Politically, these missionaries saw that with the rise of Indian nationalism, Christianity would do well to sever ties with Western culture. Thus Rev. Charles Freer Andrews of the SPG and the Cambridge University Mission in Delhi (and later advocate of the Indian National Congress) argued that links between Christianity and Western culture be dissolved lest Christianity be implicated in imperial oppression: "The wave of reaction has come and the Church presents the picture, not of 'emancipation' but of [Indian] 'denationalisation'" (14).[5] Echoing this opinion, Slater noted that because of its association with the West, conversion to Christianity in India was regarded as tantamount to anti-national feeling: "Whatever comes, Hindus *must not denationalize themselves* by accepting a religion from the West" (Bangalore 15). Fueling these sentiments was growing disillusionment with Western culture. The refusal of the British government to declare India a Christian nation in the mid-nineteenth century had convinced many evangelicals that Britain was not the Christian nation it claimed itself to be, and by the end of the century, missionary writing exhibited a "sense of betrayal by the Christian state" (Walls, *Cross-Cultural* 44). Missionaries, moreover, expressed growing unease with what appeared an insuperable divide between Christian values and the seemingly unprecedented materialism of Western capitalist society. It was in this spirit that N. C. Mukerjee of Allahabad Christian College and the North India American Presbyterian Mission argued in his testimony, "The life of the West to that of the New Testament [is] a far off cry" (3), and Rev. Mathers expressed hope that an "Eastern" iteration of Christianity would address the "limitations" of Western culture: "Perhaps in the unworldliness of their ideals we shall find the antidote to that spirit of worldliness which we all deplore in these days in the life of the West" (25–26).

Theologically, the popularity of "fulfillment theory" among late nineteenth-century missionaries helped loosen ties between Christianity and Western culture.[6] Fortified by their confidence that Christianity would "fulfill"

---

5. Andrews and his fellow missionary Susil Kumar Rudra would play central roles in the development of Gandhi's theological and political thought. After Andrews's death, Gandhi would call Andrews in a speech before the All India Congress Committee in 1942 his "closest friend" (qtd. in Gandhi 16).

6. Fulfillment theory provided the theological backbone for the discipline that Masuzawa calls "comparative theology." Yet there is a chance of confusion surrounding Masuzawa's term. For what she calls "comparative theology," missionaries (many of whom subscribed to fulfillment theology) called "comparative religion." Take, for instance, the Anglican missionary

and eventually triumph over all other religions, some missionaries argued that non-Christian religions all contained elements of the divine, which would contribute to the Christian universalism to come.[7] This "fulfillment" thus necessitated a broadening of Christian thought and dogma to accommodate other national and religious traditions—an accommodation all the more striking when one compares it to the culturally chauvinistic attitudes that motivated the first missionaries and their early nineteenth-century successors.[8] Andrews, for instance, claimed in his testimony for Commission 4 that understanding "a recognised place for Hindu religious thought and life in past ages" had brought about in him "a weakening (or perhaps the truer word would be a 'widening') of the dogmatic side of the faith" (19, 22). "I have a conscious desire to stretch all dogmas to their widest limits," he wrote. "I now find the anima Christiana in Guru Nanak, and Yulsi Das, and Kabir (according to S. John I. 9) in a way I never did before and I cannot use the word 'heathen' as I used to do" (22).[9] This "widening" eventually led Andrews to see the Gospels as "exhort[ing] believers to depart from the possessive claims of inherited or received identity and belonging" to embrace more "cosmopolitan" forms of fellowship, as Leela Gandhi notes (17). And, throughout his life, he would put these theological commitments into action. Meeting Mohandas Gandhi in South Africa in 1914, for instance, Andrews was so impressed by the lawyer that he aided him in organizing an ashram in Natal and publishing his magazine, *The Indian Opinion*.[10]

Arthur Lloyd, who defined "comparative religion" as the duty "to separate from the teaching of [the] great non-Christian Saints all that is spurious accretion only fit to be cast away and burned, all that is local and temporary and that will pass away, and to find and gather that precious residuum of Universal Faith" (17).

7. In his contribution to the Edinburgh 2010 report on *Mission Then and Now*, Vinoth Ramachandra remarks, "The language of 'fulfilment' *vis a vis* the relationship between Christianity and other Faiths surfaces especially in the sections on Hinduism," and he notes that the term "fulfilment" was probably first coined by Keshub Chunder Sen rather than by Protestant missionaries (142).

8. This is not to say that these missionaries did not reproduce culturally chauvinistic attitudes in other ways. Indeed, two native Indian readers of Commission 4's report "objected to [it] as being inattentive to the view of Indian converts" on the grounds that the insider's experience of Hinduism was "not as 'roseate' as that of the missionaries who often only had contact with the 'best' of Hinduism" (Ramachandra 142). Ramachandra argues that in making these arguments, the native readers not only illuminated these missionaries' unconscious complicity in perpetuating an oppressive caste system but also "pre-figur[ed] Dalit consciousness which champions Jesus as a fellow Dalit" (142).

9. In the final published report of Commission 4, these statements as well as other missionaries' statements to similar effects were anonymized. I imagine that this anonymity was granted to shield these missionaries from potential retribution.

10. My argument thus overlaps with Gandhi's treatment of Andrews, in which she shows how the missionary's theological commitments to an "affective cosmopolitanism" led him to

Of course, as Tomoko Masuzawa notes, fulfillment theory still amounted to "Christian absolutism" (102). Yet it is worth underscoring that "Christian absolutism" was (and is) not homogenous in the forms it takes. Where early and mid-nineteenth-century missionaries saw Christian truth inhering in British cultural norms or the saving graces of Western commerce, these late-century missionaries envisioned a form of Christian absolutism distinct from Western (and even moral) absolutism. As Walls observes, this strain of thinking stressed adaptation and modification on the part of the missionary, who was encouraged to understand Christian affirmations from the points of view of cultural Others and to "set [these affirmation] free to move within new systems of thought and discourse" (*Cross-Cultural* 40, 42). Slater represents a compelling case of this broadening in missionary thinking. Take, for instance, his position on suttee (sati). At an earlier moment, missionaries had drawn on graphic descriptions of suttee to demonstrate Hinduism's moral depravity and argue for the necessity of Western Christian intervention. Slater took a different tone. Missionary work, he claimed, had for too long ignored "*underlying truth*" in favor of "outward expression," which had blinded them to the fact that "it was the belief in a mystic union of souls that was the underlying motive of *Sati*" (Bangalore 54). This attitude permeated Slater's many works on "Indian theism," including his lengthy study, *Keshab Chandra Sen and the Brahma Samaj* (1888), in which he claimed that Keshub Chunder Sen's Brahmo Samaj brought up a series of questions central to Christian theology. "Why should one form of Christian thought and government prevail for the millions of our race?" wondered Slater. "Why may not the Gospel, when it comes to a foreign land, especially to the East, react upon the Christian Church, by discovering to it the many-sidedness of its Divine revelation, by bringing into prominence, points that have been missed or unapprehended in the past?" (iii). Again, I recognize the temptation to interpret these sentiments as nothing more than the missionary wish to assimilate the Other into British Christianity. Srinivas Aravamudan, for one, attributes missionaries' interest in Keshub to their hopes of converting the Hindu reformer to Christianity (51). But he overlooks that by the time of *Keshab Chandra Sen*'s publication, Keshub had already been dead for four years, a fact that not only complicates Aravamudan's reading of missionary motivations but also suggests the earnestness

---

adopt an anti-imperialist politics that "eschew[ed] ties of race, nation, class, and religion" (17). The example of Andrews and other like-minded missionaries challenges and complicates Masuzawa's claim that Christian universalist rhetoric amounted to little more than an effort to naturalize European Christian norms under the guise of universalism.

with which missionaries like Slater tried to envision a Christian universalism fundamentally composed of "foreign" religious and cultural influences.[11]

Thus in the scatterplot of missionary writing leading up to the World Missionary Conference, we see some of the ways that political exigency combined with theological commitments to yield a universal Christianity *freed* from Western culture, the practices, governance, and "points" of which (as missionaries freely admitted) could not be anticipated or fully envisioned. From the collapse of their Enlightenment faith in universal humanity, then, some missionaries reconstructed a "cosmopolitan spirituality"—one not unlike the new religious universalisms envisioned by movements such as Theosophy, neo-Hindu reform, and Paramhansa Yogananda's Self-Realization Fellowship (Van der Veer 173–79; Aravamudan 58; Werner). This cosmopolitan spirituality asserted the ability of religion to *accommodate,* so as to transcend, all other categories of racial, ethnic, and cultural identity.

In this moment of missionary work, then, we find a self-conscious spiritual universalism, which meditates on religion's cultural embeddedness, but precisely to uncouple itself all the better from any one culture. Surprisingly, this is a dynamic that bears some similarities to Lecourt's description of the unexpected relativism yielded by mid- to late-century polygenism. Because grounded in essentialist theories of human difference, the relativism of Richard Burton and other social scientists ends up approaching "a cosmopolitanism of sentiments: an openness to the lived experience of others that ends up being more tolerant than a classical liberal 'cosmopolitanism of reason'" (*Cultivating* 56). The shift away from Enlightenment assumptions of human similitude to recognition of the irreducibility of culture provides new resources for imagining human unity through cultural relativism. But where Lecourt locates this dynamic among *scholars* of religion, I find this movement among religious *practitioners*. Therein lies the crucial difference. For, in the eyes of these Christian universalists, if culture was irreducible, then religion would have to be all the more radically unmoored from and endlessly accommodating of every culture. Adopting cultural relativism necessitated envisioning better, more savvy forms of religious universalism.

Insofar as it commemorated the global triumph of missionary enterprises, the 1910 World Missionary Conference constituted "the high point of the modern Western missionary movement" (Walls, *Cross-Cultural* 53). But the conference also marked "the point from which [the movement] declined" (53). Two world wars quickly shattered dreams of world unity under the ban-

---

11. For a related discussion on the tensions between Christian universalism and "local culture" in the twentieth-century Dutch missionary context, see Keane 106–12.

ner of shared religion. In the words of the prominent and divisive Anglican evangelical John Stott, "These devastating conflicts sapped the moral as well as the financial strength of the west, and signaled to the rest of the world the collapse of western culture and of its foundation of Christianity" (qtd. in Escobar 190).[12] Yet, as we have seen, percolating among some missionaries was an anticipation of this cultural collapse, as well as an effort to envision something of a corrective in their universalist religion. Theirs was a vision of a Protestant Christianity radically decentered from its Western origin—a "glimpse," as Walls puts it, "of what a world church would be like" (*Cross-Cultural* 53).

Going "Glocal": Missionary Cosmopolitanism in Edinburgh 2010

The Centenary of the World Missionary Conference, held from June 2 to June 6, 2010, in Edinburgh, testified to this transformation of Christianity and missionary work.[13] The attendees of the 1910 conference could have little anticipated that a mere hundred years later, missionaries, missiologists, and theologians would widely proclaim that "the Christian faith is no longer a European or American phenomenon" (Jørgenson 6).[14] Nor, one imagines, could they have imagined that Western countries would become the new "mission fields" of the twenty-first century (6, 11). The relocation of the locus of Protestant missionary work from the West into the Global South has brought with it new theologies and new discursive formations, which have modified without abandoning the dream of a realizable Christian universalism. Building on the conviction that Christianity, to be universal, must be unmoored from any *cultural* universalism, the Christian universalism of the World Missionary Conference of 2010 stressed dialogue between the authority of the Bible and local context; listening (or "witnessing") rather than preaching; recognizing the missionary's shared "vulnerability" with those to whom

---

12. Brian Stanley notes that the "collapse of the Enlightenment inheritance and the emergence of a postmodern worldview" has constituted a crisis especially among *Protestant* missions; because they were "much more active apostles of modernity than Catholic ones . . . they have felt more acutely the challenge of disintegrating confidence in modernity" ("Christian Missions" 2).

13. This is not to say that positions of various historians, church leaders, missionaries, and theologians are univocal across these reports and position papers. Rather, it is to tease out significant strands of contemporary missionary and missiology thought in order to show their convergence with the new cosmopolitanisms.

14. Jørgenson notes, for instance, that whereas "in 1910 the number of Christians in Africa was 9.4% of the population . . . by 2010 the total has risen to 47.9%" (6).

he evangelizes; and particular focus on living with and tending to the needs of the oppressed, marginalized, and impoverished.

Theologically, the participants of Edinburgh 2010 generally appear to have taken to heart the realization that whatever the universal truths of the gospel may be, such truths only emerge from within the context of a given local culture. "1910 still believed that Western theology was universally valid and based on the ecclesiastical confessions," notes Jørgenson, but the Christianity of the Global South has "reversed the order" (8). Instead, the Christianity of the Global South argues that "Scripture should not be read as the revelation of transcendent truths (that are then applied in action), but as the story of Israel's struggle for justice and truth" (8). As such, it "implies that mission no longer begins with a transcendent truth (that demands action) but with action, modelled on Scripture (e.g. the Exodus event), which then discovers the truth of the gospel in the actual context" (8). The "universal dimension of theology" thus originates not from a set of given transcendent truths, applicable no matter the situation or person, but instead from the recognition that religious truth is inevitably provisional, born of "an on-going dialogue between text and context" (8).

The theological shift is reflected in a discursive shift. No longer the martial metaphors of Christian "conquest." Instead, new emphasis is placed on the power that inheres in *powerlessness*. This is the rhetoric of what Jørgenson calls "Vulnerable Mission," missionary work built on an emphasis of God's vulnerability by taking incarnate form in his Son, which directs its attention to the poor and oppressed as well as to the importance of the missionary making himself "vulnerable" (9). Again and again, what is stressed is the essential orientation of Christianity toward those who are sick, poor, and suffering, as well as the Christian's own stance as one of radical humility, an epistemological and rhetorical stance that the reports of Edinburgh 2010 often contrast with the missionary attitudes of the nineteenth century. "There have been times when we as European missionaries have presented the global truth in triumphant ways," writes missiologist Ingrid Eskilt. "That era is definitely put to an end. . . . The global truth must be presented in a humble incarnate manner, mostly in the form of a witness, and most of all through transformed Christlike disciples" (Eskilt 187). Thus the Danish scholar and missionary Mogens Mogenson reminds would-be missionaries that by "opening your arms—listening deeply to the other—you are also opening yourself to be changed by what you hear. You make yourself vulnerable and you have to live with the indeterminate nature of the outcome" (196).

"Vulnerable mission," too, positions itself as the corrective to missionaries' historical collusion with imperial power in the nineteenth century. Writing from a postcolonial perspective, the prominent Argentinean theologian Néstor O. Miguez decries this past partnership as a severe misreading of the Biblical mandate "to go and make disciples" (87). Noting that the injunction was delivered to "eleven humble, doubting men taken by surprise in a rural environment in the immensities of a hostile empire" and *not* to "an imperial potentate which would use all its force, its arms and tools of dominance," Miguez argues, "missionary texts [must be] read from positions of non-power, from weakness," as "a message that restores threatened dignity, that brings confidence in the sense of divine mercy to the humble poor, affirms the power of life over death" (87). In other words, missionaries must live *among*, not *above*, those they seek to convert—a dictate that demands not only the missionary's physical presence in a society but also his keen, unceasing emotional identification with the sufferings of those living in that society. Moreover, writing on missionary praxis in the context of postcolonial South Africa, R. Simangaliso Kumalo (drawing some inspiration from the example of Desmond Tutu) contends that a missionary Christianity focused on liberation and self-transformation plays a key role in democratization and social justice—a project, he implies, that is beset by the twin obstacles of rapid secularization, on the one hand, and Christian fundamentalism, on the other (110). Reasserting the global provenance of Christianity despite its past associations with Western imperialism (i.e., missionaries "need to be open about the fact that the Bible was once used for disempowerment and oppression in South Africa, and that it is still able to be used in that way," but they must also recognize "that to the African people, the Bible is a central book and has been so before the colonial era" [103, 105]), Kumalo testifies to a growing conviction in "post-Western" missionary work: The power of mission (and its ability to attract converts) hinges on the missionary's ability to demonstrate that "the reign of God begins with freedom from social oppression and exclusion today" (Wild-Wood and Rajkumar 244).

This is missionary work gone "glocal," to borrow the terminology of one of the reports written for Edinburgh 2010. In these theological and discursive shifts, missionary Christianity resembles—far more than it departs from—the "secular" cosmopolitanisms of today. Rather than being the dogmatic imposition of one set of (Eurocentric) values upon the world, missionary Christianity *and* the new cosmopolitanisms both argue that genuine universal values arise not from a privileged "view from above" but from the ongoing negotiation between universal claims and "rooted" experiences. Robbins characterizes the "actually existing cosmopolitanisms" of today as built on an assumption that "any cosmopolitanism's normative or idealizing power must acknowledge the actual historical and geographic contexts from which it emerges" ("Introduction" 2)—a characterization of cosmopolitanism that sounds suspiciously like the missionary spirit of the twenty-first century, as expressed in the 2010 reports. Just as the new cosmopolitanisms abandoned certain Enlightenment assumptions to rehabilitate the emancipatory potential of the cosmopolitan ideal, so, too, has missionary Protestantism divorced itself from aspects of Enlightenment humanism to better realize distinctly Enlightenment projects.

To be clear, I point out these similarities not to celebrate such changes in missiology and missionary praxis. The spirit of missionary work, of course, never entails a full-scale embrace of relativism or pluralism as a normative ideology, as to do so would negate the point of evangelizing in the first place.[15] To missionaries, after all, Christianity is still absolute and infallible, even if its human practitioners are inevitably limited and flawed. Rather, I make note of these strands of missionary work—its conceptual flexibility, its spirit of accommodation, its remarkable ability to adapt and readapt in the face of contemporary exigencies and a reckoning with its role in historical injustices—to make two points. First, the beliefs, theologies, and practices underwriting the new Christian universalism in no small way resemble the values and methods espoused by the modern cosmopolitanisms. And second, this resemblance suggests that the project of imagining a moral universalism in the age of globalization is not the sole demesnes of the new cosmopolitanisms but also, unexpectedly, the *very* territory staked out by missionary Christianity.

Yet, as I discuss in my introduction, the new cosmopolitanisms have not been able to conceive of religious movements as capable of or interested in doing this sort of actual or imaginative work. Rather than recognizing the ambitions and tactics of the new Christian universalism, the new cosmopolitanisms still tend to be governed by one of the key assumptions of nineteenth-century liberalism, that religion is "a category of identification," alongside other categories including "ethnicity, race, . . . and culture" (Viswanathan xii; Brown qtd. in Lecourt, *Cultivating* 15). Thus religion is considered one among several forms of localized identity to be managed instead of a rival universalist project in its own right. In this manner, the new cosmopolitanisms have continued in the wrong-minded project of affirming "religion's rootedness in cultural or racial identity" (Lecourt, *Cultivating* 15) instead of fully apprehending the degree to which missionary Christianity has abandoned—and, moreover,

---

15. For example, Eskilt rejects pluralism on the grounds that it would undermine "our commitment to Jesus Christ as the one Lord and Savior for all humankind" (Netland qtd. in Eskilt 189). Thus, while "we positively acknowledge the descriptive fact of plurality in our world," she writes to fellow missiologists and theologians, "we must reject pluralism as a normative ideology" (186).

has predicated the success of its endeavors precisely on abandoning—cultural particularism.

I find this blind spot in cosmopolitanism troubling. My hope is that in writing this coda, laying out the twentieth- and twenty-first-century afterlives of missionary cosmopolitanism, I help in showing why and the extent to which (in Craig Calhoun's words) religious projects today so often "are the direct competitors to secular cosmopolitanism" ("Cosmopolitanism"). For, instead of evangelical religion being the ideological antithesis to cosmopolitanism, the two prove inextricable, mutually informing, quick to espouse surprisingly similar values, and quick to implement surprisingly similar strategies for negotiating differences. It turns out that to understand each, we might do well to consider them together.

WORKS CITED

Ablow, Rachel. *The Marriage of Minds: Reading Sympathy in the Victorian Marriage Plot.* Stanford: Stanford UP, 2007.

Additional Thoughts of a Barrister, to Those of the Rev. Mr. O'Callaghan, on the Dangerous Tendency of Bible Societies. Dublin: W. Folds, 1816.

"An Address to Christians, Recommending the Distribution of Religious Tracts." *The Anti-Jacobin Review: And Protestant Advocate* 54.13 (1802): 431–36.

Agathocleous, Tanya. "'The Coming Clash of East and West': Syncretism, Cosmopolitanism, and Disaffection in the Colonial Public Sphere." *Textual Practice* 31.4 (2016): 661–85.

———. "Cosmopolitanism and Literary Form." *Literature Compass* 7.6 (2010): 452–66.

———. *Urban Realism and the Cosmopolitan Imagination in the Nineteenth Century: Visible City, Invisible World.* Cambridge: Cambridge UP, 2011.

Agathocleous, Tanya, and Jason R. Rudy. "Victorian Cosmopolitanisms: Introduction." *Victorian Literature and Culture* 38.2 (2010): 389–97.

Ahmed, Siraj. "'An Unlimited Intercourse': Historical Contradictions and Imperial Romance in the Early Nineteenth Century." *Praxis Series.* Ed. Daniel O'Quinn. Nov. 2000. *Romantic Circles.* 15 June 2018. <https://www.rc.umd.edu/praxis/containment/ahmed/ahmed.html>.

Alban, Donald Jr., Robert H. Woods Jr., and Marsha Daigle-Williamson. "The Writings of William Carey: Journalism as Mission in a Modern Age." *Mission Studies* 22.1 (2005): 89–113.

Albert (Prince Consort). "Speech at the Third Jubilee of the Society for the Propagation of the Gospel in Foreign Parts, June 16, 1851." *The Principal Speeches and Addresses of His Royal Highness, the Prince Consort.* London: John Murray, 1862. 131–35.

Albrecht, Thomas. "'The Balance of Separateness and Communication': Cosmopolitan Ethics in George Eliot's *Daniel Deronda*." *ELH* 79.2 (2012): 389–416.

WORKS CITED

Anderson, Amanda. "Cosmopolitanism, Universalism, and the Divided Legacies of Modernity." *The Way We Argue Now: A Study in the Cultures of Theory*. Princeton: Princeton UP, 2006. 69–92.

———. *The Powers of Distance: Cosmopolitanism and the Cultivation of Detachment*. Princeton: Princeton UP, 2001.

Anderson, Misty G. *Imagining Methodism in Eighteenth-Century Britain: Enthusiasm, Belief & the Borders of the Self*. Baltimore: Johns Hopkins UP, 2012.

Anderson, Rufus. "Introductory Essay to the American Edition." *Memoir of Mrs. Mary Mercy Ellis, Wife of Rev. William Ellis, Missionary in the South Seas, and Foreign Secretary of the London Missionary Society*. Boston: Crocker & Brewster, 1836. vii–xxii.

Andrews, Charles Freer. SPG and Cambridge University Mission (Delhi, No. 123). MS3291/2. Notes for Commission IV: The Missionary Message in Relation to Non-Christian Religions—Hinduism. 1910 World Missionary Conference. Special Libraries and Archives. Aberdeen University.

Andrews, Stuart. *Robert Southey: History, Politics, Religion*. New York: Palgrave Macmillan, 2011.

Appiah, Kwame Anthony. *Cosmopolitanism: Ethics in a World of Strangers*. New York: Norton, 2006.

Aravamudan, Srinivas. *Guru English: South Asian Religion in a Cosmopolitan Language*. Princeton: Princeton UP, 2006.

"Art. I. *Vindicae Christianae: A Comparative Estimate of the Genius and Temper of the Greek, the Roman, the Hindu, the Mahometan, and the Christian Religions*." *The Christian Remembrancer* 1.9 (Jan. 1827): 1–9.

"Art. II—Beppo, A Venetian Story." *The British Review* 11.22 (1818): 327–33.

"Art. VIII. Hints to the Public, and the Legislature, on the Nature and Effect of Evangelical Preaching." *Monthly Review, or, Literary Journal* 57 (Oct. 1808): 180–89.

"Art X. *A Sermon Occasioned by the Death of the Rev. Joseph Towers, L. L. D. Delivered at Newington Green, June 2, 1799*." *The Anti-Jacobin Review* 4 (1800): 303–7.

"Art. XII—The Missionary, an Indian Tale." *The Critical Review, or, Annals of Literature* 23.2 (June 1811): 182–95.

Azim, Firdous. *The Colonial Rise of the Novel*. New York: Routledge, 2002.

Bain, Alexander. *James Mill: A Biography*. London: Longmans, Green, and Co., 1882.

A Barrister. *Lay Thoughts on the Indian Mutiny*. 2nd ed. London: H. Sweet, 1858.

Barruel, Abbé Augustin. *Memoirs Illustrating the History of Jacobinism: A Translation from the French of the Abbé Barruel*. London: T. Burton & Co., 1797.

Baucom, Ian. *Out of Place: Englishness, Empire, and the Locations of Identity*. Princeton: Princeton UP, 1999.

"Benevolent Institutions." *The Scourge; or, Monthly Expositor of Imposture and Folly* 3 (Feb. 1812): 132–35.

Berman, Carolyn Vellenga. *Creole Crossings: Domestic Fiction and the Reform of Colonial Slavery*. Ithaca: Cornell UP, 2005.

Bernhardt-Kabisch, Ernest. *Robert Southey*. Boston: Twayne Publishers, 1977.

Best, Stephen, and Sharon Marcus. "Surface Reading: An Introduction." *Representations* 108.1 (Fall 2009): 1–21.

Bewell, Alan. "A 'True Story . . . of Evils Overcome'": Sacred Biography, Prophecy, and Colonial Disease in Southey's *Tale of Paraguay.*" *Nineteenth-Century Contexts* 26.2 (2004): 97–124.

Bizup, Joseph. *Manufacturing Culture: Vindications of Early Victorian Industry.* Charlottesville: U of Virginia P, 2003.

Blair, Kirstie. *Form and Faith in Victorian Poetry and Religion.* Oxford: Oxford UP, 2012.

Bonfiglio, Richard. "Cosmopolitan Realism: Portable Domesticity in Brontë's Belgian Novels." *Victorian Literature and Culture* 40 (2012): 599–616.

Bogue, David. "A Circular Letter from the Associated Ministers of the Gospel." *The Missionary Magazine* (1804): 1–8.

———. "Objections Against a Mission to the Heathen, Stated and Considered." *Sermons, Preached in London, at the Formation of the Missionary Society, September 22, 23, 24, 1795.* Newburyport: Barrett & March, 1797.

Bolton, Carol. *Writing the Empire: Robert Southey and Romantic Colonialism.* London: Pickering & Chatto, 2007.

Bosch, David J. *Transforming Mission: Paradigm Shifts in Theology of Mission.* Maryknoll, NY: Orbis, 2011.

Bradley, Ian C. *The Call to Seriousness: The Evangelical Impact on the Victorians.* New York: Macmillan, 1976.

Branch, Lori. "Postsecular Studies." *The Routledge Companion to Literature and Religion.* Ed. Mark Knight. Abingdon: Routledge, 2016. 91–101.

Brantlinger, Patrick. *Rule of Darkness: British Literature and Imperialism, 1830–1914.* Ithaca: Cornell UP, 1988.

———. *Taming Cannibals: Race and the Victorians.* Ithaca: Cornell UP, 2011.

———. *Victorian Literature and Postcolonial Studies.* Edinburgh: Edinburgh UP, 2009.

Brennan, Timothy. *At Home in the World.* Cambridge: Harvard UP, 1997.

Brewer, Luther A. *Leigh Hunt and Charles Dickens: The Skimpole Caricature.* New York: Haskell House Publishers, 1971.

Brontë, Charlotte. *Jane Eyre.* New York: Penguin Books, 2003.

———. "The Missionary." *The Poems of Charlotte Brontë: A New Text and Commentary.* Ed. Victor A. Neufeldt. London: Routledge, 2015. 291–94.

———. *Selected Letters.* Ed. Margaret Smith. Oxford: Oxford UP, 2007.

Brown, William. *The History of the Propagation of Christianity Among the Heathen Since the Reformation.* Vol. 2. Edinburgh: A. Fullarton & Co., 1823.

Burder, George. "An Address to the Serious and Zealous Professors of the Gospel, of Every Denomination, Respecting an Attempt to Evangelize the Heathen." *Sermons, Preached in London, at the Formation of the Missionary Society, September 22, 23, 24, 1795.* Newburyport: Barrett & March, 1797.

Burges, Mary Anne. *The Progress of the Pilgrim Good-Intent, in Jacobinical Times.* London: John Hatchard, 1800.

Burgess, Miranda. "Sydney Owenson's Tropics." *European Romantic Review* 26.3 (2015): 281–88.

Burke, Edmund. "Edmund Burke to Abbé Barruel, May 1, 1797." *The Correspondence of Edmund Burke.* Ed. Thomas W. Copeland. Vol. 9. Cambridge: Cambridge UP, 1978. 319–20.

———. *A Letter from Mr. Burke, to a Member of the National Assembly; in Answer to Some Objections to His Book on French Affairs.* Paris: J. Dodsley, 1791.

Burton, Robert. *The Anatomy of Melancholy.* Ed. Holbrook Jackson. New York: New York Review of Books, 2001.

Buzard, James. *Disorienting Fiction: The Autoethnographic Work of Nineteenth-Century British Novels.* Princeton: Princeton UP, 2005.

Byron, George Gordon. *The Works of Lord Byron.* Vol. 4. London: John Murray; New York: Charles Scribner's Sons, 1903.

Calhoun, Craig. "Cosmopolitanism and the Ideal of Postsecular Public Reason." *The Immanent Frame: Secularism, Religion, and the Public Sphere.* Feb. 11, 2008. <http://blogs.ssrc.org/tif/2008/02/11/cosmopolitanism-and-the-ideal-of-postsecular-public-reason>.

———. "Secularism, Citizenship, and the Public Sphere." *Rethinking Secularism.* Ed. Craig Calhoun, Mark Juergensmeyer, and Jonathan VanAntwerpen. Oxford: Oxford UP, 2011. 75–91.

Calhoun, Craig, Mark Juergensmeyer, and Jonathan VanAntwerpen. "Introduction." *Rethinking Secularism.* Ed. Craig Calhoun, Mark Juergensmeyer, and Jonathan VanAntwerpen. New York: Oxford UP, 2011. 3–30.

"A Call to More Importunate Prayer for the Success of Missions." *Evangelical Magazine and Missionary Chronicle* 25 (Jan. 1817): 5–10.

Canuel, Mark. *Religion, Toleration, and British Writing, 1790–1830.* Cambridge: Cambridge UP, 2002.

Caputo, John D., and Michael J. Scanlon, eds. *God, the Gift, and Postmodernism.* Bloomington: Indiana UP, 1999.

Carens, Timothy L. *Outlandish English Subjects in the Victorian Domestic Novel.* Basingstoke: Palgrave Macmillan, 2005.

Carey, Hilary. *God's Empire: Religion and Colonialism in the British World, c. 1801–1908.* Cambridge: Cambridge UP, 2011.

Carpenter, Mary Wilson. "From Treasures to Trash, or, the Real History of 'Family Bibles.'" *Constructing Nineteenth-Century Religion: Literary, Historical, and Religious Studies in Dialogue.* Ed. Joshua King and Winter Jade Werner. Columbus: The Ohio State UP, 2019. 115–38.

Carson, Penelope. "The British Raj and the Awakening of the Evangelical Conscience: The Ambiguities of Religious Establishment and Toleration, 1698–1833." *Christian Missions and the Enlightenment.* Ed. Brian Stanley. Cambridge: William B. Eerdsmans, 2001. 45–70.

———. *The East India Company and Religion, 1698–1858.* Woodbridge: Boydell & Brewer, 2012.

Carté Engel, Katherine. "The SPCK and the American Revolution: The Limits of International Protestantism." *Church History* 81.1 (2012): 77–103.

Çelikkol, Ayşe. "Form and Global Consciousness in the Victorian Period." *Literature Compass* 10.3 (2013): 269–76.

Chakravarty, Gautam. *The Indian Mutiny and the British Imagination.* Cambridge: Cambridge UP, 2005.

Chatterjee, Partha. *The Nation and Its Fragments.* Princeton: Princeton UP, 1993.

Cheah, Pheng, and Bruce Robbins, eds. *Cosmopolitics: Thinking and Feeling Beyond the Nation.* Minneapolis: U of Minnesota P, 1998.

"Christianity and Mohammedanism." *The Eclectic Review* 7 (June 1854): 641–54.

"A Citizen of the World." *The Anti-Jacobin Review* 1.5 (1799): 593.

Clayton, John. "The Final Triumph of the Church over Her Enemies, an Encouragement to the Zealous Exertions of Her Friends." *Four Sermons, Preached in London, at the Fifteenth General Meeting of The Missionary Society.* London: Townsend, Powell & Co., 1809. 25–45.

Cleall, Esme. *Missionary Discourses of Difference: Negotiating Otherness in the British Empire, 1840–1900.* Basingstoke: Palgrave Macmillan, 2012.

Comaroff, John L., and Jean Comaroff. *Of Revelation and Revolution.* 2 vols. Chicago: U of Chicago P, 1997.

"A Copy of the Original Minutes of the Missionary Deputies Held in the Orphan House, Cape of Good Hope." 12–22 August 1817. South Africa, Incoming Correspondence, Box 7, Folder 2, Jacket C. CWM/LMS Archive. SOAS Archives and Special Collections, School of Oriental and African Studies, London.

Corbett, Mary Jean. *Family Likeness: Sex, Marriage, and Incest from Jane Austen to Virginia Woolf.* Ithaca: Cornell UP, 2008.

Cox, Jeffrey. *The British Missionary Enterprise Since 1700.* New York: Routledge, 2008.

———. *Imperial Fault Lines: Christianity and Colonial Power in India, 1818–1940.* Stanford: Stanford UP, 2002.

Cox, Jeffrey N. "Cockney Cosmopolitanism." *Nineteenth-Century Contexts* 32.3 (Sept. 2010): 245–59.

Craig, David. *Robert Southey and Romantic Apostasy: Political Argument in Britain, 1780–1840.* Woodbridge: Royal Historical Society and Boydell Press, 2007.

"Critical Remarks on 1 Thess. v.23." *The Beauties of the Evangelical Magazine.* Vol. 2. Philadelphia: William Woodward, 1803. 126–28.

Cunningham, Valentine. "'God and Nature Intended You for a Missionary's Wife': Mary Hill, Jane Eyre and Other Missionary Women in the 1840s." *Women and Missions: Past and Present Anthropological and Historical Perceptions.* Ed. Fiona Bowie, Deborah Kirkwood, and Shirley Ardener. Oxford: Berg, 1993. 85–105.

"Death of Catherine Lawrie." *The Missionary Magazine* 88.8 (1803): 397–401.

"Delhi." *The Church Missionary Gleaner* 7 (Sept. 1857): 99–100.

De Quincey, Thomas. "Idea of a Universal History on a Cosmopolitical Plan: A Translation from Kant." *The Collected Writings of Thomas De Quincey.* Ed. David Masson. Vol. 9. London: A. & C. Black, 1897. 428–44.

Derrida, Jacques. *Acts of Religion.* Ed. Gil Anidjar. New York: Routledge, 2002.

———. "Globalization, Peace, and Cosmopolitanism." *Negotiations: Interventions and Interviews, 1971–2001.* Ed. and trans. Elizabeth Rottenberg. Stanford: Stanford UP, 2002. 371–86.

Dickens, Charles. *Bleak House.* New York: Norton, 1977.

———. *The Letters of Charles Dickens.* Ed. Georgina Hogarth and Mary Dickens. London: Macmillan and Co., 1893.

———. "Review: *Narrative of the Expedition Sent by Her Majesty's Government to the River Niger in 1841, Under the Command of Captain H. D. Trotter, R. N.*" *Examiner* (19 Aug. 1848): 531–33.

Dixon, W. Hepworth, ed. *Lady Morgan's Memoirs: Autobiography, Diaries and Correspondence.* 3 vols. Leipzig: Bernhard Tachnitz, 1863.

Donovan, Julie. *Sydney Owenson, Lady Morgan and the Politics of Style.* Palo Alto: Academica Press, 2009.

Douglas, Mary. *How Institutions Think*. Syracuse: Syracuse UP, 1986.

Dwight, Timothy. "Appendix A." *Counsels to a Newly-Wedded Pair; A Companion to the Honeymoon and a Remembrancer for Life*. By John Morison. London: F. Westley and A. H. Davis, 1830. 73–76.

Edelstein, Dan. "Enlightenment Rights Talk." *The Journal of Modern History* 86.3 (2014): 530–65.

Edmond, Rod. *Representing the South Pacific: Colonial Discourse from Cook to Gauguin*. Cambridge: Cambridge UP, 1997.

Elbourne, Elizabeth. *Blood Ground: Colonialism, Missions, and the Contest for Christianity in the Cape Colony and Britain, 1799–1853*. Montreal: McGill-Queen's University, 2002.

Ellis, John Eimeo. *Life of William Ellis: Missionary to the South Seas and to Madagascar*. London: John Murray, 1873.

Ellis, William. *The History of the London Missionary Society*. Vol. 1. London: John Snow, 1844.

———. *Polynesian Researches: During a Residence of Nearly Six Years in the South Sea Islands, Including Descriptions of the National History and Scenery of the Islands, with Remarks on the History, Mythology, Traditions, Government, Arts, Manners, and Customs of the Inhabitants*. 2 vols. London: Fisher, Son, & Jackson, 1829.

Escobar, Samuel. "Mission from Everywhere to Everyone: The Home Base in a New Century." *Mission Then and Now*. Ed. David A. Kerr and Kenneth R. Ross. Oxford: Regnum, 2009. 185–98.

Eskilt, Ingrid. "Can We—and Dare We—Present a Global Truth in a Pluralistic Age? A Response to Stefan Gustavsson." *The Church Going Glocal: Mission and Globalisation*. Ed. Tormod Engelsviken, Erling Lundeby, and Dagfinn Solheim. Oxford: Regnum, 2011. 185–89.

"Foreign Intelligence: India-Church Missionary Society." *The Missionary Register* (Nov. 1816): 440–56.

Foster, John. "Essay IV. On Some of the Causes by Which Evangelical Religion Has Been Rendered Less Unacceptable to Persons of Cultivated Taste." *Essays in the Series of Letters to a Friend*. Vol. 2. Andover: Mark Newman, 1826. 98–297.

Foucault, Michel. *The Archaeology of Knowledge*. London: Tavistock, 1972.

Fox, Joseph. *An Appeal to the Members of the London Missionary Society, Against a Resolution of the Directors of That Society, Dated March 26, 1810*. London, 1810.

Franklin, Michael J. "'Passion's Empire': Sydney Owenson's 'Indian Venture,' Phoenicianism, Orientalism, and Binarism." *Studies in Romanticism* 45.2 (2006): 181–97.

Freeman, Kathryn. "'Eternally Disunited': Gender, Empire, and Epistemology in Sydney Owenson's *The Missionary*." *Wordsworth Circle* 36.1 (2005): 21–28.

Frykenberg, Robert Eric. "Introduction: Dealing with Contested Definitions and Controversial Perspectives." *Christians and Missionaries in India: Cross-Cultural Communication since 1500*. Ed. Robert Frykenberg. Grand Rapids: Wm. B. Eerdmans, 2003. 1–32.

Fulford, Tim. "Blessed Bane: Christianity and Colonial Disease in Southey's *Tale of Paraguay*." *Romanticism on the Net* 24 (Nov. 2001). <http://id.erudit.org/iderudit/005998ar>.

Fulford, Tim, and Debbie Lee. "The Jenneration of Disease: Vaccination, Romanticism, and Revolution." *Studies in Romanticism* 39.1 (2000): 139–63.

Fulford, Tim, Debbie Lee, and Peter J. Kitson. *Literature, Science and Exploration in the Romantic Era: Bodies of Knowledge*. Cambridge: Cambridge UP, 2004.

Gallagher, Catherine. *The Body Economic: Life, Death, and Sensation in Political Economy and the Victorian Novel*. Princeton: Princeton UP, 2006.

Galperin, William H. "Anti-Romanticism, Victorianism, and the Case of Wordsworth." *Victorian Poetry* 24.4 (1986): 357–71.

Gandhi, Leela. *Affective Communities: Anticolonial Thought, Fin-de-Siècle Radicalism, and the Politics of Friendship*. Durham: Duke UP, 2006.

Gaskell, Elizabeth. *The Life of Charlotte Brontë*. New York: Harper & Brothers Publishers, 1900.

Gibson, Mary Ellis. "Henry Martyn and England's Christian Empire: Rereading *Jane Eyre* Through Missionary Biography." *Victorian Literature and Culture* (1999): 419–42.

Gillespie, William. *An Exposure of the Unchristian Principles Set Forth in Mr George Combe's Work Entitled, "The Constitution of Man, Considered in Relation to External Objects;" Being an Antidote to the Poison of That Publication*. Edinburgh: Thomas Clark, 1836.

Gledstone, J. P. "A Visit to an English Roman Catholic College." *Evangelical Magazine and Missionary Chronicle* 11 (Nov. 1881): 730–36.

Glen, Heather. *Charlotte Brontë: The Imagination in History*. Oxford: Oxford UP, 2002.

Goodlad, Lauren M. E. *The Victorian Geopolitical Aesthetic: Realism, Sovereignty, and Transnational Experience*. Oxford: Oxford UP, 2015.

Goodlad, Lauren M. E., and Andrew Sartori. "The Ends of History: Introduction." *Victorian Studies* 55.4 (2013): 591–614.

Goodlad, Lauren M. E., and Julia Wright. "Introduction and Keywords: Victorian Internationalisms." *Romanticism and Victorianism on the Net* 48 (Nov. 2007). <http://www.erudit.org/revue/ravon/2007/v/n48/017435ar.html>.

"The Good Pastor." *The Evangelical Magazine* (Jan. 1806): 12–13.

Gottlieb, Evan. *Romantic Globalism: British Literature and the Modern World Order, 1750–1830*. Columbus: The Ohio State UP, 2014.

Greatheed, Samuel. "A Mission to the Heathen, Founded upon the Moral Law." *Sermons, Preached in London, at the Formation of the Missionary Society, September 22, 23, 24, 1795: To Which Are Prefixed, Memorials, Respecting the Establishment and First Attempts at That Society*. Newburyport: Barrett & March, 1797.

Griffiths, Devin. *The Age of Analogy: Science and Literature Between the Darwins*. Baltimore: Johns Hopkins UP, 2016.

———. "The Comparative History of *A Tale of Two Cities*." *ELH* 80.3 (2013): 811–38.

Gunson, Neil. *Messengers of Grace: Evangelical Missionaries in the South Seas, 1797–1860*. Melbourne: Oxford UP, 1978.

Habermas, Jürgen. "Secularism's Crisis of Faith: Notes on a Post-Secular Society." *New Perspectives Quarterly* 25 (2008): 17–29.

Haddad, Samir. "Derrida and Democracy at Risk." *Contretemps* 4 (Sept. 2004): 29–44.

Hall, Catherine. *Civilising Subjects: Metropole and Colony in the English Imagination 1830–1867*. Chicago: U of Chicago P, 2002.

Heady, Emily. "The Polis's Different Voices: Narrating England's Progress in Dickens's *Bleak House*." *Texas Studies in Literature and Language* 48.4 (2006): 312–39.

Herbert, Christopher. *Culture and Anomie: Ethnographic Imagination in the Nineteenth Century*. Chicago: U of Chicago P, 1991.

———. *War of No Pity: The Indian Mutiny and Victorian Trauma*. Princeton: Princeton UP, 2008.

Herppich, Birgit. *Pitfalls of Trained Incapacity: The Unintended Effects of Integral Missionary Training in the Basel Mission on Its Early Work in Ghana (1828-1840)*. Cambridge: James Clarke & Co., 2016.

Hey, John. "The Fulness of Times." *Sermons, Preached in London, at the Formation of the Missionary Society, September 22, 23, 24, 1795*. Newburyport: Barrett & March, 1797.

Hilton, Boyd. *The Age of Atonement: The Influence of Evangelicalism on Social and Economic Thought, 1795-1865*. Oxford: Oxford UP, 1988.

Hoffman, C. "The Missionary Bride." *Bentley's Miscellany: Vol. IV.* London: Richard Bentley, 1838. 330–37.

Hogg, Thomas. *Life of Percy Bysshe Shelley*. Vol. 1. London: Edward Moxon, 1858.

Hole, Charles. *The Early History of the Church Missionary Society for Africa and the East to the End of A. D. 1814*. London: Church Missionary Society, 1896.

Hollander, Rachel. *Narrative Hospitality in Late Victorian Fiction: Novel Ethics*. New York: Routledge, 2013.

Hollinger, David A. "Not Universalists, Not Pluralists: The New Cosmopolitans Find Their Own Way." *Conceiving Cosmopolitanism: Theory, Context, and Practice*. Ed. Steven Vertovec and Robin Cohen. Oxford: Oxford UP, 2002. 227–39.

"Home Proceedings: Society for Promoting Christian Knowledge. Archdeacon Middleton's Charge to Rev. C. A. Jacobi." *The Missionary Register for the Year 1814: Containing an Abstract of the Proceedings of the Principal Missionary and Bible Societies Throughout the World*. Vol. 2. London: Ellerton and Henderson, 1814. 11–20.

Hopkins, Dwight N. "The Religion of Globalization." *Religions/Globalizations: Theories and Cases*. Ed. Dwight N. Hopkins, David Batstone, Lois Ann Lorentzen, and Eduardo Mendieta. Durham: Duke UP, 2001. 7–32.

"India." *The Missionary Magazine and Chronicle* 21.258 (Nov. 1857): 682–87.

"Inquisition in Goa, in the East Indies." *Evangelical Magazine* 19 (1811): 351.

"Introduction." *The Scottish Missionary Register for 1832* 13 (1832): iii–v.

[Jackson, John]. *Church Missions. Speech of the Right Rev. the Lord Bishop of Lincoln, at a Public Meeting, Held at Nottingham, June 30, 1856*. London: Bell and Daldy, 1856.

Jager, Colin. "Introduction." *Praxis Series*. Ed. Colin Jager. *Romantic Circles*. Aug. 2008. <https://www.rc.umd.edu/praxis/secularism/jager/jager_intro.html>.

Jeal, Tim. *Livingstone*. New Haven; London: Yale UP, 2013.

"Jesus Wept." *The Baptist Magazine* 1 (Nov. 1826): 503–7.

Johnston, Anna. *Missionary Writing and Empire, 1800–1860*. Cambridge: Cambridge UP, 2003.

Johnston, H. H. (Harry). "British Missions and Missionaries in Africa." *The Nineteenth Century* 22 (July–Dec. 1887): 708–24.

Jørgensen, Jørgen. *State of Christianity in the Island of Otaheite, and a Defence of the Pure Precepts of the Gospel, Against Modern Antichrists, with Reasons for the Ill Success Which Attends Christian Missionaries in Their Attempts to Convert the Heathens*. Reading: Snare and Man, 1811.

Jørgenson, Knud. "Edinburgh 2010 in Global Perspective." *The Church Going Glocal: Mission and Globalisation*. Ed. Tormod Engelsviken, Erling Lundeby, and Dagfinn Solheim. Oxford: Regnum, 2011. 3–19.

J. R. "Reflexions on the Conversion of the Natives of India to Christianity." *The Monthly Magazine and Universal Register* 2.7 (Aug. 1814): 28–33.

Judson, Barbara. "Under the Influence: Owenson, Shelley, and the Religion of Dreams." *Modern Philology* 104.2 (2006): 202–23.

Kale, Madhavi. *Fragments of Empire: Capital, Slavery, & Indian Indentured Labor in the British Caribbean*. Philadelphia: U of Pennsylvania P, 1998.

Kant, Immanuel. "An Answer to the Question: 'What Is Enlightenment?'" *Kant: Political Writings*. Trans. H. B. Nisbet. Ed. H. S. Reiss. Cambridge: Cambridge UP, 1991. 54–60.

———. "Idea for a Universal History with a Cosmopolitan Purpose." *Kant: Political Writings*. Trans. H. B. Nisbet. Ed. H. S. Reiss. Cambridge: Cambridge UP, 1991. 41–53.

———. "Perpetual Peace: A Philosophical Sketch." *Kant: Political Writings*. Trans. H. B. Nisbet. Ed. H. S. Reiss. Cambridge: Cambridge UP, 1991. 93–115.

Kaplan, Cora. "'A Heterogeneous Thing': Female Childhood and the Rise of Racial Thinking in Victorian Britain." *Human, All Too Human*. Ed. Diana Fuss. New York: Routledge, 1996. 169–202.

Kauffman, Michael W. "The Religious, the Secular, and Literary Studies: Rethinking the Secularization Narrative in Histories of the Profession." *New Literary History* 38.4 (2007): 607–28.

Keane, Webb. *Christian Moderns: Freedom & Fetish in the Mission Encounter*. Berkeley: U of California P, 2007.

Keirstead, Christopher M. "Cosmopolitan Soul: Travels in Body and Spirit with Browning's Cleon and Karshish." *LIT: Literature Interpretation Theory* 27.1 (2016): 7–28.

———. *Victorian Poetry, Europe, and the Challenge of Cosmopolitanism*. Columbus: The Ohio State UP, 2011.

Kennedy, James. *The Great Mutiny of 1857: Its Causes, Features, and Results*. London: Ward and Co., 1858.

Kidd, Colin. *The Forging of Races: Race and Scripture in the Protestant Atlantic World, 1600–2000*. Cambridge: Cambridge UP, 2006.

King, Joshua, and Winter Jade Werner. "Introduction." *Constructing Nineteenth-Century Religion: Literary, Historical, and Religious Studies in Dialogue*. Columbus: The Ohio State UP, 2019. 1–21.

Kleingeld, Pauline. "Six Varieties of Cosmopolitanism in Late Eighteenth-Century Germany." *Journal of the History of Ideas* 60.3 (1999): 505–24.

Knight, Mark, and Emma Mason. *Nineteenth-Century Religion and Literature: An Introduction*. Oxford: Oxford UP, 2006.

Kumalo, R. Simangaliso. "The Bible in and Through Mission and Mission in the Bible in Postcolonial Africa." *Foundations for Mission*. Ed. Emma Wild-Wood and Peniel Rajkumar. Oxford: Regnum, 2013. 96–110.

Kurnick, David. "Unspeakable George Eliot." *Victorian Literature and Culture* 38.2 (2010): 489–509.

Leask, Nigel. *British Romantic Writers and the East: Anxieties of Change*. Cambridge: Cambridge UP, 1992.

Lecourt, Sebastian. *Cultivating Belief: Victorian Anthropology, Liberal Aesthetics, and the Secular Imagination*. New York: Oxford UP, 2018.

———. "Matthew Arnold and Religion's Cosmopolitan Histories." *Victorian Literature and Culture* 38.2 (2010): 467–87.

Ledger-Lomas, Michael. "Introduction." *The Oxford History of Protestant Dissenting Traditions*. Ed. Timothy Larsen and Michael Ledger-Lomas. Vol. 3. Oxford: Oxford UP, 2017. 1–36.

Lennon, Joseph. *Irish Orientalism: A Literary and Intellectual History*. Syracuse: Syracuse UP, 2004.

[Lewis, Sarah]. *Woman's Mission*. 4th ed. London: John W. Parker, 1839.

Lichtenstein, Henry. *Travels in South Africa, in the Years 1803, 1804, 1805, and 1806*. Trans. Anne Plumptre. London: Henry Colburn, 1812.

Liebau, Heike. "Country Priests, Catechists, Schoolmasters, and the Tranquebar Mission." *Christians and Missionaries in India: Cross-Cultural Communication Since 1500*. Ed. Robert Eric Frykenberg. Grand Rapids, MI: William B. Eerdmans, 2003. 70–92.

Lindsay, James. *A Sermon, Occasioned by the Death of the Rev. Joseph Towers, LL. D. Delivered at Newington Green, June 2d, 1799, by the Rev. James Lindsay, to Which is Added the Oration, Delivered at His Internment, by the Rev. Thomas Jervis*. London: J. Johnson, 1799.

Livingstone, David. *Dr. Livingstone's Cambridge Lectures*. Ed. Rev. William Monk. London: Bell and Daldy, 1860.

Lloyd, Arthur. *The Wheat Among the Tares: Studies of Buddhism in Japan*. London: Macmillan and Co., 1908.

"Luxima, the Prophetess." *Calcutta Review* 33.64 (1859): i–v.

Madsen, Emily. "William Ellis's 'A Journal of a Tour Around Hawai'i, the Largest of the Sandwich Islands': Writings from Britain's Anglican and Evangelical Missionaries in Hawai'i." NAVSA Conference, St. Petersburg, FL, Oct. 11–14, 2018. Unpublished conference paper.

Malchow, Howard. *Gothic Images of Race in Nineteenth-Century Fiction*. Stanford: Stanford UP, 1996.

Marcus, Sharon. *Between Women: Friendship, Desire, and Marriage in Victorian England*. Princeton: Princeton UP, 2007.

Martyn, Henry. *The Life and Letters of the Rev. Henry Martyn, B. D. 1837*. Ed. John Sargent. 10th ed. London: Seeley, Jackson, and Halliday, 1862.

Marx, Karl. Letter to Frederic Engels, Jan. 24, 1852. *Marx-Engels Correspondence 1852. Marx & Engels Internet Archive*. <https://marxists.catbull.com/archive/marx/works/1852/letters/52_01_24.htm>.

Masuzawa, Tomoko. *The Invention of World Religions: Or, How European Universalism Was Preserved in the Language of Pluralism*. Chicago: U of Chicago P, 2005.

Mathers, James. (Bangalore, S. India, No. 203). MS3291/2. Notes for Commission IV: The Missionary Message in Relation to Non-Christian Religions—Hinduism. 1910 World Missionary Conference. Special Libraries and Archives, Aberdeen University.

Maurice, Frederick Denison. *The Indian Crisis: Five Sermons*. Cambridge: Macmillan and Co., 1857.

McCaw, Neil. *George Eliot and Victorian Historiography: Imagining the National Past*. Basingstoke: Palgrave Macmillan, 2000.

McClintock, Anne. *Imperial Leather: Race, Gender, and Sexuality in the Colonial Contest*. New York: Routledge, 1995.

McCracken, John. *Politics & Christianity in Malawi 1875–1940: The Impact of the Livingstonian Mission in the Northern Province*. 3rd ed. Cambridge: Cambridge University Press, 1977. Rpt. Zomba, Malawi: Kachere Series, 2000.

McKee, Patricia. "Racial Strategies in *Jane Eyre*." *Victorian Literature and Culture* 37 (2009): 67–83.

McMurran, Mary Helen. "The New Cosmopolitanism and the Eighteenth Century." *Eighteenth-Century Studies* 47.1 (2013): 19–38.

McParland, Robert. *Charles Dickens's American Audience*. Plymouth: Lexington Books, 2010.

Memoir of the Rev. J. T. Van Der Kemp, M. D. Late Missionary in South Africa. 3rd ed. London: J. Dennett, 1812.

"Memoirs of a Missionary. Fragment III." *The Satirist, or, Monthly Meteor* 8 (Aug. 1810): 281–87.

Mendieta, Eduardo. "Society's Religion: The Rise of Social Theory, Globalization, and the Invention of Religion." *Religions/Globalizations: Theories and Cases*. Ed. Dwight N. Hopkins, David Batstone, Lois Ann Lorentzen, and Eduardo Mendieta. Durham: Duke UP, 2001. 46–65.

Messmore, J. H. Foreign Board of Missions, Methodist Episcopal Church (Pauri, Garhael, India, No. 203A). MS3291/2. Notes for Commission IV: The Missionary Message in Relation to Non-Christian Religions—Hinduism. 1910 World Missionary Conference. Special Libraries and Archives, Aberdeen University.

Meyer, Susan. "Colonialism and the Figurative Strategy of *Jane Eyre*." *Victorian Studies* 33.2 (Winter 2009): 247–68.

Miguez, Néstor. "Biblical Foundations for Liberative Mission from Latin America." *Foundations for Mission*. Ed. Emma Wild-Wood and Peniel Rajkumar. Oxford: Regnum, 2013. 85–95.

Mill, John Stuart. *Principles of Political Economy with Some of Their Applications to Social Philosophy*. Ed. J. M. Robson. Toronto: U of Toronto P, 1965.

"Minutes August 5th, 1799." CMS/G/C/1. CMS Archives. Cadbury Research Library. University of Birmingham.

"Minutes May 4th, 1802." CMS/G/C/1. CMS Archives. Cadbury Research Library. University of Birmingham.

"Minutes Nov 4th, 1799." CMS/G/C/1. CMS Archives. Cadbury Research Library. University of Birmingham.

"Missionary Conference at Benares." *The Church Missionary Intelligencer* 8 (1857): 260–64.

"Missionary Conference in Edinburgh." *The Mercury* (16 June 1910): 5.

"Missionary Contributions, from the 1st to the 30th of November, 1842, Inclusive." *The Evangelical Magazine and Missionary Chronicle* 21 (Jan. 1843): 51–52.

"Missionary Contributions, from the 1st to the 31st of December, 1842, Inclusive." *The Evangelical Magazine and Missionary Chronicle* 21 (Jan. 1843): 153–55.

Mitchell, John Murray. *Indian Missions; Viewed in Connexion with the Mutiny and Other Recent Events*. London: James Nisbet and Co., 1859.

Mitford, Mary Russell. *Recollections of a Literary Life; or, Books, Places, or People*. 1852. Vol. 2. London: Richard Bentley, 1857.

"Modern Visionaries." *The Evangelical Magazine and Missionary Chronicle* 13 (1805): 40–41.

Mogenson, Mogens. "A Missiology of Listening for a Folk Church in a Postmodern Context." *Foundations for Mission*. Ed. Emma Wild-Wood and Peniel Rajkumar. Oxford: Regnum, 2013. 190–204.

Moore, Grace. *Dickens and Empire: Discourses of Class, Race and Colonialism in the Works of Charles Dickens*. Aldershot: Ashgate, 2004.

Mott, John R. "The Coming World Missionary Conference." *The Missionary Review of the World* 31 (Dec. 1908): 927–36.

Mukerjee, N. C. (Allahabad, No. 208). MS3291/2. Notes for Commission IV: The Missionary Message in Relation to Non-Christian Religions—Hinduism. 1910 World Missionary Conference. Special Libraries and Archives, Aberdeen University.

Mullens, Joseph. *Ten Years Missionary Labour in India Between 1852 and 1861*. London: James Nisbet & Co., 1863.

Murray, Jocelyn. "Anglican and Protestant Missionary Societies in Great Britain: Their Use of Women as Missionaries from the Late 18th to the Late 19th Century." *Exchange* 21.1 (Apr. 1992): 1–28.

"Necessity of Greatly-Enlarged Liberality." *Missionary Register* 16 (June 1828): 271–72.

Neill, Stephen. *A History of Christian Mission*. 2nd ed. London: Penguin, 1990.

Neufeldt, Victor A. "Introduction." *The Poems of Charlotte Brontë: A New Text and Commentary*. Ed. Victor A. Neufeldt. London: Routledge, 2015. xxi–xlvii.

"New Publications." *The Asiatic Journal and Monthly Miscellany* 19 (1825): 269.

Nussbaum, Martha. "Kant and Cosmopolitanism." *Perpetual Peace: Essays on Kant's Cosmopolitan Ideal*. Ed. James Bohmann and Matthias Lutz-Bachmann. Cambridge: MIT Press, 1997. 25–58.

———. "Patriotism and Cosmopolitanism." *For Love of Country?* Ed. Joshua Cohen. Boston: Beacon Press, 2002. 3–20.

Odie, Geoffrey A. "Constructing 'Hinduism': The Impact of the Protestant Missionary Movement on Hindu Self-Understanding." *Christians and Missionaries in India: Cross-Cultural Communication Since 1500*. Ed. Robert Eric Frykenberg. Grand Rapids: William B. Eerdsmans, 2003. 155–82.

Oldham, D. "On the Peace Movement, with Some Account of the Late Peace Congress, at Paris.—IX." *The Methodist New Connexion Magazine, and Evangelical Repository* 53 (June 1850): 261–65.

Oliphant, Margaret. "Mill on *The Subjection of Women*." *Blackwood's Edinburgh Review* 130 (Oct. 1869): 572–602.

Olmanson, Eric D. *The Future City on the Inland Sea: A History of the Imaginative Geographies of Lake Superior*. Athens: Ohio UP, 2007.

"On Marriage." *The Evangelical Magazine and Missionary Chronicle* 24 (Feb. 1816): 46–49.

"Otaheitean Journals." *Transactions of the Missionary Society* 1 (1804): 1–258.

Owenson, Sydney (Lady Morgan). *Lady Morgan's Memoirs: Autobiography, Diaries and Correspondence*. Ed. W. Hepworth Dixon. 3 vols. Leipzig: Bernhard Tachnitz, 1863.

———. *Luxima, the Prophetess: A Tale of India*. London: Charles Westerton, 1859.

———. *The Missionary: An Indian Tale*. Ed. Julia M. Wright. Toronto: Broadview, 2002.

———. *The O'Briens and the O'Flahertys*. Ed. Julia M. Wright. Toronto: Broadview, 2013.

Parrinder, Patrick. *Authors and Authority: English and American Criticism, 1750–1990*. New York: Columbia UP, 1991.

Parsons, Cóilín. "'Greatly Altered': The Life of Sydney Owenson's Indian Novel." *Victorian Literature and Culture* 38 (2010): 373–85.

Patton, Cornelius H. "World Missionary Conference: Report of Meeting in Edinburgh." *The Missionary Herald Containing the Proceedings of the American Board of Commissioners for Foreign Missions* 106 (Aug. 1910): 351–54.

"The Peace." *Evangelical Magazine and Missionary Chronicle* 22 (Oct. 1814): 391–93.

Perera, Suvendrini. *Reaches of Empire: The English Novel from Edgeworth to Dickens*. New York: Columbia UP, 1991.

Perry, Ruth. *Novel Relations: The Transformation of Kinship in English Literature and Culture, 1748–1818*. Cambridge: Cambridge UP, 2006.

Peterson, Linda H. *Traditions of Victorian Women's Autobiography: The Poetics and Politics of Life Writing*. Charlottesville: U of Virginia P, 1999.

Philip, Robert. *The Life, Times, and Missionary Enterprises of the Reverend John Campbell*. London: John Snow, 1841.

Plasa, Carl. "Silent Revolt: Slavery and the Politics of Metaphor in *Jane Eyre*." *The Discourse of Slavery: Aphra Behn to Toni Morrison*. Ed. Carl Plasa and Betty Joan Ring. New York: Routledge, 1994. 64–93.

Pocock, J. G. A. *Barbarism and Religion: The Enlightenments of Edward Gibbon, 1737–1764*. Vol. 1. Cambridge: Cambridge UP, 1999.

Pope, Norris. *Dickens and Charity*. New York: Columbia UP, 1978.

Porter, Andrew. "An Overview, 1700–1914." *Missions and Empire*. Ed. Norman Ethrington. New York: Oxford UP, 2005. 40–63.

———. *Religion Versus Empire? British Protestant Missionaries and Overseas Expansion, 1700–1914*. Manchester: Manchester UP, 2004.

Pratt, Lynda. "Introduction: Robert Southey and the Contexts of English Romanticism." *Robert Southey and the Contexts of English Romanticism*. Ed. Lynda Pratt. London: Routledge, 2006. xvii–xxix.

Price, Richard. *Making Empire: Colonial Encounters and the Creation of Imperial Rule in Nineteenth-Century Africa*. Cambridge: Cambridge UP, 2008.

Price, Richard. *Observations on the Nature of Civil Liberty, the Principles of Government, and the Justice and Policy of the War with America*. Philadelphia: John Dunlap, 1776.

Prichard, James Cowles. *Researches into the Physical History of Mankind*. 4th ed. Vol. 1. London: Houlston and Stoneman, 1851.

"Professor Lichtenstein Corrected in Regard to Dr. Van der Kemp." *The New Monthly Magazine and Universal Register* 2.12 (Jan. 1815): 518–19.

Rajan, Balachandra. *Under Western Eyes: India from Milton to Macauley*. Durham: Duke UP, 1999.

Ramachandra, Vinoth. "A World of Religions and a Gospel of Transformation." *Edinburgh 2010: Mission Then and Now*. Ed. Donald A. Kerr and Kenneth R. Ross. Oxford: Regnum, 2009. 139–51.

Rangarajan, Padma. *Imperial Babel: Translation, Exoticism, and the Long Nineteenth Century*. New York: Fordham UP, 2014.

Reiss, H. S. "Introduction." *Kant: Political Writings*. Trans. H. B. Nisbet. Ed. H. S. Reiss. Cambridge: Cambridge UP, 1991. 1–40.

Report of Commission IV: The Missionary Message in Relation to Non-Christian Religions. Edinburgh and London: Oliphant, Anderson & Ferrier; New York, Chicago, Toronto: Fleming H. Revell Company, [1910].

Report of the Directors to the Twenty-Seventh General Meeting of The Missionary Society, Usually Called The London Missionary Society, on Thursday, May 10, 1821. London: F. Westley, J. Nisbet; Bristol: A. Browne and T. D. Clarke; Manchester: M. Richardson; Edinburgh: Oliphant, Waugh, and Innes; Dublin: La Grange, 1821.

"Review: Modern Literature: A Novel in Three Volumes." *The Anti-Jacobin Review* 75.19 (1804): 44–55.

Reynolds, Nicole. "Suicide, Romance, and Imperial Rebellion: Sati and the Lucretia Story in Sydney Owenson's *The Missionary: An Indian Tale*." *Literature Compass* 12.12 (2015): 675–82.

Rice, Benjamin. "Letter from Rev. Benjamin Rice, Bangalore, Sept. 23rd." *The Missionary Magazine and Chronicle* 21.256 (Dec. 1857): 267.

Ritson, J. H. *Records of Missionary Secretaries, an Account of the Celebration of the Centenary of the London Secretaries' Association*. London: United Council for Missionary Education, 1920.

Robbins, Bruce. "Afterword: Secularism, Cosmopolitanism, and Romanticism." *Praxis Series*. Ed. Colin Jager. *Romantic Circles*. Aug. 2008. <https://www.rc.umd.edu/praxis/secularism/robbins/robbins.html>.

———. "Introduction Part I: Actually Existing Cosmopolitanism." *Cosmopolitics: Thinking and Feeling Beyond the Nation*. Ed. Pheng Cheah and Bruce Robbins. Minneapolis: U of Minnesota P, 1998. 1–19.

Robert, Dana L. "Introduction." *Converting Colonialism: Visions and Realities in Mission History, 1706–1914*. Ed. by Dana L. Robert. Grand Rapids: William B. Eerdmans, 2008. 1–20.

Roberts, Daniel Sanjiv. "Beneath High Romanticism: 'Southeian' Orientations in De Quincey." *Robert Southey and the Contexts of English Romanticism*. Ed. Lynda Pratt. Aldershot: Ashgate, 2006. 37–48.

Robison, John. *Proofs of a Conspiracy Against All the Religions and Governments of Europe, Carried on in the Secret Meetings of Free Masons, Illuminati, and Reading Societies*. New York: George Forman, 1798.

Ross, Kenneth R., and David A. Kerr. "The Commissions After a Century." *Mission Then and Now*. Ed. David A. Kerr and Kenneth R. Ross. Oxford: Regnum, 2009. 307–17.

Rutz, Michael A. *The British Zion: Congregationalism, Politics, and Empire, 1790–1850*. Waco: Baylor UP, 2011.

———. "The Politicizing of Evangelical Dissent, 1811–1813." *Parliamentary History* 20.2 (2001): 187–207.

Salesa, Damon. *Racial Crossings: Race, Intermarriage, and the Victorian British Empire*. Oxford: Oxford UP, 2011.

Schaffer, Talia. *Romance's Rival: Familiar Marriage in Victorian Fiction*. Kindle ed. New York: Oxford UP, 2016.

Schlereth, Thomas. *The Cosmopolitan Ideal in Enlightenment Thought: Its Form and Function in the Ideas of Franklin, Hume, and Voltaire, 1694–1790*. Notre Dame: U of Notre Dame P, 1977.

Scott, J. Barton. *Spiritual Despots: Modern Hinduism & the Genealogies of Self-Rule*. Chicago: U of Chicago P, 2016.

Scrivener, Michael. *The Cosmopolitan Ideal*. Abingdon: Routledge, 2015.

Sedgwick, Adam. "A Prefatory Letter." *Dr. Livingstone's Cambridge Lectures*. London: Deighton, Bell, & Co., 1860. 49–136.

Seed, John. *Dissenting Histories: Religious Division and the Politics of Memory in Eighteenth-Century England*. Edinburgh: Edinburgh UP, 2008.

"A Sermon Preached at the Parish Church of St. Andrew by the Wardrobe and St. Anne, Blackfriars, on Tuesday in Whitsun Week, May 26, 1801, Before the Society for Missions to Africa and the East, Instituted by Members of the Established Church, Being their First Anniversary." *Proceedings of the Society for Missions to Africa and the East, Instituted by Members of the Established Church. From the Formation of the Society to Whit-Tuesday, 1805*. London: Jaques and Co., 1801–1805. 1–111.

Sharpe, Charles Kirkpatrick. *Letters from and to Charles Kirkpatrick Sharpe*. Ed. Alexander Allardyce. Vol. 1. Edinburgh: William Blackwood and Sons, 1858.

Sharpe, Jenny. *Allegories of Empire: The Figure of Woman in the Colonial Text*. Minneapolis: U of Minnesota P, 1993.

Shenk, Wilbert R. *Henry Venn: Missionary Statesman*. Eugene: Wipf and Stock Publishers, 1983.

Sivasundaram, Sujit. *Nature and the Godly Empire: Science and the Evangelical Mission in the Pacific*. Cambridge: Cambridge UP, 2005.

Slater, Thomas Ebenezer. (Bangalore, No. 229). MS3291/2. Notes for Commission IV: The Missionary Message in Relation to Non-Christian Religions—Hinduism. 1910 World Missionary Conference. Special Libraries and Archives, Aberdeen University.

———. *Keshab Chandra Sen and the Brahma Samaj*. Calcutta: Thacker, Spink and Co.; London: James Clarke and Co., 1884.

Smith, Anthony D. *Nations and Nationalism in a Global Era*. Cambridge: Polity, 1995.

Smith, George. *The Life of William Carey, D. D.: Shoemaker and Missionary*. London: John Murray, 1885.

Smith, Sydney. "India Missions (Edinburgh Review, 1808)." *The Works of the Rev. Sydney Smith*. Philadelphia: Carey and Hart, 1848. 48–61.

Smith, Vanessa. *Literary Culture and the Pacific: Nineteenth Century Textual Encounters*. Cambridge: Cambridge UP, 1998.

"Some Moral Aspects of the Great Exhibition." *Economist* 9 (17 May 1851): 531–32.

Sorkin, David. *The Religious Enlightenment: Protestants, Jews, and Catholics from London to Vienna*. Princeton: Princeton UP, 2008.

"South African Mission." *Transactions of the Missionary Society* 1 (1804): 323–507.

Southey, Robert. "Art. I—*Polynesian Researches, During a Residence of Nearly Six Years, in the South Sea Islands*." *The Quarterly Review* 43.85 (May 1830): 1–54.

———. "Art. II. Transactions of the Missionary Society." *The Annual Review and History of Literature* 3 (Jan. 1804): 621–34.

———. "Art. II. Transactions of the Missionary Society in the South Sea Islands." *Quarterly Review* 2.3 (Aug. 1809): 24–61.

———. "Art. LXIV. Transactions of the Missionary Society." *The Annual Review and History of Literature* 2 (Jan. 1803): 189–201.

———. "Art. LXXI: Periodical Accounts Relative to the Baptist Missionary Society." *The Annual Review and History of Literature* 1 (Jan. 1802): 207–18.

———. "Art. XVII. Periodical Accounts Relative to the Baptist Missionary Society." *The Quarterly Review* 1.1 (Feb. 1809): 193–226.

———. Letter to Bertha Southey, May 1, 1820. *Romantic Circles*. <www.rc.umd.edu/editions/southey_letters/Part_Six/HTML/letterEEd.26.3474.html>.

———. Letter to Henry Herbert Southey, Dec. 4, 1804. *Romantic Circles*. <https://romantic-circles.org/editions/southey_letters/Part_Three/HTML/letterEEd.26.995.html>.

———. Letter to James Montgomery, March 26, 1812. *Romantic Circles*. <https://www.rc.umd.edu/editions/southey_letters/Part_Four/HTML/letterEEd.26.2066.html>.

———. *Life and Correspondence of Robert Southey*. Ed. Charles Cuthbert Southey. 6 vols. London: Longman, Brown, Green, and Longmans, 1850.

———. *Sir Thomas More: Colloquies on the Progress and Prospects of Society*. 2 vols. London: John Murray, 1829.

———. *A Tale of Paraguay*. Boston: S. G. Goodrich, 1827.

Speck, W. A. *Robert Southey: Entire Man of Letters*. New Haven: Yale UP 2006.

Spivak, Gayatri. "Three Women's Texts and a Critique of Imperialism." *Critical Inquiry* 12.1 (1985): 243–61.

Stanley, Brian. "An Ardour of Devotion: The Spiritual Legacy of Henry Martyn." *India and the Indianness of Christianity: Essays on Understanding—Historical, Theological and Bibliographical—In Honor of Robert Eric Frykenberg*. Ed. Richard Fox Young. Grand Rapids: William B. Eerdsmans, 2009. 108–26.

———. *The Bible and the Flag: Protestant Missions and British Imperialism in the Nineteenth and Twentieth Centuries*. Leicester: Apollos, 1990.

———, editor. *Christian Missions and the Enlightenment*. Grand Rapids: Wm. B. Eerdsmans, 2001.

———. "Christian Missions and the Enlightenment: A Reevaluation." *Christian Missions and the Enlightenment*. Ed. Brian Stanley. Grand Rapids: Wm. B. Eerdsmans, 2001. 1–21.

———. "'Commerce and Christianity': Providence Theory, the Missionary Movement, and the Imperialism of Free Trade, 1842–1860." *The Historical Journal* 26.1 (1983): 71–94.

———. "From 'the Poor Heathen' to 'the Glory and Honour of All Nations': Vocabularies of Race and Custom in Protestant Missions, 1844–1928." *International Bulletin of Missionary Research* 34.1 (Jan. 2010): 3–10.

———. *The World Missionary Conference: Edinburgh 1910*. Grand Rapids: Wm. B. Eerdsmans, 2009.

Stanton, Domna C. "Presidential Address 2005: On Rooted Cosmopolitanism." *PMLA* 121.3 (May 2006): 627–40.

Steiner, F. George. "A Preface to *Middlemarch*." *Nineteenth-Century Fiction* 9.4 (Mar. 1955): 262–79.

Stock, Eugene. *The History of the Church Missionary Society: Its Environment, Its Men and Its Work*. Vol. 1. London: Church Missionary Society, 1899.

Stocking, George. "Franz Boas and the Culture Concept in Historical Perspective." *American Anthropologist* 68.4 (1966): 867–82.

———. *Victorian Anthropology*. New York: The Free Press, 1987.

Stoler, Ann Laura. *Carnal Knowledge and Imperial Power: Race and the Intimate in Colonial Rule*. Berkeley: U of California P, 2002.

Storey, Mark. *Robert Southey: A Life.* Oxford: Oxford UP, 1997.

"Thirty-Third General Meeting of the London Missionary Society, Held on the 9th, 10th, and 11th days of May, 1827." *Evangelical Magazine and Missionary Chronicle* 5 (June 1827): 265–66.

Thom, Georges. "Statement of A/cs.&Details of Letters Sent Home. Re: the Meeting at C. Town & General State of Mission." South Africa, Incoming Correspondence, Box 7, Folder 2, Jacket B. CWM/LMS Archive. SOAS Archives and Special Collections, SOAS, London.

Thomas, Sue. *Imperialism, Reform and the Making of Englishness in* Jane Eyre. Houndsmills: Palgrave Macmillan, 2008.

Thormählen, Marianne. *The Brontës and Religion.* Cambridge: Cambridge UP, 1999.

Thorne, Susan. *Congregational Missions and the Making of an Imperial Culture in Nineteenth-Century England.* Stanford: Stanford UP, 1999.

Timpson, Thomas. *Memoirs of British Female Missionaries: With a Survey of the Condition of Women in Heathen Countries.* London: William Smith, 1841.

"To the Editor of the Christian Observer." *The Christian Observer* 16.6 (June 1817): 368–71.

Tretrail, Frederick. "Doc. VIII.17: Frederick Tretrail on Native Churches, 1860." *Protestant Nonconformist Texts, Volume 3: The Nineteenth Century.* Ed. David Bebbington. Aldershot: Ashgate, 2006. 381–84.

Ullbrecht, Messer, Brownlee, Evans, and Hooper. "Minutes of Conversation at B. Amongst Writers. Insufficiency of Allowances. Change of Rules. Vergood's Name Should be off LMS Lists. Wimmer's Case to Be Considered." 5 June 1817. South Africa, Incoming Correspondence, Box 7, Folder 2, Jacket A. CWM/LMS Archive. SOAS Archives and Special Collections, SOAS, London.

Van der Veer, Peter. *Imperial Encounters: Religion and Modernity in India and Britain.* Princeton: Princeton UP, 2001.

[Vason, George]. *An Authentic Narrative of Four Years' Residence at Tongataboo, One of the Friendly Islands, in the South Sea, by*———. London: Longman, Hurst, Rees, and Orme, 1810.

Vertovec, Steven, and Robin Cohen. "Introduction: Conceiving Cosmopolitanism." *Conceiving Cosmopolitanism: Theory, Context and Practice.* Ed. Steven Vertovec and Robin Cohen. Oxford: Oxford UP, 2002. 1–22.

Viswanathan, Gauri. *Outside the Fold: Conversion, Modernity, and Belief.* Princeton: Princeton UP, 1998.

von Kotzebue, Otto. *A New Voyage Round the World, in the Years 1823, 1824, 1825, and 1826.* 2 vols. London: Henry Colburn and Richard Bentley, 1830.

Wakefield, Gilbert. *An Enquiry into the Expediency and Propriety of Public or Social Worship.* London: Deighton, 1792.

Walls, Andrew. *The Cross-Cultural Process in Christian History.* Maryknoll: Orbis, 2002.

———. "The Eighteenth-Century Protestant Missionary Awakening in Its European Context." *Christian Missions and the Enlightenment.* Ed. Brian Stanley. Grand Rapids: Wm. B. Eerdsmans, 2001. 22–44.

Wanhalla, Angela. *Matters of the Heart: A History of Interracial Marriage in New Zealand.* Auckland: Auckland UP, 2013.

———. "'The Natives Uncivilize Me': Missionaries and Interracial Intimacy in Early New Zealand." *Missionaries, Indigenous People, and Cultural Exchange.* Ed. Patricia Grimshaw and Andrew May. Eastbourne: Sussex Academic Press, 2010. 24–36.

Ward, W. R. *The Protestant Evangelical Awakening*. Cambridge: Cambridge UP, 1992.

Watson, Richard. "Sermon V.—The Religious Instruction of the Slaves in the West India Colonies Advocated and Defended." *Sermons and Sketches of Sermons*. Vol. 1. New York: G. Lane & C. B. Tippett, 1848. 63–88.

Wells, Julia C. "The Suppression of Mixed Marriages Among LMS Missionaries in South Africa Before 1820." *South African Historical Journal* 44 (May 2001): 1–20.

Werner, Winter Jade. "'Altogether a Different Thing': The Emerging Social Sciences and the New Universalisms of Religious Belief in *Kim*." *Nineteenth-Century Literature* 73.3 (2018): 293–325.

"What Else Doth Hinder?" *The Baptist Reporter and Missionary Intelligencer*. Ed. Joseph Foulkes Winks. London: Simpkin, Marshall, and Co.; Leicester: J. F. Winks, 1846. 153–55.

Whish, J. C. *The Great Exhibition Prize Essay: Non sine Deo*. London: Longman, Brown, Green and Longmans, 1851.

White, Daniel E. *Early Romanticism and Religious Dissent*. Cambridge: Cambridge UP, 2006.

———. *From Little London to Little Bengal: Religion, Print, & Modernity in Early British India, 1793–1835*. Baltimore: Johns Hopkins UP, 2013.

———. "'A Little God Whom They Had Just Sent Over': Robert Southey's *The Curse of Kehama* and the Museum of the Bristol Baptist College." *Nineteenth-Century Contexts* 32.2 (2010): 99–120.

Whitehead, William Bailey. *A Letter to the Rev. Daniel Wilson, A. M. Minister of St John's Chapel, Bedford Row, London, in Reply to His Defence of the Church Missionary Society, and in Vindication of the Rev. the Archdeacon of Bath, Against the Censures Contained in That Publication*. Bath: Barratt and Son, 1818.

Wilberforce, William. *A Practical View of Christianity*. Ed. Kevin Charles Belmonte. Peabody: Hendrickson Publishers, 1996.

———. Wilberforce, William to William Ellis (June 4, 1832), William Ellis Papers. Box 5, Personal, Home. CWM/LMS Archive. SOAS Archives and Special Collections, SOAS, London.

Wild-Wood, Emma, and Peniel Rajkumar. "Conclusion: Setting Sail for the Future." *Foundations for Missions*. Ed. Emma Wild-Wood and Peniel Rajkumar. Oxford: Regnum, 2013. 239–53.

Wilks, John. *An Apology for the Missionary Society*. London: Chapman, 1799.

Williams, John. *A Narrative of Missionary Enterprises in the South Sea Islands with Remarks Upon the Natural History of the Islands, Origin, Languages, Traditions, and Usages of the Inhabitants*. New York: D. Appleton & Co., 1837.

Williams, Raymond. *Culture and Society: 1780–1950*. New York: Columbia UP, 1958.

Wilson, Ben. *Decency and Disorder: The Age of Cant 1789–1837*. London: Faber and Faber, 2007.

Wisnicki, Adrian S. "Interstitial Cartographer: David Livingstone and the Invention of South Central Africa." *Victorian Literature and Culture* 37 (2009): 255–71.

Wohlgemut, Esther. *Romantic Cosmopolitanism*. New York: Palgrave MacMillan, 2009.

"A Woman's Luncheon." *The Atlantic Monthly* 76.454 (August 1895): 194–205.

Woodward, Wendy. "The Petticoat and the Kaross: Missionary Bodies and the Feminine in the London Missionary Society 1816–1828." *Kronos* 23 (1996): 91–107.

Wright, Julia M. "Introduction." *The Missionary: An Indian Tale*. Ed. Julia M. Wright. Toronto: Broadview, 2002. 9–57.

———. *Ireland, India, and Nationalism in Nineteenth-Century Literature.* Cambridge: Cambridge UP, 2007.

Young, Paul. *Globalization and the Great Exhibition: The Victorian New World Order.* Houndsmills: Palgrave Macmillan, 2009.

INDEX

Addison, Joseph, 39, 44, 75
Adorno, Theodor W., 8
Agathocleous, 5n3, 20, 21, 22, 22n27, 29, 24n31, 32, 59, 63, 64, 67, 121, 153n20
Albert, Prince, 59
Alley, Jerome, 122
Anatomy of Melancholy (Burton), 117
Anderson, Amanda, 1, 19, 21, 24n31
Anderson, Rufus, 130, 131, 133
Andrews, Charles Freer, 24, 172, 172n5, 173, 173–74n10
Anglicanism, 7n6, 11. *See also* Church of England
Annual Review, 84, 85, 85n16
Anti-Jacobin Review, 47, 50, 51, 52, 53, 55, 74
Apology for the Missionary Society, An (Wilks), 54
Appiah, Kwame Anthony, 19, 142
Aravamudan, Srinivas, 24n31, 32, 174
Arnold, Matthew, 61
Asad, Talal, 25
Asiatic Journal and Monthly Miscellany, The, 48, 48n7

At Home in the World: Cosmopolitanism, Now (Brennan), 19
Atlantic, The, 64

Ballantyne, Robert M., 2n2, 5, 131
Baptist Magazine, 119, 122
Baptist Missionary Society (BMS), 2, 7, 10, 11, 60, 75, 78, 79, 85–86, 89, 96, 119, 156, 160, 161
Baptist Reporter and Missionary Intelligencer, The, 14
Barruel, Augustin, 47
Beauties of the Evangelical Magazine, The, 164
benevolence, 39; expansion of, 42, 58, 83; universal, 49, 50
Beppo, A Venetian Story (Byron), 58
Bewell, Alan, 94
Bleak House (Dickens), 5, 29, 30, 37, 61, 65n19, 110n3; cosmopolitan idea and, 43, 44, 58–68
Bogue, David J., 10n10, 11, 14, 49, 50, 52n10, 54, 62, 151
Bolton, Carol, 70, 85n16
Bosch, David J., 7

Branch, Lori, 25
Brantlinger, Patrick, 2n2, 17, 17n20
Brennan, Timothy, 19
British and Foreign Bible Society, 53, 155
British Critic, The, 74, 79
British Review, 58, 67
Brontë, Charlotte, 6, 28, 36, 71, 111, 113, 114, 118, 132, 134; family ties and, 115; kinship and, 119, 120n12, 136; missionary work and, 131, 131n23
Brontë, Patrick, 132, 132n24
Brooke, Graham Wilmot, 141
Brooke, Greville Lord, 96
brotherhood, 64, 111n4; common, 43, 63, 161; universal, 44, 46, 53, 67
Browning, Elizabeth Barrett, 22, 23n29
Bunyan, John, 47
Burges, James Bland, 47
Burges, Mary Anne, 47
Burke, Edmund, 20, 39, 40, 47, 63, 111
Burns, Robert, 14
Burton, Richard, 175
Burton, Robert, 117
Buxton, Thomas Fowell, 61, 62, 145n6
Byron, Lord, 20, 51, 58, 59, 67

Caird, Edward, 8
Calhoun, Craig, 22n26, 74, 180
Calvinists, 74n2, 88–89
capitalism, 21, 23, 25, 44, 57, 57n13, 172
Caputo, John, 25
Carey, Hilary, 7, 16, 33, 89
Carey, William, 10, 79, 86
Carson, Penny, 14, 51n9, 76n7
Carstone, Richard, 67
Casanova, Jose, 25
Casaubon, Isaac, 101
Castlereagh, Lord, 139
Catholics, 5, 13, 71; Dissenters and, 144, 145, 145n7
Cecil, Richard, 132
Çelikkol, Ayşe, 4
Chakravarty, Guatam, 148, 149, 157n25

Chalmers, Thomas, 14
Cheah, Pheng, 19
Childe Harold's Pilgrimage, 58
Chisholm, Caroline, 61
Christian Socialism, 70
Christianity, 3, 11, 15, 32, 95, 102, 103, 160, 164, 166, 167, 168, 174; advantages of, 107; British, 72, 122, 154; cosmopolitan, 171; doctrines of, 159; Eastern, 171; embracing, 131, 165; European culture and, 24; evangelical, 10, 23, 59; expansion of, 107; forces of, 170; functional, 101; global, 17, 25, 89, 160n26; introduction of, 62, 100, 176; missionary, 17, 23, 29, 178, 179; Protestant, 57, 154; true, 55, 61; universal, 18, 175; Western, 32, 171, 172, 174
Church Missionary Society (CMS), 7, 11, 48, 59, 60, 79, 132; British rule and, 91; evangelicals and, 144n6; LMS and, 12
Church of England, 11, 13, 53, 84, 132. *See also* Anglicanism
citizen of the world, 3, 21, 39, 41, 45, 46, 50, 52, 68
civil rights, 15, 82, 107
civilization, 32, 62, 92, 156, 168; colonization and, 91; Western, 9n9, 170
Clapham Sect, 10, 132
Cleall, Esme, 16, 33, 125
Cockney School, 51, 58, 65, 67
Cohen, Robin, 22n26, 142
Coleridge, Samuel Taylor, 70, 83n15, 159
Collins, Wilkie, 52
colonialism, 21, 31, 54, 91, 92, 96, 144; British, 85, 108; Christian, 33, 36n36, 72, 73, 83, 93, 105, 107, 108; Enlightenment values and, 95; as natural plan, 93, 102, 103, 105; vaccination as, 95–96
colonization, 84, 93, 97, 100; British, 90, 90n20; Christian, 72, 89n19, 92, 100, 107n28, 146; civilization and, 91; missionaries and, 90n20, 91, 92; paternalist, 96
Comaroff, Jean and John L., 16
Combe, George, 153
Commission 4 (World Missionary Conference), 173, 173n8, 173n9; report of, 170, 171n3
Committee for Promoting Christianity in the East, 53

Congregationalism (Independency), 10, 11
conversions, 129, 131, 141, 165, 166
Cook, Captain, 64, 78, 87, 91
Coral Island, The (Ballantyne), 5
Corbett, Mary Jean, 111, 135
cosmo-political idea, 47, 104, 107, 108
cosmopolitan idea, 18, 40, 46; historiography of, 58–68
cosmopolitanism, 12, 18–25, 31, 32, 41, 42, 71, 72, 105, 168, 169, 170, 173, 175; actually existing, 19n22, 20, 178; affective, 24n31, 173n10; antinationalist, 58; Burkean denouncements of, 60; changing views of, 143; characterization of, 108, 179; Christian, 23, 23n29, 31, 58, 62, 73; controversies, 47–57; culture and, 39, 142; domestication of, 104; eighteenth-century, 44–46; Enlightenment, 4, 15, 18, 28, 29, 30, 45, 46, 83, 111, 140, 141, 151, 156; European, 40; evangelical religion and, 180; feelings, 6, 111; genealogy of, 23, 25; historiography of, 43, 44; history of, 2–3; hostility for, 40, 47; human form of, 61; imperialism and, 3, 18; invocation of, 30, 48; Kantian, 22, 44, 73, 84, 104; meanings of, 35, 43; missionary, 1, 3–4, 9, 25–26, 29, 30–31, 33, 37, 43, 49, 50, 52, 62, 63, 93, 112, 113, 142, 150, 162, 168, 180; missionary societies and, 4, 31, 41, 53, 54–55, 170; moral, 45, 111; nationalism and, 20, 22, 83; new, 4, 19, 24, 33, 141–42, 162, 171, 178, 179; perspectives, 22, 48; philosophy of, 63, 111; politicized, 30, 40, 46, 50; post-Mutiny, 4, 141, 157–62; radicals and, 83–84; reinvention of, 30; religion and, 3, 5, 23n29; secular, 178, 180; socialism and, 22; spiritual, 24, 24n31, 159; sympathies, 42, 57; tenets of, 30, 36; term, 20n25, 23–24, 35, 57; thought, 22n26, 153; understanding of, 1, 29, 37, 42, 45, 58, 60, 68, 111, 142; vague, 152–57; visions, 168
cosmopolite, 3, 39, 39n1, 40, 41, 44, 45, 45n5, 46, 50, 60, 104; Enlightenment, 151; idealized, 48; noisy, 69; self-proclaimed, 51
Cosmopolitics: Thinking and Feeling Beyond the Nation (Cheah and Robbins), 19
Council for a Parliament of the World's Religions, 26
Cox, Jeffrey N., 16, 33, 51, 58, 130, 155
Cruikshank, George, 53
Crystal Palace, 60, 65n19

Cultivating Belief (Lecourt), 28, 152, 154, 175, 179
cultural difference, 24, 111, 124, 161, 168
culture, 2, 32, 120, 161, 162, 175n11; British, 35–36; cosmopolitanism and, 142; dissenting, 12; European, 24; forces of, 162n28; Hindu, 153n21, 163; Indian, 153; indigenous, 156, 158; literary, 33; non-Christian, 9; Western, 32, 160, 171, 172, 175, 176
Culture and Anarchy (Arnold), 61
Culture and Society: 1790–1950 (Williams), 70
Cuvier, Georges, 155

De Quincey, Thomas, 70, 104
de Staël, Madame, 20
Derrida, Jacques, 26, 27
devotion, rational/elevated, 73–83
Dickens, Charles, 2n2, 6, 29, 30, 36n36, 43, 61, 62, 64, 64n17, 65n18, 67
Diderot, Denis, 50, 56n12
Diogenes, 44
discourse, 33, 176; civilizational/universalist, 155; cosmopolitan, 23, 24, 29; missionary, 160, 167, 168
disease, 97n23, 99; cure of, 96–97; vaccination and, 92, 96
Dissent, 6, 7n6, 14, 31, 54, 75n6; evangelical, 71, 74, 75; radical, 13, 56
Dissenters, 10n11, 12, 28, 51n9, 84, 132n24, 144, 145, 145n6, 155; Catholics and, 144, 145n7; free conscience and, 90. *See also* Nonconformists
Dobrizhoffer, Martin, 93, 94, 95, 98–99, 100
Douglas, Mary, 93
Dundas, David, 88
Dwight, Timothy, 123, 123n14

East India Company, 54, 60, 76, 76n7, 89, 89n19, 147, 154, 160n27
Eclectic Review, The, 155, 156, 159
Eclectic Society, 132
Economist, The, 40
Ecumenical Association of Third World Theologians (EATWOT), 26
Edinburgh Review, 2

Edinburgh (Scotland) Missionary Society, 7
Elbourne, Elizabeth, 16, 33
Ellis, John Eimeo, 69, 70, 73, 82, 108
Ellis, William, 7, 69, 73, 78n10, 80, 154
Encyclopédie (Diderot), 50
Engels, Friedrich, 59
Enlightenment, 4, 12, 15, 20, 22, 25, 31, 49, 50, 55, 58, 72, 73, 82, 83, 84, 93, 101, 105, 107, 108, 140, 151, 152, 153, 156, 168, 171, 175, 179; Eurocentric normativity of, 142–43; evangelicalism and, 74; idea, 31, 58, 72, 73; Kantian, 23; missionary movement and, 7–10; Protestantism and, 8, 9; Scottish, 65; secular, 6
Enquiry into the Expediency and Propriety of Public or Social Worship (Wakefield), 75
enthusiasm, 6, 15n16, 15n18, 31, 61, 71, 72, 72n1, 74, 78, 79, 84, 86, 93, 101, 102, 104, 135, 147, 148
Eskilt, Ingrid, 177, 179n15
Eurocentrism, 4, 17, 142, 156, 178
Evangelical Magazine and Missionary Chronicle, 48, 78, 79, 118, 120, 122, 123n14, 125, 145, 152n19, 164
evangelical movement, 14, 82, 144, 145, 168
Evangelical Revival, 7n6, 34n34, 169
evangelicalism, 141, 145; Enlightenment and, 74; global, 4, 6, 51; politicization of, 146; secularizing, 84; stereotypes of, 73–74; utilitarianism and, 9n8
evangelicals, 15n18, 55, 140, 144, 144n6, 146n9, 153, 154, 158; Anglican, 51n9
Exeter Hall, 60, 61, 62, 64n17
Exposure of the Unchristian Principles Set Forth in Mr. George Combe's Work, An (Gillespie), 153
Eyre, Jane: feminist agency of, 112n5; kinship and, 111, 114, 115, 116, 119; Rochester and, 117, 118, 121, 122, 136; St. John and, 5, 109, 110, 110n3, 113, 115, 116, 117, 117n9, 119, 133n28, 134, 135, 136, 136n29

For Love of Country? (Nussbaum), 19
Foster, John, 75, 75n5, 79
Foucault, Michel, 35–36
Fountain, John, 156
Franciscans, 148, 148n15

French Revolution, 7, 47, 51, 61
fulfillment theory, 172, 172n6, 174
Fulford, Tim, 70, 86, 94, 95, 96, 97n23

Gallagher, Catherine, 70
Gandhi, Leela, 24, 24n31, 173, 173n10
Gandhi, Mohandas, 24, 32, 172, 173
Gilchrist, John Borthwick, 48
Gillespie, William, 153
Glasgow Missionary Society, 7
Gledstone, J. P., 145, 145n7
globalization, 5, 6, 21, 22, 25–29
Goodlad, Lauren, 5n3, 20n34, 21, 57
Great Exhibition (1851), 15, 30, 40, 41, 42, 57n14, 60, 61, 64; characterization of, 44; cosmopolitanism and, 43, 59; nationalism of, 65
Greatheed, Samuel, 49, 62, 153
Grenfell, Lydia, 133
Griffiths, Devin, 66
Gunson, Neil, 76, 52n10, 90n21

Habermas, Jürgen, 82, 104
Haddad, Samir, 27
Hall, Catherine, 16, 33
Hardcastle, Joseph, 12n14, 124
Hartwig, Peter, 11
Hastings, Selina, Countess of Huntingdon, 144
Haweis, Thomas, 52n10, 76, 77n8, 124
Hayford, Mark C., 170
Heady, Emily, 65n19, 66
Herbert, Christopher, 2n1, 16, 16n19, 126, 148, 152, 162n28
Hilarion, 146n9, 147, 147n14, 150, 151, 163, 164, 167; colonial power and, 148; colonial unrest and, 148n15; Luxima and, 143, 165, 166; religious liberty and, 152n19
Hill, Rowland, 144
Hilton, Boyd, 23
Hindley, Charles, 57, 57n14
Hinduism, 5, 154, 164–65, 167, 173, 173n7, 173n8; genuine character of, 159; moral depravity of, 174; spirit and, 164

Hindus, 87, 88, 143, 146, 147, 148, 154, 155, 156, 159, 161, 163, 168, 172, 174
Historia de Aponibus (Dobrizhoffer), 93, 102
History of Henry Esmond, The (Thackeray), 110n3
History of the London Missionary Society (Ellis), 14, 78n10
Home, Henry, 124
Homer, 75
Horkheimer, Max, 8
Hottentots, 14, 88, 128, 128n19, 129, 130n22
humanism, 3, 12, 16, 26, 39, 44, 57, 87, 91; Christian, 71, 72; cosmopolitan, 50; Enlightenment, 9, 13, 32, 153, 168, 179
humanity, 88, 141, 153; common, 154; Enlightenment, 32, 142–43; genuine, 156; shared brotherhood of, 161; universal, 24, 32, 113, 142, 152, 155, 157, 168, 175

"Idea for a Universal History with a Cosmopolitan Purpose" (Kant), 18n21, 45, 72
"Idea of a Universal History on a Cosmo-Political plan" (Kant), 108
identity, 137, 153; British national, 41; development of, 162; emotional, 178; individual, 142; non-religious, 28; racial, 179
imperialism, 2, 23, 24, 57, 92, 101, 107, 120, 147; British, 142, 150, 157; cosmopolitanism and, 3, 18; evangelism and, 149; jingoistic, 29; mentality, 16–18; missionaries and, 3, 16–18, 90n20, 155, 177–78; missionary work and, 146n9; opposition to, 90n20; triumphalist, 150; understandings of, 37; Victorian, 21; Western, 17, 178
Indian Missions; Viewed in Connexion with the Mutiny and Other Recent Events (Mitchell), 159
Indian "Mutiny" (1857), 2–3, 29, 35, 140, 143, 149–52, 157, 157n25, 158, 160, 161, 163, 164; anti-imperialism and, 149; cataclysm of, 32, 34
Indian National Congress, 172
Indian Opinion, The, 173
intermarriage, 31, 108, 112, 113, 131–37; cultural boundaries and, 133; ending, 129, 130; in mission field, 121–31; missionaries and, 129n21, 130, 132, 135; morality/advisability of, 131
Irvine, Judith, 42

Jackson, John, 60
Jacomb, Nathaniel Pierce, 120
Jager, Colin, 17, 25
Jane Eyre (Brontë), 6, 29, 31, 37, 111, 112, 113–14, 120, 121, 123, 131, 135, 137; feminist readings of, 112n5; kinship/marriage in, 114–19; marriage and, 35, 118–19, 133, 136; missionary plotline of, 113
Jefferson, Thomas, 44
Jellyby, Mrs., 5, 30, 43, 60, 62, 64, 65, 146; cosmopolitanism of, 66; mission of, 61, 67; philanthropy and, 63; Skimpole and, 67, 68
Jenner, Edward, 95, 96, 98, 100
Jervis, Thomas, 51
Jesuits, 94, 95, 148, 148n15
Johnston, Anna, 12
Jørgensen, Jørgen, 76
Jorgenson, Knud, 176n14, 177
Juergensmeyer, Mark, 74

Kale, Madhavi, 121
Kames, Lord, 124
Kant, Immanuel, 8, 20, 23, 42, 46, 100, 194; cosmo-political plan of, 72, 93, 102, 103, 104, 105, 108; cosmopolitanism and, 45, 50; international federation and, 40; providentialism and, 108; secularism of, 105; Universal History and, 102, 106
Keane, Webb, 8, 16, 25, 41, 42n3
Keats, John, 51
Keirstead, Christopher M., 20n25, 22, 23n29
Kennedy, James, 158, 160
Keshab Chandra Sen and the Brahma Samaj (Slater), 174
Keshub Chunder Sen, 173n7, 174
Kidd, Colin, 155–56
King, Joshua, 37
kinship: evangelical scheme of, 122; feeling, 111, 120, 122; global, 121; ideal of, 116, 136; language of, 116, 131; marriage and, 114–19, 136; missionary movement and, 112; missionary work and, 119–21; notion of, 111n4, 114, 141; race and, 114; universal, 6, 31, 33, 35, 108, 111, 112, 113, 114, 119–21, 120n12, 131, 134, 135, 137
Kitson, Peter J., 86

Kleingeld, Pauline, 45, 111n4
Kumalo, R. Simangaliso, 178

language: cosmopolitan, 41, 42, 51; Enlightenment, 71; Hindu, 163; missionary, 28, 77; peculiarity of, 79; vernacular, 153
language ideology, 41–42, 71
Lawrie, Catherine, 79
Lay Thoughts on the Indian Mutiny (Nisbet), 159
Le Cosmopolite (Montbron), 58
Lecourt, Sebastian, 23, 25, 32, 61, 151n18, 175
Lee, Debbie, 86, 97n23
Leigh Hunt, James Henry, 30, 51, 60, 65
Letter 35 (Burke), 39
Letter to the Rev. Daniel Wilson (Whitehead), 48
Lewis, Sarah, 123, 123n15
Lewis, Thomas, 126, 127, 129; excommunication of, 125; Hastings and, 143
liberality, cosmopolitan, 58, 59, 60, 61, 67
Lichtenstein, Henry, 127n18, 129n21
Liebau, Heike, 120
Lindsay, James, 51, 52
Livingstone, David, 15, 57n13, 61, 80, 133n27, 141, 150, 153, 157, 157n24; expedition of, 34
London Critical Journal, 58
London Missionary Society (LMS), 2n1, 7, 10, 11, 14, 15, 17, 34, 49, 54, 55, 56, 60, 69, 75, 76, 77, 78, 79, 80, 85, 86, 87, 88, 89, 94, 119, 124, 125, 127; CMS and, 12; intermarriage and, 128, 129, 130; public image of, 79n12; report by, 158; Seidenfadden and, 129n22
London Secretaries' Association, 60
Long, Edward, 124, 155
Luther, Martin, 101
Luxima, 140, 148, 167; displacement of, 149–50; Hilarion and, 143, 165, 166; post-Mutiny, 166
Luxima, the Prophetess: A Tale of India (Owenson), 29, 32, 140, 142, 143, 149, 150, 163, 164, 165, 166, 167; Enlightenment sensibility and, 152; inspiration for, 148; revision of, 140n3, 149n16, 149n17

Macaulay, Thomas Babington, 100, 160n27

mankind, 1; brotherhood of, 111n4; civilization of, 61; equality/kinship of, 6; oneness of, 137; origin of, 125
Marcus, Sharon, 35
marriage: bond of, 122; Christian, 123; interracial, 112, 131, 136, 148; kinship and, 114–19, 136; missionary, 6, 112, 126, 127, 134, 136; patriarchal nature of, 112; Victorians and, 122
Martyn, Henry, 35, 132, 132n26, 134
Marx, Karl, 21, 44, 59, 64
Mason, Bertha, 112n5; Rochester and, 31, 112–13, 116, 117–18, 120n12, 127, 134, 135, 136
Masuzawa, Tomoko, 33, 172n6, 174, 174n10
Mathers, James, 171, 172
Maurice, Frederick Denison, 158
McCaw, Neil, 65
McKee, Patricia, 117
McMurran, Helen, 39n1, 44, 45
Memoir of Mrs. Mary Mercy Ellis, Wife of Rev. William Ellis (Anderson), 130
Memoir of the Rev. J. T. Van Der Kemp, 81
Memoirs Illustrating the History of Jacobinism (Barruel), 47
Mendieta, Eduardo, 25, 26, 27
Mercury, The, 169, 170
Messmore, J. H., 171
Methodist Episcopal Church, 171
Methodists, 11, 15n18, 74, 86, 87, 88, 132
Middlemarch (Eliot), 116
Middleton, Thomas Fanshaw, 154, 159
Miguez, Néstor O., 178
Mill, John Stuart, 21
missionaries, 18, 25, 77, 79, 84, 96, 111, 121, 123, 124, 125, 153, 160, 170, 172, 173, 174; Baptist, 88, 147, 147n12, 147n13; Catholic, 90; Christianity and, 179; colonization and, 90n20, 91, 92, 93; Congregational, 90n20; Dissenting, 85–86, 148; dual identity of, 147n14; European, 177; family history and, 24n30; human family, 137; as humanists, 2; imperialism and, 17, 90n20, 155, 177–78; indigenous culture and, 156; interest in, 108; intermarriage and, 130, 132, 135; Jesuit, 106; marginality/insanity of, 2; marriages of, 6, 112, 124, 126, 127, 130, 132, 134, 135, 136; politics

INDEX • 207

and, 89–90, 90n21; pre-Mutiny, 159–60; progress of, 162–63; proselytization by, 89, 94; protecting, 130–31; Protestant, 153; South Sea, 88, 91, 127n19; Tahitian, 126; theology and, 33, 34; universalist concerns of, 29

"Missionary, The" (Brontë), 113n7, 131, 131n23, 133

Missionary, The (Owenson), 29, 32, 37, 139–40, 142, 143, 144, 146, 149, 163, 164, 166, 167; critical readings of, 149n16, 150; Enlightenment sensibility and, 151, 152; mutiny and, 35

Missionary Enterprises, 81

Missionary Magazine, 49, 165

missionary movement, 1, 3, 6–15, 24, 28, 49, 107, 175; ethos of, 152, 152n19; evangelical, 10, 147; goal of, 72; ideological foundation of, 15; indigenous culture and, 156; kinship and, 112; modern, 6–15, 42, 56, 58, 68, 90; Protestant, 31; Southey and, 71, 83–93

Missionary Register, 48, 83

missionary societies, 12, 25, 56, 67, 68, 79, 82, 84–85, 107, 111, 112, 124, 126, 133, 154, 160; binary of, 74; challenges for, 152; cooperation/coordination among, 6; cosmopolitanism and, 4, 31, 41, 53, 54–55, 170; dissenting, 51n9, 71; fund-raising by, 76; history of, 2–3, 33, 34; interdenominational/undenominational, 10n11; intermarriages and, 131; kinship and, 121, 136; marriage and, 134; public image of, 73; rhetoric of, 86; sentiments of, 144; textual output of, 6; universalizing theories and, 157

Missionary Society, 7, 11, 18, 52, 53, 55, 77, 86n17

missionary thought, 141, 142, 152–57, 162, 168

Missionary Travels and Researches in South Africa (Livingstone), 150, 157n24

missionary work, 1, 16, 31, 73, 82, 104, 112, 124, 141, 142, 170, 174, 176, 179; condemnation of, 51–53, 61; histories of, 14, 33, 34, 78n10; imperialism and, 146n9; kinship and, 119–21; post-Western, 178

missionary writing, 18, 35, 78, 78n1, 119, 152, 175; literature and, 33

Missionary's Portable Christmas Box, and Cosmopolitan's Seasonable New Year's Gift, The (Gilchrist), 48

Mitchell, John Murray, 159, 160

Mitford, Mary Russel, 65

modernity, 7, 8, 19, 22; confidence in, 176n12; myths of, 22n27; secular, 72n1

Mogenson, Mogens, 177

Montbron, Fougeret de, 44, 58, 60

Montesinos, 103, 104, 105, 106; optimism of, 101–2

Montesquieu, 50

Monthly Meteor, 74, 78

Monthly Review, 75

morality, 46, 125; Christian, 42, 72, 85

More, Sir Thomas, 101, 101n25, 102, 104, 106

Morton, Agnes, 5

Morton, Colin, 5

Mott, John R., 169

Mukerjee, N. C., 172

Narrative of Missionary Enterprises in the South Sea Islands, A (Williams), 1, 11, 81

Narrative of the Niger Expedition, Dickens review of, 62

nationalism, 23, 49, 65, 107; blind, 44; British, 30, 40, 111; cosmopolitanism and, 20, 22; Indian, 24, 172

Nature, 89n19, 92, 106; hidden plan of, 105, 108; vaccination and, 93

New Ground (Yonge), 5

New Monthly Magazine and Universal Register, 127, 128

Newton, John, 10

Niger Expedition, 61, 63

Nisbet, James, 159

Nonconformists, 15n18, 144, 145n6, 145n7; Catholics and, 145. *See also* Dissenters

North India American Presbyterian Mission, 172

Nussbaum, Martha, 19, 104

Nussey, Ellen, 118

O'Briens and the O'Flahertys, The (Owenson), 145

O'Connell, Daniel, 145, 145n7

Observations on the Nature of Civil Liberty (Price), 13

Odie, Geoffrey A., 162

Oliphant, Margaret, 116

Oliver, Rosamond, 110, 131, 133n28

Owen, John, 53

Owenson, Robert, 143

Owenson, Sydney (Lady Morgan), 5, 6, 29, 32, 36, 139, 140, 142, 150, 162–68; awareness/sensitivity of, 168; conservatives and, 146n8; evangelicalism and, 146; inspiration for, 143; missionaries and, 146, 147, 151, 152, 168; Mutiny and, 148; political savvy of, 146n9; politics of religion and, 143–48, 148n15; rebellions and, 149; revisions by, 140, 149n16, 163–64

Paley, William, 103

Parminedes, 86

Parsons, Cóilín, 149, 150, 166

Periodical Accounts Relative to the Baptist Society (Southey), 72, 85, 88

Perry, Ruth, 122

philanthropy, 15n16, 30; telescopic, 5, 64, 67

philosophes, 58, 74, 103, 111n4

Pietism, 8, 9n7

Pilgrim's Progress, The (Bunyan), 47

Pocock, J. G. A., 8

politics, 26–27, 40, 54, 56, 88, 91; colonial, 148; missionaries and, 89–90, 90n21; native, 90n21; particularities of, 168; radical, 41; religion and, 143–48

Polynesian Researches (Ellis), 7, 69, 82, 107n28, 154

Pope, Alexander, 75, 81

Porter, Andrew, 33, 60n16, 162

Powers of Distance: Cosmopolitanism and the Cultivation of Detachment (Anderson), 1, 19

Practical View of Christianity, A (Wilberforce), 55

Pratt, Lynda, 70

Price, Richard, 13, 52n10

Prichard, James Cowles, 103, 124

Priestley, Joseph, 84

Progress of the Pilgrim Good-Intent, in Jacobinical Times, The (Burges), 47

Protestantism, 6, 11, 15, 176, 179; British, 74n3, 123; denomination of, 82; Enlightenment and, 8, 9

providentialism, 93, 102, 105; cosmo-political, 103; secular, 107–8

Quarterly Review, The, 58n15, 70, 75, 84, 85, 88, 107n28, 139

race, 4, 17, 31, 87, 94, 112, 113n7, 129, 136, 137, 153, 156, 161, 170; kinship and, 111, 114, 121

radicalism, 30, 53, 58, 83–84

rationality, 14, 25, 28, 77

Read, James, 127, 128n20, 129n21, 132, 132n26, 133n27, 134

Reasons for the Ill Success Which Attends Christian Missionaries (Jørgensen), 76

Recollections of a Literary Life (Mitford), 65

Reductions, 94, 95, 99

Reed, Eliza, 114

Reed, Georgiana, 114

religion, 3, 5, 6, 24, 32, 105, 170; freedom of, 55, 84, 85, 146; globalization and, 25–29; literature and, 23; politics of, 142, 143–48, 148n15; universality of, 151n18, 176

Renner, Melchior, 11

Researches into the Physical History of Man (Prichard), 124

revivalism, 15, 28, 37, 74, 83

Rivers, St. John: fixation of, 110–11; intermarriage and, 131–37; Jane and, 5, 109, 110, 110n3, 113, 115, 116, 117, 117n9, 119, 133n28, 134, 135, 136, 136n29; kinship and, 111, 114, 115, 134; missionary history and, 109–10; missionary plotline and, 111, 113

Robbins, Bruce, 16–17, 19, 19n42, 142, 162, 178

Roberts, Daniel Sanjiv, 83, 103

Robinson, Robert, 13, 47

Rochester, 114; Bertha and, 31, 112–13, 116, 120n12, 127, 134, 135, 136; Jane and, 117, 118, 121, 122, 136

Roman Catholic Relief Act (1829), 145

Romantic Cosmopolitanism (Wohlgemut), 20, 40, 46, 83, 101n25, 103, 104

Romantic period, 20, 22, 35, 35n35, 51, 61, 67

Rousseau, Jean-Jacques, 8, 40, 42, 51

Rutz, Michael A., 14, 15n18, 16, 51, 144

Salesa, Damon, 124

Samaj, Brahmo, 174

Santon Barissa, 128

Satirist, The, 74, 78

Scanlon, William, 25

Schaffer, Talia, 110, 110n3, 133n28

Schlereth, Thomas, 13, 18n21, 39, 44, 45, 50, 111n4, 151, 152, 156–57

Schroder, Sarah, 120

Schwartz, Regina Mara, 25

Scott, J. Barton, 8, 9n8

Scott, Thomas, 10

Scottish Missionary Register, 119

Scourge; or, Monthly Expositor of Imposture and Folly, 53

Scrivener, Michael, 22

secularism, 18, 26, 28, 73, 74, 103, 105, 107n28, 178; ideology of, 17; logic of, 25

Sedgwick, Adam, 153

Seidenfadden, Johannes, 128, 129, 129–30n22

self-determination, 14, 41, 55n11

Self-Realization Fellowship, 175

Sermon Occasioned by the Death of the Rev. Joseph Towers, LL. D., A (Lindsay and Jervis), 51

sexual relations, 110, 118n11, 135–36

Sharpe, Charles Kirkpatrick, 139

Shelley, Percy Bysshe, 51, 139

Sidmouth, Lord, 15n18, 144

Sir Thomas More: Colloquies on the Progress and Prospects of Society (Southey), 29, 31, 37, 71, 72, 83, 92, 93, 96, 97, 103, 105, 106, 107, 107n28; cosmopolitanism and, 84; Macaulay review of, 100; providentialism and, 102; vaccination/Nature and, 108; writing of, 101

Sivasundaram, Sujit, 74

Skimpole, Harold, 30, 43, 60, 62, 63, 64, 65, 65n18; cosmopolitanism of, 66; Jellyby and, 67, 68

Slater, Thomas Ebenezer, 171, 172, 174

slavery, 61, 63, 120n13, 128, 129, 155; war and, 14

smallpox, 94, 96, 97–98, 97n24

Smith, Christian, 25

Smith, Sydney, 2, 50, 147n12

Society for Missions to Africa and the East, 7. *See also* Church Missionary Society

Society for Promoting Christian Knowledge (SPCK), 6, 10n11, 59, 60, 154, 156

Society for the Propagation of the Gospel in Foreign Parts (SPG), 6, 24, 59, 60, 60n16, 63, 76n6, 172

Socinianism, 13

Sorkin, David, 8

South Sea Islands, 17, 64, 76, 77n8, 79, 87, 88, 97, 111, 123, 125, 129n21, 143

Southcott, Joanna, 78

Southey, Robert, 6, 29, 31, 51, 68, 70, 72, 78, 82, 95–96, 98–99, 101; colonization and, 89n19, 98, 100, 107; cosmo-political scheme of, 107; cosmopolitanism and, 31, 83, 84, 93, 104; Dissenting missionaries and, 85–86; Ellis and, 69; global Christianity and, 89; goal of, 94–95; humanitarianism and, 87; imagination of, 104; journalism of, 92, 94; Kant and, 105; missionary movement and, 71, 73, 83–93; proper position and, 108; as social commentator, 70; vaccination and, 96–97, 97n24, 98; van der Kemp and, 86, 86n17

Stanley, Brian, 9n9, 10, 16, 33, 92, 132, 168, 169, 170, 176n12; on missionary societies, 34; theological shift and, 141

Stapleton, Sir Thomas, 139

Steiner, George, 116

Stoler, Ann Laura, 33, 134

Stott, John, 176

Summerson, Esther, 63, 68

Tale of Paraguay, A (Southey), 29, 31, 36–37, 73, 92, 93–100, 106, 107; smallpox and, 97; source material for, 93; vaccination/Nature and, 93, 97–98, 108

Tale of Two Cities, A (Dickens), 66

Taming Cannibals (Brantlinger), 17

Taylor, Charles, 25, 28

theology, 103, 176, 179, 179n15; Christian, 174; missionary, 33, 34; universal dimension of, 177

Theology; Explained and Defended (Dwight), 123

Theosophy, 175

Thom, George, 129

Thomas, Sue, 117, 118, 120n12

Thorne, Susan, 33

tolerance, 21, 25, 41, 71, 82, 85, 124, 156; political, 28, 73; religious, 13, 55n1, 82, 84

Toleration Acts (1689 and 1779), 144

Towers, Rev., 52, 52n10

Transactions of the Missionary Society, 77, 80, 127n19; Southey review of, 72, 86, 87, 88

Tretrail, Frederick, 161

Tutu, Desmond, 178

Unitarianism, 13, 52

universalism, 18; Christian, 29, 125, 171, 172–76, 175n11, 179; cosmopolitanism and, 18n21; cultural, 176; enlightened, 170; humanist, 24; moral, 45, 179; religious, 171, 175; spiritual, 175

Urban Realism and the Cosmopolitan Imagination in the Nineteenth Century (Agathocleous), 4, 5, 20, 22, 63, 64, 67, 121, 142

vaccination, 93, 96–97, 98, 100, 108; colonialism and, 95–96

Van der Kemp, Johannes, 79, 86, 88, 127, 132, 134; intermarriage and, 130; LMS and, 80–81; marriage of, 128; Martyn and, 132n26

VanAntwerpen, Jonathan, 74

Vason, George, 126, 127, 127n17, 131

Vellore Massacre (1806), 35, 146, 147, 147n14, 148, 149–52

Venn, John, 10

Vertovec, Steven, 22n26, 142

Victorian period, 2n1, 3n2, 20, 21, 22, 35, 35n35, 43, 65, 111, 112, 135, 140, 141n4

Vindiciae Christianae (Alley), 122

Viswanathan, Gauri, 31, 135, 149–50

Voltaire, 8, 42, 51

Wakefield, Gilbert, 75

Wallenstein, 159

Walls, Andrew, 8–9n7, 33, 34, 90, 174, 176

Waterhouse, Joseph, 17, 17n20

Watson, Richard, 153

Wells, Julia, 123, 124

Wesleyan Methodist Missionary Society, 60

Whish, John Charles, 59

White, Daniel, 13n15, 70, 74n2, 156

Whitehead, William, 48

Wieland, Christoph Martin, 111

Wilberforce, William, 10, 34n34, 55, 74, 82, 90n21, 91, 145n6

Wild Irish Girl, The (Owenson), 139

Wilks, John, 54

Williams, John, 1, 11, 80, 81

Williams, Robert, 70

Williams, Thomas, 2n1, 17, 17n20, 162n28

Wilson, Ben, 74

Wilson, W., 92

Wimmer, Michael, 128, 129, 129n21, 133n27

Wimmer, Susannah, 128

Wisnicki, Adrian, 141

Wohlgemut, Esther, 20, 40, 46, 83, 101n25, 103, 104

Woman's Mission (Lewis), 123, 123n15

Wordsworth, William, 70

World Council of Churches (WCC), 26

World Missionary Conference (1910), 169, 170, 170n2, 172–76

World Missionary Conference (2010), 32, 176–80

Wright, Julia, 21, 139, 140, 146n8, 149, 151, 152, 156, 167

Yogananda, Paramhansa, 175

Yonge, Charlotte, 2n2, 5

LITERATURE, RELIGION, AND POSTSECULAR STUDIES
LORI BRANCH, SERIES EDITOR

Literature, Religion, and Postsecular Studies publishes scholarship on the influence of religion on literature and of literature on religion from the sixteenth century onward. Books in the series include studies of religious rhetoric or allegory; of the secularization of religion, ritual, and religious life; and of the emerging identity of postsecular studies and literary criticism.

Missionary Cosmopolitanism in Nineteenth-Century British Literature
WINTER JADE WERNER

Constructing Nineteenth-Century Religion: Literary, Historical, and Religious Studies in Dialogue
EDITED BY JOSHUA KING AND WINTER JADE WERNER

Good Words: Evangelicalism and the Victorian Novel
MARK KNIGHT

Enlightened Individualism: Buddhism and Hinduism in American Literature from the Beats to the Present
KYLE GARTON-GUNDLING

A Theology of Sense: John Updike, Embodiment, and Late Twentieth-Century American Literature
SCOTT DILL

Walker Percy, Fyodor Dostoevsky, and the Search for Influence
JESSICA HOOTEN WILSON

The Religion of Empire: Political Theology in Blake's Prophetic Symbolism
G. A. ROSSO

Clashing Convictions: Science and Religion in American Fiction
ALBERT H. TRICOMI

Female Piety and the Invention of American Puritanism
BRYCE TRAISTER

Secular Scriptures: Modern Theological Poetics in the Wake of Dante
WILLIAM FRANKE

Imagined Spiritual Communities in Britain's Age of Print
JOSHUA KING

Conspicuous Bodies: Provincial Belief and the Making of Joyce and Rushdie
JEAN KANE

Victorian Sacrifice: Ethics and Economics in Mid-Century Novels
ILANA M. BLUMBERG

Lake Methodism: Polite Literature and Popular Religion in England, 1780–1830
JASPER CRAGWALL

Hard Sayings: The Rhetoric of Christian Orthodoxy in Late Modern Fiction
THOMAS F. HADDOX

Preaching and the Rise of the American Novel
DAWN COLEMAN

Victorian Women Writers, Radical Grandmothers, and the Gendering of God
GAIL TURLEY HOUSTON

Apocalypse South: Judgment, Cataclysm, and Resistance in the Regional Imaginary
ANTHONY DYER HOEFER